Colorado's Landmark Hotels

Linda R. Wommack

Filter Press, LLC
Palmer Lake, Colorado

ISBN: 978-0-86541-129-6
Library of Congress Control Number: 2012953521
Copyright © 2012 Linda R. Wommack. All rights reserved.

P.O. Box 95 • Palmer Lake, CO 80133
888-570-2663
FilterPressBooks.com
Printed in the United States of America

CONTENTS

FOREWORD

Historic properties across the state of Colorado, including hotels, are more often than not identified, listed, and preserved by landmark status through programs such as the National Trust for Historic Preservation, the National Register of Historic Places, and Colorado Preservation, Inc. *Colorado's Landmark Hotels* features the thirty hotels in the state of Colorado that meet the criteria and historic distinction necessary for landmark designation. All but three of these hotels are at least one hundred years old and have operated as hotels for the past fifty years.

At the time of their construction, these historic hotels exhibited not only the latest architectural styles, but also the latest technology and creature comforts. For example, architectural advances such as the steel skeleton and the skylit atrium lobby were introduced by Frank Edbrooke's Brown Palace Hotel in 1892.

Hotels have long been the heart of Colorado communities. Indeed, Colorado's historic hotels not only lent advances in architectural design and comfortable accommodations for the guests, but also provided a place for social interaction. It was often at these hotels that the community celebrated their triumphs, birthday parties, debutante balls, and weddings while graciously accommodating distinguished travelers, investors, and prospective newcomers.

Between the 1880s and 1920s, Coloradans built their grand hotels: The Broadmoor in Colorado Springs, The Oxford and The Brown Palace in Denver, the Strater in Durango, the Hotel Colorado in Glenwood Springs, the Beaumont in Ouray, and the Grand Imperial in Silverton. In these palaces, guests availed themselves of luxuries such as fine haircuts and snappy shoeshines, iced drinks and gourmet meals in sumptuous surroundings. They gawked at such wonders as elevators and telephones, hot water, and flush toilets. Later, such comforts as air-conditioning and room service delighted guests.

Hotels, of course, were prime spots for affairs of the heart and the murders they sometimes triggered. Here ordinary folks might catch a glimpse, or even sleep in the beds, of the rich and infamous.

I've had the pleasure of working with Linda Wommack on cemetery tours, history talks, and excursions over many years. Along with writing six books on Colorado history, Linda is a contributing editor for *True West* magazine and contributes a monthly column for *Wild West* magazine. She has served as a consultant and researcher for many state and national organizations, including the national Wild West History Association and the new (2007) Lawman & Outlaw Museum in Cripple Creek, Colorado. Linda's involvement with various landmark destinations attracted her to the rich history of Colorado's hotels.

Through crackerjack research, personal visits, and extensive interviews with hotel owners, Linda not only takes the reader back in time, but also brings each hotel story up-to-date by noting such modern conveniences as online booking and Wi-Fi access. The "Fun Facts" in each entry add a delightful bit of trivia about each hotel, ranging from ghostly apparitions to little-known historic facts—including prized hotel guest registers with the signatures of US presidents, lesser known politicos, Hollywood movie stars, and even notorious criminals.

This book is an important contribution to the fabric of our state's history, both in social terms and the rich Victorian architecture preserved by their historic landmark status.

—*Thomas J. Noel, "Dr. Colorado," Professor of History and Director of Public History, Preservation & Colorado Studies at the University of Colorado Denver*

PREFACE

We live in a time when it is easy to pass things by—to drive seventy-five miles per hour on concrete and asphalt, intent on our destination and totally impervious to the call of history. Even in Colorado, the state that represents the heart of the West and the romantic notions of the Wild West, we're generally clueless about the events that forged our home. There, at Mile Marker 41, something glorious happened in 1897. That old building downtown across from the parking garage once was the site of dazzling galas. Such things are there for us to see and celebrate, but we far too often ignore it.

Thank goodness for Linda Wommack. No one knows the state's cultural history and historical attractions in such detail, and no one can match her ability to communicate the importance of what we were in relation to what we've become. Her books are invaluable to the armchair historian and even more so to those who follow her guidance in experiencing historic Colorado. She has resurrected the lives and stories of those who rest in the state's first cemeteries in *From the Grave*, and she chronicled the heartbreaking yet fascinating lives of the state's frontier prostitutes in *Our Ladies of the Tenderloin*. Now, she brings the state's important historic hotels to life, in all their Victorian-era glory, in *Colorado's Landmark Hotels*.

Colorado's beauty, geography, and geology have always drawn those who appreciate both adventure and luxury. As increasing wealth from minerals brought more and more people to the state in the last half of the nineteenth century, the great hotels followed. Some, such as The Brown Palace, The Broadmoor, and the Hotel Jerome, became and remained famous, while some have endured rocky roads before being restored to their former grandeur. All have fantastic stories to tell.

Wommack is a terrific writer, and has done a fine job in communicating each hotel's timeline and physical attributes. But this is more than a boilerplate chronicle of when a hotel was built and who the owners were and are. She instead approaches each with an in-depth examination of its distinct personality and interaction within its community. Paupers and presidents, miners and millionaires populated these grande dames, and Wommack weaves them through the narrative, culminating with a look at each hotel's modern operations. And, given the subject matter, she even throws in a ghost story or two.

As a Colorado native who has a long-standing relationship with the historic Hotel Colorado in Glenwood Springs, I'm impressed by Wommack's command of its history. She describes its regional and national significance straightforwardly, yet with palpable affection. Those who know it well will nod their heads in appreciation, and those who don't will want to visit.

For those who count themselves as Coloradans, either geographically or in spirit, a new Linda Wommack book is a singular treat. Once again, she has written an important addition to both the historian's and the history buff's libraries.

—*Jon Chandler, award-winning novelist and singer-songwriter*

INTRODUCTION

With the discovery of gold in 1858, Colorado's Rocky Mountain region exploded in population. In time, mining camps such as Aspen, Creede, Cripple Creek, and Victor developed into towns and attracted businessmen and travelers. Hotel proprietors saw an obvious need in these bustling communities. Cities such as Boulder, Denver, Fort Collins, and Colorado Springs also built fine hotels to attract visitors, to offer a European resort experience, and to build a business clientele. Hotel proprietors built grand resorts in beautiful locales as well, such as the Redstone Inn in Pitkin County and the Hotel Colorado in nearby Glenwood Springs, which capitalized on the fabulous natural hot springs.

Primarily because of relatively inexpensive and available materials, log and wooden frame structures were the earliest hotels of Colorado. Fortunately, we have these landmark treasures today in the Peck House, the Rio Grande Southern Hotel, the River Forks Inn, the Meeker and Creede Hotels, the Goldminer Hotel, and the Western Hotel.

Later, as technology moved westward, hotels were built using the architectural designs of the time, from brick establishments that could withstand the threat of fire, such as the New Sheridan Hotel in Telluride, to the fireproof steel skeleton housing of The Brown Palace Hotel in Denver. With further improvements, hotels were able to provide guests with such comforts as private bathrooms and running water, elevators, and telephone service.

Colorado's landmark hotels not only brought a sense of refinement to their town, but often became the social hub of the town. Many of these hotels hosted celebrities, US presidents, and European royalty. These hotels brought significant economic development, social impact, and vitality to their communities.

This book attempts to bring that landmark hotel history together in one volume. The thirty hotels included in this book, are the only hotels in the state to have achieved a listing on at least one, if not all registers of preservation status: 1) the National Register of Historic Places; 2) the National Trust for Historic Preservation; 3) Colorado Preservation, Inc., with a "landmark" status; or 4) city or county historic properties listings. Requirements for such a prestigious listing on even one of these are extensive. For example, to be included in the National Trust for Historic Preservation's "Historic Hotels of America" program, a hotel must be at least fifty years old, listed on the National Register of Historic Places, and be recognized as having historic significance.

Conversely, while the National Register of Historic landmarks signifies that the building is worthy of preservation, a city approving landmark status of a building "carries much more weight than the National Register application, as it ensures that the exterior will remain the same," says Boulder County historian Silvia Pettem.

Additionally, all thirty hotels included in this book have operated as hotels for the past fifty years, and operate as hotels today. They are chronicled by the date of construction. The preservation status and/or registration number or category are also listed in each chapter.

As I did my research, I discovered many interesting tidbits of hotel information that weave in and around Colorado's history. From President Theodore Roosevelt's 1905 visit to the Hotel Colorado, which sparked the creation of the teddy bear, to the infamous 1964 visit of the Beatles to The Brown Palace Hotel, pop culture history was made at Colorado hotels. The Delaware Hotel was a place where the destitute and lonely Baby Doe Tabor often warmed herself in the manager's office. Conversely, the Redstone Inn was built by multimillionaire John C. Osgood, who had more money than he knew what to do with. Politics and labor issues became a part of hotel history at the famed Oxford Hotel as well as at the New Sheridan Hotel, whose owner had a not-so-innocent role in the various labor struggles in Telluride.

Actually, politics played a very important role in the history of hotels. The political term *lobbying* arose during President Ulysses S. Grant's term from 1869 to 1877. Congressmen, senators, and even constituents would gather in the lobby of the famed Willard Hotel in Washington, DC, in order to gain an audience with the president to present their various agendas. Grant often met with such folks in the lobby. This practice continued in one form or another in the lobbies of hotels all across America. In Colorado hotel lobbies, business deals concerning the Denver Broncos were made in The Brown Palace Hotel. Strategic decisions during the labor struggles of Telluride were made at the New Sheridan Hotel, and politicians met regularly in The Oxford Hotel lobby in Denver.

And then there are the rumors of ghosts. Many Colorado hotels are said to be haunted—from The Imperial Hotel, where the owner mysteriously fell down the back stairs to his death, to The Stanley Hotel, where ghosts have reportedly roamed since long before Stephen King's visit that resulted in the best-selling novel *The Shining*.

These tidbits and more are included throughout the historical thread that binds these landmark hotels to the history of Colorado. I cannot recommend a better way to get to know the history of Colorado than to visit the state's grand historic hotels.

– *Linda Wommack*

Landmark Hotels by Region

Northern Foothills

Boulder
Hotel Boulderado – 1909

Denver
The Oxford Hotel – 1891
The Brown Palace Hotel – 1892

Drake
River Forks Inn – 1905

Eldora
Goldminer Hotel – 1897

Estes Park
The Stanley Hotel – 1909

Fort Collins
Armstrong Hotel – 1923

Central Mountains

Aspen
Hotel Jerome – 1889

Empire
The Peck House – 1862

Glenwood Springs
Hotel Colorado – 1893
The Hotel Denver – 1915

Leadville
Delaware Hotel – 1886

Meeker
Meeker Hotel – 1883

Pitkin County
Redstone Inn – 1902

Southern Foothills

Cripple Creek
The Imperial Hotel and Casino – 1896
The Hotel St. Nicholas – 1898

Colorado Springs
The Broadmoor – 1918

Manitou Springs
The Cliff House – 1874

Victor
Victor Hotel – 1899

Southern Mountains and Southwest

Creede
The Creede Hotel – 1892

Dolores
The Rio Grande Southern Hotel – 1893

Durango
Strater Hotel – 1887
Rochester Hotel – 1892
General Palmer Hotel – 1898

Ouray
Beaumont Hotel – 1886
Western Hotel – 1892
St. Elmo Hotel – 1898

Silverton
Grand Imperial Hotel – 1883
The Teller House Hotel – 1896

Telluride
New Sheridan Hotel – 1891

THE PECK HOUSE – 1862
A PIONEER ON THE FRONTIER

I t's been said that the California gold rush of 1849 hastened westward migration by fifteen years. If so, then the Pikes Peak gold rush of 1858–1859 sealed that fate. "Pikes Peak or Bust" was the slogan on covered wagons headed west for new beginnings and a chance at striking it rich. That first gold rush to the Rocky Mountain region brought thousands of eager men and a few women to the Colorado Territory. The mountains held a wealth of gold, and mining camps sprang up all over the Rockies. As gold was found in nearly every camp, prosperity followed and towns were formed.

The front porch and entry to the Peck House in Empire remains largely unchanged from James and Mary Peck's original construction.
Landmark Register:
NR 5CC.183

Not far from the first major gold discoveries, at Russell Gulch (Central City) in 1858 and Payne's Bar (Idaho Springs) in 1859, a group of prospectors on their way toward today's Berthoud Pass discovered rich gold deposits in the rocks of Silver Mountain. By

1860 the mining camp of Empire City, named by prospectors from New York and soon known simply as Empire, was a bustling mining community.

While the mining history of this mountain town has been overshadowed by a few richer gold strikes, Empire maintains the distinction of being one of Colorado's oldest gold camps and lays claim to the state's oldest landmark hotel—The Peck House.

The Beginning

The summer of 1860 saw a new wave of prospectors arrive in Empire. Among them were a successful Chicago merchant, James Peck, and his three teenage sons. By the end of the summer, Peck had discovered another rich vein of ore on Silver Mountain and later constructed the Peck Mill, an ambitious structure with twelve stamps.

With his great success, Peck purchased a prime piece of hillside property with a stunning view of the valley and the breathtaking Rocky Mountains in the distance. It was here that he and his sons built a fine, modest four-room wood-framed home. Satisfied with his prospects and feeling optimistic about the future, Peck sent for his wife, Mary Grace Parsons Peck, and their daughters in 1862. The arrival of Mrs. Peck brought a sense of charm and warmth that James Peck welcomed wholeheartedly. She decorated her new mountain home with the nice maple, oak, and walnut furniture as well as the china, silver, and linens that she had brought from Chicago. Their home, the finest in Empire, became the place where eastern mine investors and associates of Mr. Peck stayed.

Soon word spread of the Peck hospitality, as well as their kindness and generosity. With the home's growing popularity, Peck added a stone foundation and a second story. The stairway banister was hewn from a single pine tree.

James and Mary Peck opened their home to travelers, who fondly referred to it as The Peck House. The name stuck. As more travelers arrived in the area, The Peck House also served as a stage stop on the Georgetown–Middle Park run over Berthoud Pass and the four-mile run over Union Pass to Georgetown. As a stage stop, The Peck House was hailed as "one of the finest hostelries of its day—a landmark of hospitality, comfort and good living."

Guests at The Peck House have enjoyed the inviting front porch and views of mountain scenery for 150 years.

Photo courtesy of hotel proprietor, Sally St. Clair

Emma Shepard Hill wrote of her adventures as a young girl who arrived with her family in Empire in 1864. Traveling for several months across the wind-driven plains, the Hill family arrived at their destination and the hospitality of The Peck House. Emma recounted the story in her 1928 book, *Empire City in the Sixties*:

```
The welcome received upon our arrival
at Empire has lingered in my memory to
this day. A large living room with open
fireplace, piled high with blazing logs,
dimming the light of the several kerosene
lamps, and a glimpse into the room beyond
where a bounteous meal was spread on a
table; a real table, around which one
could sit in a real chair, not on a box or
a wagon seat as we had done for the past
ten weeks.
```

Emma's recollections also included that James Peck helped in the purchase of the "story and a half log house" that she and her family lived in after they arrived in Empire. Such was the kindness and generosity of James Peck and his family.

Glory Days

By 1872, mining in the Empire area was in an economic slump. James and Mary Peck suffered as well. For years, they had welcomed travelers to their home. In an effort to increase their income, they turned The Peck House into a fine mountain hotel. The Peck House was remodeled, updated, yet still offered the same hospitality the Pecks' were known for, but now for a modest charge.

A new two-story section extended the length of the house. Peck added a veranda that wrapped around the front of the hotel. There, guests could take in the incredible mountain views that had always been one the great features of The Peck House.

The hotel was equipped with running water made possible by thousands of one-inch pieces of aspen trees. By hollowing out the pieces with a hot poker and linking them together, Peck created a wooden pipeline that ran from a nearby spring to the hotel. Running water was a luxury in a town where everyone carried buckets to a hundred-foot well in the middle of town to draw their daily water.

Electricity was another luxury. Peck designed and built a waterwheel and a powerhouse to supply electricity not just for The Peck House but for the entire town of Empire. At night the front porch lit up with red, white, and blue lights, creating a festive setting for grand parties. When the lights at The Peck House went out, the town fell dark.

Three times a day, Mrs. Peck and her daughter-in-law prepared meals and served them in the large dining room on the main floor. To announce mealtime as well as stage arrivals, a large ship's bell rang out from the veranda. Meals cost from forty cents to a dollar. The Peck House, always popular in town, soon became well known across the northern mountain mining region.

Over the years, James Peck was postmaster and mayor of Empire. Then in 1880, he died from complications of injuries he sustained when thrown from his buggy while crossing Union Pass. His eldest son, Frank, moved from Georgetown to join his mother in operating the hotel. The younger Peck wasted no time in making improvements, building another addition that included entertainment rooms.

The original four-room house, on the west side of the hotel, became the kitchen and bar, and another two-story, side-gabled section added twelve more guest rooms upstairs. On the main floor, a billiard room, a library, and a women's parlor room offered entertainment and relaxation. With a shiny white paint job, the long two-story clapboard hotel was very attractive and brought in even more guests to the fashionable Peck House.

Guests signing the black oilcloth register (on display today) included General Grenville M. Dodge, a Civil War Union army officer, US congressman, railroad executive, and one of the founders of the General Mills Corporation. Two other Union army officers, General William Tecumseh Sherman and General John A. Logan, stayed at the hotel as did the great American showman Phineas T. Barnum.

By 1882 a telephone had been installed in the hotel, adding to the amenities of the glamorous atmosphere. One night in Georgetown, located four miles away on the other side of Union Pass, the townspeople gathered around the receiving end of a telephone call to dance and cheer the sounds of the Silver Coronet Band playing on the front porch of The Peck House.

The 1898 Empire Business Directory printed this description of the hotel:

```
Peck House Has water piped through the
house and is supplied with electric lights
and long distance telephone. Middle Park
Stage for Hot Sulphur Springs and Grand
Lake leaves the House daily.
```

The Rest Is History

In the 1940s, the last of the Peck family passed away. After nearly ninety years of family ownership, The Peck House was sold in 1955 to two Colorado gals who brought a proud heritage of their own to the hotel. They were Margaret Collbran and Louise Harrison, granddaughters of Adolph Coors, the founder of the Coors Brewery in Golden.

The women, with their energy and lofty ideas, are largely responsible for the many restorations that hotel guests enjoy today. Everything was updated, from electrical wiring to plumbing, and private bathrooms were added. Extensive restoration enlarged many of the guest rooms, and a new kitchen and dining room were added to the west wing. The hotel was renamed Hotel Splendide, after an establishment that author Sandra Dallas described as a "grand imitation of its former fashionable self" in her 1967 book, *No More Than Five in a Bed.*

An article in a 1956 issue of the *Georgetown Courier* described the newly decorated hotel this way:

```
Going back thru the hall into the formal
dining room—it was the ladies' parlor room
in the old days—you admire the gold-leaf
frame of the mirror, and the walnut tables.
Then you enter the Ice Cream Parlor Café.
The theme set by the candy-striped pink and
white wallpaper and the genuine ice cream
tables and chairs is cool and delightful.
```

In 1980 Gary and Sally St. Clair honeymooned at Hotel Splendide. Enchanted, they returned each year, and in 1984 they purchased the property. They paid $300,000 for the hotel, making this one of the largest real estate transactions ever recorded in Clear Creek County. Just as James Peck had brought his three teenage sons to Empire in 1864, the St. Clairs brought their three teenage children to the hotel more than a century later.

The St. Clairs did their own renovating, adding bathrooms and a large hot tub. They restored furniture, replaced carpet in period-correct style, and added a lovely landscape full of wildflowers as well as a large garden where herbs and vegetables are grown for the freshly prepared meals. Most importantly, the name The Peck House was restored.

Photo courtesy of hotel proprietor, Sally St. Clair

Today, the interior of The Peck House conveys the Victorian charm of yesteryear.

The Hotel Today

For more than thirty years now, the St. Clairs have succeeded in providing tradition and pride as well as the hotel's historic qualities and service as did the original owners, the Pecks. The elegance of yesteryear is evident in the ten antique-filled guest rooms, with no televisions or telephones, and a parlor room for visiting or reading. The Garden Room features the maple bedroom suite that belonged to Mary Peck and an antique footed bathtub; the room has a separate entrance leading to the gardens. The Governor's Quarters, an elegant parlor-style room has a reading corner and a beautiful mountain view. Several of the rooms on the second floor share a hall bathroom, another feature that will take you back in time. The dining room offers award-winning dishes including Raspberry Duck and Steak Béarnaise, all prepared by Gary St. Clair.

As Emma Shepard Hill stated so eloquently, The Peck House remains a place to rest, enjoy the simple life, and take in the beauty of the Rocky Mountains at a place that was once a pioneer on the frontier.

Today, as Colorado's oldest landmark hotel, there is little doubt the tradition and history will continue.

FUN FACTS

- In 1872, The Peck House was the first establishment in the area to have running water.

- The telephone installed in The Peck House in 1882 was the first in Empire.

- The globe lights adorning the hall and cocktail room are the original gas jets that provided the light for the Colorado State Capitol and are decorated with the state seal and motto.

- The historic hotel register contains the signature of Ulysses S. Grant, Civil War Commander of the Union Army and the 18th President of the United States. However, there is no official record of Grant ever visiting Empire or the hotel.

- In 1885 the Pecks' fourteen-year-old granddaughter, Gracie, died of tuberculosis in the hotel. Since then, guests and employees of the hotel have reported hearing strange noises and feeling a ghostly presence and restless spirits in the hotel, particularly in room 5.

Contact Information: The Peck House, 83 Sunny Avenue, Empire, Colorado 80438 www.thepeckhouse.com 303.569.9870

THE CLIFF HOUSE - 1874
OVERFLOWING WITH CHARM

Native American tribes—primarily the Ute, Cheyenne, Lakota, Shoshone, and Comanche—headed into the foothill valleys and box canyons at the base of Pikes Peak every spring to enjoy great hunting. They had long called this land home. Before traveling up Ute Pass, the trail they had made, they paused for spiritual guidance and rejuvenation at the sacred boiling waters that flowed up from the ground in what is now Manitou Springs. They believed these waters held spiritual powers. For centuries, the Utes had regarded the area with the boiling springs sacred and named it Manitou, meaning "great spirit." This was the site of all things spiritual, all things holy to the Indian culture.

A sense of enchantment awaits visitors to The Cliff House at the foot of Pikes Peak in Manitou Springs.
Landmark Register: NR 5EP.192

Into this Indian sacred land of the Manitou and Shining Mountain, later renamed Pikes Peak by the white man, came explorers, trappers, traders, and eventually, settlers. The main trail used by these men was the trail made by the Ute Indians, which is today called Ute Pass. Following a few famous westward expeditions such as Lewis and Clark in 1803 and Lieutenant Zebulon Montgomery Pike's southwest exploration in 1806, a steady stream of explorers and travelers, including John C. Fremont, the "Pathfinder of the West," passed through the area on what is now known as Fremont's Trail. Reports of the spring waters and their medicinal qualities brought many travelers, including frontiersman Daniel Boone's grandson, Colonel A. G. Boone, who spent the winter of 1833 in the area specifically for the natural spring waters.

The Beginning

In 1858, gold was discovered in the Rocky Mountains and the great slogan "Pikes Peak or Bust" brought a whole new round of prospectors and settlers to the area of the Manitou waters, despite the fact that the main gold strikes were a few mountain peaks to the north and west. A few stayed and made the area home.

By 1868, general interest in both the area and the natural mineral waters brought a surveying crew for the Kansas Pacific Railway. Leading the group was Civil War veteran General William Jackson Palmer and his right-hand man, Dr. William A. Bell. The duo realized the advantages of the region and the obvious draw of the natural spring waters. By 1872, Palmer had formed the Fountain Colony and began drawing up plans for the future town of Colorado Springs. Bell, meanwhile, built a home up Ute Pass and soon began buying large plots of land, planning his own layout of a town. Bell first called the health resort he envisioned Villa La Fonte, then La Font, but the name Manitou Springs finally prevailed.

Built in 1874, The Cliff House originally welcomed guests who sought cures and better health in the bubbling springs nearby.

> At La Fount [sic], near Colorado City,
> Governor Hunt is building a handsome
> cottage. The place really has greater
> attraction than Mount Washington.
> — *The Greeley Tribune*, September 13, 1871

On a hill overlooking the new town, a boardinghouse with twenty rooms was built to serve the travelers along the stage line between Colorado City and Leadville. The owners, listed in the 1876 Manitou Business Directory as Maison Doree and Numa Vidal, called their establishment The Inn. When it opened in May 1874, travelers, trappers, and hunters enjoyed quiet evenings on one of the many porches or relaxing games of pool in the billiard hall. Hotel furnishings consisted of handmade log furniture and a few blankets in the sleeping rooms, although buffalo hides kept the guests warm on winter nights.

Business for both The Inn and the stage line greatly improved with the silver strikes in Leadville in 1876. As more and more miners traveled through, tents were often erected on The Inn's grounds to handle the overflow of guests. Soon, mine owners traveling on the stage line stopped at the hotel as well. Many invested in the growing town and health resort of Manitou Springs. New enterprises, including water bottling, as well as the railroad brought even more business to The Inn.

Glory Days

Edward Erastus Nichols was one of many to take advantage of the crisp, clean mountain air and healing spring waters during the 1870s in Manitou Springs. Stricken with tuberculosis, he spent considerable time at the new mountain resort town, taking in the air and the natural waters. When his illness went into remission, he remained in Manitou Springs and made it his home. He became active in the community and served several terms as mayor.

In 1886 Nichols bought The Inn and renamed it The Cliff House. When the Denver & Rio Grande Railroad arrived in Manitou Springs, travelers and a new group known as tourists stayed at the enlarged Cliff House, which had become a resort hotel. Interest in the town's ancient mineral springs began to increase. The fresh cool water tasted good, and the high concentration of minerals had a proven healing benefit for the body and soul. Nichols, realizing the advantage of a new tourist trade, capitalized on the sparkling waters. He advertised the Cliff House location as "within a few yards of those wonderful mineral springs, Shoshone, Navaho, Manitou, and Comanche."

His success led to a massive expansion of The Cliff House that elevated it to national prominence. A wing was added to each end, extending the number of guest rooms to fifty-six. Further expansion included a beautiful four-story sandstone building complete

with all the modern conveniences, minus the buffalo hides for warmth. Visitors and guests were greeted by an inviting cast-iron water fountain in the front entrance. The stunning lobby, with high arched doorways and windows, brought in the natural light, gracing the dark Victorian furniture. Long, stretching verandas provided exquisite views of the mountains.

Guests of The Cliff House received personalized attention expected of a premier resort. Entertainment and relaxation were provided by a library, billiard room, sitting rooms for the ladies, and smoking rooms for the gentlemen. The enormous dining room, which seated four hundred, had a large brick fireplace and served nightly formal dinners followed by dessert and friendly conversation. Concerts were held on the grounds each evening, after which the guests were encouraged to cross the street to the natural Soda Springs for a glass of fresh spring water as a nightcap.

Within ten years, Nichols had made The Cliff House the most popular hotel in the Colorado Springs region. Over the next ten years, the hotel gained worldwide recognition. It attracted guests such as famed photographer William Henry Jackson, P. T. Barnum, J. Paul Getty, Theodore Roosevelt, Thomas Edison, F. W. Woolworth, Charles Dickens Jr., Henry Ford, Clark Gable, and Ferdinand, the crown prince of Austria.

Always looking to improve both The Cliff House and the town of Manitou Springs, Nichols partnered with Oliver H. Shoup (who would later be elected Colorado's governor) in 1914 to form the Manitou Bath House Company, which provided private accommodations for those seeking medicinal cures from the benefits of the natural spring waters. The new Queen Anne–style structure brought folks from all over the country, seeking a natural cure for many afflictions. Dr. Harriet Leonard, who specialized in Russian vapor baths, served as the resident physician at the Bath House for several years. In turn, The Cliff House received the benefit of an increased guest registry. The hotel was once again expanded and remained a popular resort well into the twentieth century.

The Rest Is History

Over the next thirty years, Nichols expanded the hotel into a fine resort, with two additional dining rooms, a ballroom, two hundred guest rooms, and eighty-six private bathrooms. During the summer tourist season, entire families arrived with wardrobe trunks and spent the summer at The Cliff House. A story is often told of hotel bellboys who would walk to the spring and return with bottles of natural mineral water to fill the glasses of guests. Hack drivers offered buggy rides to local sights such as Pikes Peak, Garden of the Gods, and Cave of the Winds.

Nichols and his son, E. E. Nichols Jr., successfully ran The Cliff House for nearly seventy years. Through the economic downturns of the late nineteenth century, The Cliff House remained a steady enterprise in Manitou Springs. However, with the death of E. E. Nichols Jr. in 1945, the hotel was sold and went through a series of owners for several years.

In 1981, James S. Morley, a California real estate developer, bought The Cliff House with the intention of turning it into residential housing. However, the hotel suffered a major fire in March 1982. The water damage from the fire was severe: floors were ruined, walls were warped, plumbing was damaged, and furnishings were lost. Because The Cliff House was on the National Register of Historic Places, immediate action was taken to preserve the structure.

The Hotel Today

Historic Preservation, Inc. and local citizen groups voiced their desire to restore the historic hotel. In 1997, Morley committed $9 million to extensive restoration, preserving the hotel's Victorian architecture and charm while incorporating state-of-the-art technology and amenities.

Today, the hotel's beautiful restoration work in the four-and-a-half story building is evident in the fifty-five guest rooms that boast, among other things, bathrooms with towel and toilet seat warmers. Several oil paintings were hung in the dining area, depicting distinctive geological features of the Pikes Peak region.

Courtesy of The Cliff House Collections

The Buffalo Bill Room is one of the many western theme rooms at Cliff House.

The Cliff House stands today, still offering spectacular views of Pikes Peak and the Rocky Mountains, with first-rate modern accommodations and services.

Indeed, the past remains in The Inn, now brought forward with modern conveniences

in The Cliff House. Seventeen celebrity-themed suites are named for one of the many famous historic personalities who stayed at The Cliff House during its nearly 140-year existence. Included are rooms named for Henry Ford, Thomas Edison, Clark Gable, and Buffalo Bill Cody (which is a tipi-style suite). All guest rooms have complimentary wireless Internet, cable television, and DVD players, with free DVDs in the hotel library. Suites are available with the choice of either a double spa tub or a stream shower with body sprays. The hotel also offers a sauna room, an exercise room, and a swimming pool.

FUN FACTS

- There are seven springs in Manitou Springs, all close to Fountain Creek, which flows through the town. They were created during the same geological eruption that brought about Pikes Peak. Water from natural aquifers deep below the ground's surface rises naturally, absorbing minerals in high concentrations. As the water bubbles to the surface, the sulfur-like smell meets the air, caused by high levels of carbonic acid, creating the natural carbonation.

  The Cliff House at one time had underground tunnels leading from the hotel to the natural spring spa across the street.

- Horace and Augusta Tabor camped in Manitou Springs on their wagon journey to Oro City (later Leadville) and eventual riches in silver mining.

- Beginning with the Pikes Peak gold rush of 1859, and continuing through the next ten years, the soda springs and surrounding valley were purchased through various land deals by nearly a dozen people, including the infamous Colonel John M. Chivington, who led the Sand Creek Massacre. Chivington believed he was a victim of land fraud and took his case to court, eventually losing the case. Not satisfied, he took the case to the Colorado Supreme Court, where he again lost in 1886.

- When the Denver & Rio Grande Railroad arrived in Manitou Springs in 1882, former president Ulysses S. Grant dedicated the railroad depot.

Contact Information: The Cliff House at Pikes Peak
306 Canon Avenue, Manitou Springs, Colorado 80829,
www.thecliffhouse.com 719.785.1000 or 888.212.7000

Grand Imperial Hotel – 1883
Silver Queen of the Rockies

Photo courtesy of David Emory

Colorado territory west of the Continental Divide belonged to Mexico until 1848, when it was ceded to the United States following the Mexican War. The divide, some 7,500 feet above sea level, is a jagged ridge running southwest through the state. It is high in these Rocky Mountains that the many rivers of Colorado are born. From peaks over 14,000 feet high flow the waters of the Platte, the San Juan, the Rio Grande, and the great rapids of the Arkansas and Colorado Rivers. The rugged Rockies are rich with minerals, ores, granite, and marble. Mineral veins of untold value run through the rock formations. They also produced hopes and dreams to thousands of early prospectors and pioneers.

Grand Imperial Hotel in Silverton combines history and comfort with spectacular views of the San Juan Mountains. Landmark Register: NHL 5SR.59

Settlements in the San Juan Mountain region, in the southwestern part of the state, grew slowly but steadily. It was a high, often snowy range to cross and, once crossed, very isolated. While experienced miners realized the potential there, others claimed the area "did not look right for gold." Eventually, a few gold mines did make a promising profit, but it was the discovery of silver that brought a throng of prospectors to the San Juans. The 1870s became Colorado's silver era, with mining camps springing up across the range. The San Juan Mountains seemed to open up and pour forth their

riches. Places like Ouray and Silverton became legendary as they made millions and millionaires.

The Beginning

Nestled in the San Juan Mountains, Silverton's abundant caches of silver ore caused a massive population boom by 1874. In the early years, Silverton, as with many mountain mining towns, was a clash of cultures. Miners headed to Blair Street every Saturday night. Lined with saloons and bordellos, Blair Street became the most infamous mountain red-light district in all of Colorado. The town depended on miners spending their time and, more importantly, their money there, and so it tolerated the business nature of Blair Street. As the population grew and businessmen and even miners thought of raising families in Silverton, the town began a slow and steady change.

Silverton grew with a sense of optimism and confidence about the future not typically found in most early mining towns. This positive attitude led to churches and schools being given the same importance as the businesses. All were prominent and successful within two years of Silverton's beginnings. However, there seemed to be a lack of suitable lodgings for travelers.

James Hague, a well-regarded engineer, later recalled, "In this comfortless place there was no decent spot to stop in at a hotel."

The elegant lobby of the Grand Imperial Hotel is inviting, warm and cozy.

By 1880 the rooming accommodations in Silverton had improved, but not by much, according to Eben Olcott, a mining engineer, "They think you are stuck up if you ask for a bed alone, not to say a room. They open their eyes at your wanting any better place to wash than the common sink of their office."

That was about to change when an Englishman named William S. Thomson arrived in Silverton. Thomson had interests

in the nearby Martha Rose Smelter. So taken was he with the little mountain hamlet that he told the *San Juan Herald*, "I became convinced that Silverton is the best town in southern Colorado." Noting the opportunities in the bustling mining town, and the obvious lack of a fine hotel to attract visitors and investors, Thomson set about building what he called the Thomson Block. A common commercial real estate practice in small communities, the long business block would incorporate various businesses on the main floor, while providing hotel accommodations for the visitors and travelers in the upper stories.

The effort cost Thomson $60,000, an astounding amount at the time. The building was located on Greene Street, Silverton's main commercial thoroughfare, and constructed of locally quarried stone. Designed by John Griswold, the square-cut Thomson Block rose three stories on the corner lot. The first floor was inviting, with a grand entrance facing Greene Street and large French-style plate glass windows. The second story, faced in brick, was complemented with a row of arched windows all around the building, while the third story capped the building with diamond-patterned sheet metal featuring rounded dormers.

Entering the building through a beautiful door with a doorknob bearing the Colorado state seal, visitors stepped into a lobby decorated with fine paintings on walls colored in cream and dark brown. Next to the lobby was the elaborate dining room decorated with marble-topped sideboards and imported carpets. The remainder of the first floor was occupied by businesses, including a dry goods store, a gentleman's clothing store, and two hardware stores. There were more offices on the second floor, including doctors and lawyers, and the local telephone company. Later, officials of San Juan County operated from rooms located on the second floor for many years before the courthouse was constructed in 1907.

The second floor contained the Imperial Hotel sleeping rooms, featuring eighteen large, extravagantly decorated guest rooms, including one known as the bridal suite. On the third floor, an additional thirty-eight guest rooms accommodated the traveling public. Three bathrooms, advertised as "easily accessible," served the entire hotel, with hot and cold water available.

Glory Days

With the overwhelming success of the new hotel and the grand opening in the summer of 1883, the hotel was dubbed "The Grand Hotel." It wasn't long before mining engineers, such as Eben Olcott, local miners, and even Silverton's mine owners were staying at the Grand Imperial Hotel.

The hotel's management offered a wide variety of entertainments to entice customers and please their guests. Of the many entertainers the hotel hosted, none was more beloved than the famous Miss Lillian Russell. Not to be outdone, Jack Slattery, the flamboyant manager of the hotel's most popular feature, the Hub Saloon, brought in various members of major-league baseball clubs to play exhibition ball games. The

saloon moved into the hotel in 1886.

While the guests undoubtedly appreciated the entertainment and social atmosphere, there were those who enjoyed providing their own entertainment. The saloon was the site of many a boisterous event over the years. Open twenty-four hours a day, the Hub witnessed it all—from business transactions and mining deals to heavy drinking, fights, brawls, and shootings. In 1900 a jealous fit led to attempted murder when Jack Turner shot Jack Lambert after he found Lambert having a drink with his girlfriend, a Blair Street "working gal" named Blanche. Turner went to prison. Lambert recovered, but his wife divorced him.

The elegant walls of the Hub stood guard over the magnificent hand-carved mahogany bar. It was shipped from the manufacturer in three sections and arrived at the hotel on the narrow gauge Denver & Rio Grande Railroad, where it was carefully assembled inside the hotel. Behind the bar are three stunning diamond dust mirrors, set in ornate arches, all of which were designed and shipped from France.

The Rest Is History

The hotel did a brisk business, as it was strategically located one block from the Denver & Rio Grande Depot. Miners and millionaires alike stayed at the hotel, and ate, drank, and played poker in the saloon.

However, a dark horizon loomed for this twenty-year-old mining town. In 1893 Congress repealed the Sherman Silver Purchase Act, which meant that the U.S. Treasury decreased the amount of silver purchased as the monetary backing for United States currency. The entire country fell into an economic depression, and Silverton suffered a tremendous blow when the mining industry literally collapsed.

Fortunately for Silverton and all of San Juan County, the miners were a hardy lot, full of that "can do" spirit. It was gold that originally brought the miners to this area, and it was gold that again pulled the region from the brink of economic ruin. Gold production steadily increased, hitting the $1 million mark in 1898. While silver mining remained second to gold, the ore became a by-product and still produced an admirable return on the exchange.

By 1898, Silverton mines employed more than one hundred miners. The economy was recovering, and even the *Engineer & Mining Journal*, a New York publication, noted the great improvement in the San Juan area and wrote that the "area properties were in fine shape."

One of those properties was the Grand Imperial Hotel. The hotel remained open during that turbulent time in Silverton's history, but was renamed simply, the Imperial.

The Prohibition Era of the 1930s took yet another toll on the hotel. The popular Hub Saloon was shut down, and the hotel management and even ownership changed hands several times under the economic pressures.

In 1950, Winfield Morton, of Dallas, and president of the Texas Housing Company, bought the hotel and restored the name to the Grand Imperial Hotel. After a massive renovation costing nearly a half a million dollars, the hotel décor was again resplendent in Victorian charm and offered the best amenities of the day. A portion of the upper floor, an open area once used for the county court offices, was converted into individual guest rooms.

Denver Public Library, Western History Collection, X-1751

Grand Imperial Hotel today is little changed from this photograph taken more than fifty years ago.

Now the hotel guest rooms numbered forty-two, and all had private bathrooms.

The Grand Imperial Hotel enjoyed a new resurgence as travelers and tourists from all over the country came to see the beauty of the San Juans and enjoy the charm of the high mountain town.

The Hotel Today

This wonderful hotel still carries on William S. Thomson's original concept for the building. An assortment of shops and boutiques occupies the first floor, and the Hub Saloon is a favorite watering hole. A large sunroom filled with antique wicker furniture makes a pleasant place for an afternoon of relaxed socializing. Wide staircases lead upstairs, wooden floors creak with history, and guest rooms with all the modern amenities still offer spectacular views of the San Juans.

Fun Facts

- There is no elevator in the hotel or in all of Silverton for that matter!

- Portions of the 1969 movie, *Butch Cassidy and the Sundance Kid*, were filmed in Silverton. The opening scene in the film shows the Sundance Kid (played by Robert Redford) in a poker game. This scene was filmed in the Grand Imperial Hotel's Hub Saloon.

- If walls could talk! A bullet wedged in the wall of the hotel from a gunfight in 1904 is evidence of Silverton's wilder days.

- Bat Masterson was hired by the city of Silverton in 1883 to "tame the town" of the rough elements. His good friend Wyatt Earp visited him on several occasions.

- A new bartender on the night shift in the hotel's Hub Saloon accidentally turned the knob of the safe containing the cash. The hotel bar had to borrow money to operate until the manufacturer of the safe could send a representative from Denver to decipher the forgotten combination.

- Of the many hotel owners during the Depression years of the 1930s, one was Henry Frecker, who managed to hang on to the hotel until his death. Frecker had mysteriously left his family in Victor, Colorado, decades earlier. The family thought he had died until his daughter learned she had inherited the hotel upon his death.

Contact Information: Grand Imperial Hotel
1219 Greene Street, Silverton, Colorado 81433
www.grandimperialhotel.com   970.387.5527 or 800.341.3340

Meeker Hotel – 1883
Main Street in the Mountains

With the end of the Civil War, the Westward Expansion movement brought thousands of new pioneers to the prairies and mountains of the Colorado Territory. As the wagon trains stretched across the horizon, Ute Chief Ouray knew that sharing the land was the only answer for peace for his people. On March 2, 1868, he struck a deal with his friend Kit Carson, a government Indian agent. The Kit Carson Treaty gave six million acres of land on Colorado's western slope to the Utes. In return, Ouray and his people were guaranteed that "no one would pass over the remaining Ute land." The Utes, for their part, had dealt in good faith.

In ten short years, Ouray found himself explaining to his people why they must leave their land. Gold had been discovered in the Colorado Ute Territory, and the US government was pushing the Indians aside once again. The Utes were moved and confined to a reservation.

Meeker's oldest hotel has welcomed guests for 130 years. The town was named for Indian Agent Nathan Meeker who also lent his name to the Meeker Massacre.
Landmark Register: NR5RB.985

In the spring of 1878, Nathan C. Meeker was appointed Indian agent at the White River reservation in northwestern Colorado. While a kind and generous man, Meeker proved to be a poor choice as an agent, especially for White River where tensions were running high. He had formed the Union Colony, today's town of Greeley, in 1870 with help from Horace Greeley, and he operated from an agricultural mindset. Meeker believed that the Utes should be farmers. He knew nothing of the Indian way of life and was less than understanding of the Utes desire to retain their ways.

When Meeker plowed up pastures and a horse racing track used by the Utes, a subchief named Douglas fired shots at Meeker. Undaunted, Meeker was back at the pasture with his plow the next day. This time, two armed Utes, Parviet and Antelope, ordered the plowing stopped. Meeker resisted, and the two men beat him nearly unconscious. Meeker's authority became intolerable to the Utes, and further uprisings and conflicts occurred. Meeker feared violence and asked the US Army for help.

A rare 1887 photo of the original Meeker Hotel, which was built in 1883.

Meeker's tyrannical behavior and disregard for the Utes' way of life so incensed the Indians that the conflict led to his death. On September 29, 1879, the Utes turned their anger toward Meeker and the Indian agency. In a well-planned attack, several Indians gained entry to the agency storeroom and, without attracting attention, managed to take all the firearms and ammunition. The Indians took their positions and began firing, killing two agency employees. The siege lasted nearly all day. In the end, Meeker and nine agency employees were killed. Before the Utes left the agency, they set the buildings on fire and captured Mrs. Flora Ellen Price, her two infant children, Meeker's wife, Arvilla, and his daughter Josephine.

By October 3, Ute runners had conveyed the news of the uprising to Chief Ouray, who was at home on the Tabeguache Southern Ute reservation, near Ignacio. Ouray and

his wife, Chipeta, left for the northern reservation immediately. They were met by old friends Charles Adams, a former Los Piños Indian agent, and his wife. The two couples set up negotiations for the return of the women and their children. Nearly three weeks later, Adams and Chief Ouray secured the release of the captives, and Mrs. Adams and Chipeta cared for them before their return to their families. Chief Ouray and Chipeta had worked for peace but could not stop the Meeker Massacre, or the outrage that followed, as the headline, *The Utes Must Go,* in the October 30, 1879, issue of *Harpers Weekly,* clearly shows.

In the end, because of the public outcry, the government moved the Northern Utes out of Colorado and onto the Uintah Reservation in eastern Utah.

The Beginning

Following the massacre, the army moved up the White River to the present site of the town of Meeker. Here they established a permanent military camp barracks, officers' quarters, horse stables, and barns. Then in the summer of 1883, the government dismantled the military camp and auctioned off the buildings to settlers eager to homestead. Many of the buildings were auctioned for fifty to one hundred dollars each. A few remain in use today as private homes.

One of those early permanent settlers to the area was Susan C. Wright. Originally from South Carolina, Wright made her way west as many did following the Civil War. She settled in the White River valley of northwestern Colorado in 1883. In March of that year, she was the first woman to take a homestead in the area at the base of Nine Mile Hill. Then, when the military held the auction, Wright secured a loan, backed by her land, to purchase six of the buildings, including the adobe building used as the military barracks. It took time, ingenuity, and pioneer fortitude, yet Wright's strong will and attitude held out.

Glory Days

With so many settlers arriving in the valley that summer of 1883, folks decided to turn the former military camp into a permanent town. Wright was bright, good natured, and enterprising. While working to open a hotel, she accepted a position with the newly formed Town Company Association, the only female involved with the new town building group. That fall she organized a community harvest so that everyone would have enough provisions for the long winter. She also asked everyone to bring any extra corn they had to feed the livestock through the winter. With so much corn available, she made cornmeal and johnnycakes for each family.

The town of Meeker—named in honor of Nathan Meeker—was incorporated in 1885, thanks to the fine work of future town leaders William H. Clark, John C. Davis, J. W. Hugus (a future banking millionaire), Newton Major, and Susan Wright. The town became the county seat of Rio Blanco County, and for the next twenty years, Meeker

Courtesy of Kimberly Richie and Meeker Hotel Collection.

Theodore "Teddy" Roosevelt, standing beside a wagon in front of the Meeker Hotel during one of his many hunting trips in the area.

remained the only incorporated town in northwestern Colorado. In the meantime, Wright—by this time affectionately known as "the Mother of Meeker"—opened her Meeker Hotel to the public in the fall of 1883.

As the first hotel within a one hundred-mile radius, the Meeker Hotel was a welcome site and great comfort to the many settlers arriving in the area. The adobe building, originally used as a military barracks, was modestly furnished and included a small café. Although it was a small hotel, it was warm in atmosphere and hospitality. Wright was never known to turn away a traveler in need of lodging, no matter how full her hotel was. She was also known to spend considerable time in casual conversation with her guests, often while enjoying a nice mild cigar.

Wright lost her hotel partner, Charlie Dunbar, shortly after the hotel opened. Dunbar, an avid gambler, was involved in a card game gone awry that resulted in arguments, gunshots, and in the end, his death. The following year, she gained a new partner in her hotel enterprise, joining with Simp Harp, a noted stage line operator. With this new partnership and the advantage of the added stage line business, the Meeker Hotel grew and prospered, as did the community of Meeker.

The Rest Is History

> The French glass recently arrived from Denver, and has been placed behind the bar and adds greatly to the appearance of the saloon.
> —*Meeker Herald*, July 3, 1886

By 1891 Harp had sold his share of the hotel to Wright and moved on to Craig, where he again built a successful stage line enterprise. Wright brought in her brother, Rueben

22

Sanford Ball, as her new partner. Ball had arrived at Creede, Colorado, in June 1890 at the age of twenty-three and established a saloon there. When the saloon was destroyed in the great Creede fire of 1892, Ball made his way to Meeker. The two worked very well together improving the lodgings and the available amenities of the era. Unfortunately, Wright took sick in 1892. After a long year with an agonizing illness, she died in March 1893. She left all personal property, real estate, and her beloved Meeker Hotel to her brother.

In 1896, under Ball's ownership, the hotel was enlarged and gained a face-lift of sorts. Gone was the false front, and the original building was fortified with a double-brick fire wall that Ball requested and local builder I. G. Mitchell provided. Five large arched windows now graced the second story under the engraved, arched sign "Meeker Hotel." A plaque commemorating Ball was placed in the hotel entrance. Inside, the first floor contained businesses and offices, with the guest rooms on the upper floor.

In 1904–1905, Ball added on to his popular hotel. With Mitchell again hired as the builder, two two-story wings were constructed in nearly identical style and detail. They were built of brick, and their arched windows and corbeled cornices blended nicely with the original center building. The new additions, in keeping with Ball's original design, had businesses and offices on the ground floors and guest rooms on the second floors. Early businesses included the Colorado Telephone Company, Strehlke Bros. Drug Store, and Dr. Bruner's medical offices. When completed, it was proudly called the Brick Block.

Another historic change occurred in 1918, when Ball moved the café into the adjoining Vorges Building. This building has its own history. Built in 1891 of locally quarried stone, it was originally Meeker's first post office. Later, in 1904, it became the First National Bank. Throughout the many changes and businesses over the years, the café has remained a constant business and source of pride in Meeker.

Perhaps America's most enthusiastic outdoorsman, Theodore Roosevelt loved to hunt in the Colorado Rocky Mountains. In 1900, Roosevelt was the governor of New York, but he had just been elected William McKinley's vice president. Taking a little hunting vacation before being sworn in to his new duties, Roosevelt came to the White River valley and the Meeker Hotel. He spent three weeks in the area hunting mountain lions and other large game. On this particular trip, Roosevelt's hunting party included Colorado State Senator Edward Wolcott and friends Dr. Gerald C. Webb and Phillip B. Stewart, both of Colorado Springs. The *Meeker Herald* of January 12, 1901, reported:

```
Gates Keenesburg left Tuesday afternoon for
Rifle with a swell tallyho and fours handled by
the prince of jehus Ed Wolcott, for the purpose
of meeting a select party of gentlemen who had
```

previously made arrangements to enjoy a few weeks' vacation in this out-of-the-way place. It was nearly eight o'clock last evening when the rig returned to Meeker, and among its occupants were none less than Hon. Theodore Roosevelt, of Oyster Bay, N.Y. They were at once taken to St. James rectory, where the Rev. H.A. Handel had an elegant spread awaiting them. In deference to the vice-president-elect's wishes it was pre-arranged that there would be no public demonstration, but there was a general desire to meet and shake hands with the distinguished gentleman. However, it was near midnight before the party proceeded to the Meeker Hotel, where rooms were reserved for them, and but few had the pleasure of an introduction. That the famous "rough rider" will find plenty of sport in the next three weeks goes without saying.

An early photo of the growing town of Meeker.

The lobby of the Meeker Hotel shows examples of the many successful hunting adventures in the area.

Because of his own enthusiasm for hunting, as well as the added history of Roosevelt's stay at the hotel, Ball created an extraordinary hunting trophy collection. A legacy and tribute to the hotel's history, the collection is exhibited in the lobby and throughout the hotel.

In the spring of 1923, the Ball family sold the Meeker Hotel to Mr. and Mrs. Clarence P. Mathis. The hotel's charm and history remain to this day.

The Hotel Today

The historic Meeker Hotel offers twenty-four unique rooms—single, double, or adjoining. Once guests enter the lobby and their footsteps resonate against the hardwood floor, an experience in western hospitality awaits. From the hand-stitched leather chairs to the custom-forged wood-burning stove, warmth and ambiance abounds. The dining room, decorated in western oak, offers fine food all day, and at night the original chandelier glows brightly. A stay at the historic Meeker Hotel is not only a step back into history but an experience in northwestern heritage.

FUN FACTS

- In fortifying the center of the 1896 hotel structure, Ball's 1904 expansion used some 200,000 bricks in the center of the structure. Modern replacements over the years have relieved the heavy stress.

- While most historians believe Billy the Kid died by the gun of Sheriff Pat Garrett in 1881, the Meeker Hotel register of 1889 mysteriously contains the signature of William H. Bonney (a.k.a. Billy the Kid).

- There are many stories of ghostly encounters in the hotel. Room 15 is said to be the one most visited by ghosts. Several guests in the room have reported the smell of strong perfume, while others have reported the door opening or, when locked, the door knob turning. The apparition of a cowboy has been seen in both wings of the additions, as has the vision of a young, blond child in the center building of the hotel.

- Today, the town of Meeker is a summer retreat for many Americans, including billionaire Henry Kravis and the former president and COO of Goldman Sachs.

Contact Information: Meeker Hotel & Cafe
560 Main Street, Meeker, Colorado 81641
www.themeekerhotel.com 970.878.5255 or 855.878.5255

DELAWARE HOTEL – 1886
LEADVILLE'S VICTORIAN CROWN JEWEL

Courtesy of Filter Press Image Collection

The Beginning

The rush of miners, tenderfoot easterners, merchants, and fortune seekers who headed West during the Pikes Peak gold rush of 1858–1859 brought thousands to the area that would become Colorado Territory. They were known as the '59ers, pioneers who built and shaped the great state we enjoy today. Mining became the number-one industry in the state, and rich ore strikes occurred all over the state, from Central City to the San Juan Mountains, and from Creede to Leadville. The '59ers also became the leading businessmen and politicians of the new Centennial State. The most notable was undoubtedly Horace Austin Warner Tabor.

The delightful Delaware Hotel is located in the center of the National Historic District on busy Harrison Avenue in Leadville.
Landmark Register: NHL 5LK.40

But it was William H. Stevens, a name nearly lost to Colorado history, who led the first group of miners to the area where silver riches would eventually be found. It was Stevens who figured out that the dark, dingy, slimy mud that miners had to separate from the gold was actually a carbonate of silver. But that would be fifteen years in the making. Meanwhile, in the spring of 1860, Stevens and his group followed Bear Creek to the South Platte River, then headed west through the South Park region where they crossed the Mosquito Range near the present town of Granite. By April, they located the Arkansas River, which led them to the valley and dry gulches between Colorado's highest peaks, Mount Elbert, at 14,433 feet, and Mount Massive, at 14,421 feet. They followed a promising-looking stream that yielded "color" in the water in a gulch crowded between Carbonate Hill and Rock Hill to the west. It was here that Abe Lee, a member of the group, pulled a pan full of gold from the river and exclaimed, "Boys, I've got all of California in this here pan."

W. P. Jones, a member of the Stevens' group, was one of the first to write of this discovery. After Abe Lee's find, miners swarmed to the area now called California Gulch, and soon the mining camp of Oro City came to be. One of those miners was Horace A. W. Tabor. A tried-and-true '59er, Tabor brought his wife, Augusta, and their young son, Maxcy, to Payne's Bar (now Idaho Springs) in search of gold. After a few attempts at gold mining, he moved his family up the hills arriving in the Oro City settlement, such as it was, in the fall of 1860.

While Tabor set out to mine the area, Augusta saw a business opportunity and opened a bake shop. So popular was her baking—not to mention she was the only woman in the camp—that the miners built her a cabin where she could expand her cooking skills. The Tabor family stayed and helped build the community; Horace opened a general store, and Augusta managed it and served as postmistress for Oro City.

Yet no substantial gold strikes occurred during these years, and the town of Oro City barely managed to get by. In 1870, activity in the region picked up when Stevens constructed a water pipeline in the gulch about a mile below Oro City. He was convinced that the gold in the area had to be washed out by an extensive placer mining method. He spent more than $50,000 building the water pipeline, and his operation succeeded in flushing out the gold he knew was there. However, heavy black soil slowed the process and was quite a nuisance. Curious about the soil, Stevens packed up a few samples from the bedrock and the stream underlay, and headed for the local assayer. Incredibly, the black sludge turned out to be a carbonate of lead, the parent rock of silver! Stevens' few small samples assayed at two and a half pounds of silver to the ton.

The very year Colorado became a state, 1876, a new rush to the Rocky Mountains was on. Silver! The entire area swarmed almost overnight with miners in a frenzy to strike it rich. Before the year was out, $100,000 worth of silver came out of the first developed mine in California Gulch, and a new town was incorporated closer to the major mining claims. They called it Leadville.

After sixteen years of prospecting and living on a dream, Tabor's spirits lifted with this new discovery. He moved his family to Leadville, set up a new store for Augusta to run, and became postmaster, which allowed time for backslapping with businessmen and a new venture: politics. Tabor became the first mayor of Leadville on January 26, 1878. In his one-year term, he was credited with hiring lawman Martin Duggan, who succeeded three previous lawmen, all killed in the line of duty. Duggan finally cleaned out the lawless element of Leadville before he was murdered on the very streets he protected.

Instead of prospecting for himself, Tabor occasionally "grubstaked" miners. He would supply miners with equipment and needed materials in return for one-third of any silver discovery. In April 1878, two miners looking for a grubstake walked into Tabor's store, and Tabor obliged. For nearly thirty days, August Rische and George Hook dug in the hills above Leadville before they struck a massive lode of silver. They immediately filed the claim, with Tabor's name included, and called it the Little Pittsburg. In May 1878, Tabor received one-third of the richest silver strike to date in the state. The riches poured from the mine, and Tabor soon bought out Rische and Hook.

The Delaware Hotel is on the left in this view of Harrison Avenue in the late 1930s. Horace Tabor's Grand Hotel (Hotel Vendome) is across the street.

With overnight riches, Tabor couldn't spend money fast enough. He bought up mining stakes all over the gulch, and all turned profits. Tabor was soon the richest man in Colorado. Word spread, miners and investors came to Leadville, and more mines became incredible successes, including Tabor's legendary Matchless Mine. By the 1880s, Leadville literally was shining in silver.

Among those who arrived in Leadville to make their fortune were the Callaway brothers. Successful Denver merchants John, George, and William Callaway all agreed that Leadville was the place to be. The brothers established a mercantile business on Harrison Avenue, and in 1884, they bought the corner lot at 7th Street and Harrison Avenue, with the intention of building Leadville's finest hotel. They christened it the Delaware Hotel in honor of their home state.

Glory Days

George Edward King, the preeminent architect of Leadville, was hired in late 1885 to design the Delaware Hotel. King had designed and built most of Leadville's finest buildings, including the 1880 Leadville Court House (which burned in 1942), the post office building, both the Central High School and the Ninth Street School, and the 1885

Since 1886, the Delaware Hotel registration desk has been the first stop for guests.

Tabor Grand Hotel on Harrison Avenue. King built his Victorian crown jewel, the Delaware, at 701 Harrison Avenue, directly across the street from Tabor's hotel.

Completed in October 1886, at a cost of $80,000, the three-story hotel was elegance personified. The angled, recessed, corner entrance reflected the ornate French style that King favored throughout his career. The central tower extended up three stories with fanciful segmented arched windows. The French flair, the focal point of King's design, is subtle, but according to Colorado State University architectural professor Lawrence Von Bamford, it is King's "most refined work." The cornice was crowned by the mansard roof, sectioned with sheet metal and ornamental ironwork topping the engraved nameplate. The red brick building, in the Second Empire style, contained offices and businesses on the ground floor, on both Harrison and 7th Streets. The top two stories contained fifty guest rooms graced by beautiful six-foot windows. Inside, steam heat kept the guests warm, and gas lights brightened the rooms. Each room had all the amenities of the day, and a few even had water closets. Six bathrooms, three on each floor, were available for the guests in rooms without water closets. The Delaware opened in October 1886 to rave reviews.

A noticeable improvement has taken place in the character of Leadville in the past year. During the year just ended the Delaware block has been added to the business portion of the community, and it is by all odds the finest block in the city.
— *The Herald Democrat*, April 19, 1897

The Rest Is History

John Callaway remained the proprietor of both the hotel and the business block for more than two decades. He has been described by Dorthea Hougland, who spent much of her childhood at the hotel, as "a delightful man who wore Benjamin Franklin glasses, a derby hat, and a vest with his suit." Hougland's grandmother, Josephine Feller, worked for Callaway for years.

Callaway's business acumen sustained the Delaware through the economic downturn caused by the repeal of the Sherman Silver Purchase Act in 1893. The mines of Leadville closed nearly overnight, and many lost their fortunes, including town founder Horace Tabor. Yet, the Delaware remained opened. As business slowed, Callaway simply found innovative ways to retain businesses on the ground floor, while advertising lower rates to attract guests to the upper hotel rooms.

Following World War II, the Callaway heirs sold the Delaware for less than half of what it cost to build it. Yet the "Crown Jewel of Leadville" remained in operation. A $1 million restoration was begun in 1992 by then owners, Scott and Susan Brackett, with help from a grant from the Colorado Preservation Commission. The restoration converted the fifty guest rooms into thirty-six spacious rooms with baths. All were uniquely decorated with vintage furnishings.

Courtesy of Linda Jones

Stairs from the lobby lead to rooms and suites on the second and third floors. The sign on the gift counter reads, "Yes! We are an operating hotel."

The Hotel Today

The Victorian charm of Leadville's mining days is evident in every room of the Delaware Hotel. From the elegant lobby to the Callaway Restaurant, from the stairway to the guest rooms above, staying at the Delaware is a trip back in time. The hotel offers several different packages throughout the year and hosts many events, including the popular Murder Mystery event.

Hotel tour guides relate the story of a horrific murder, with a twist, that occurred at the hotel in 1889. John and Mary Coffey and their two young children had moved to Leadville from Idaho just a year earlier. John Coffey soon gained a reputation for his drunken brawls about town, and the couple was often seen quarreling in public.

He once had his wife arrested for adultery but later dropped the charge. In turn, Mrs. Coffey had her husband arrested for assault. Police officer John Morgan served the warrant on Mr. Coffey, who responded by shooting the officer twice. Mr. Coffey was immediately arrested, and Mrs. Coffey took a room with her children at the Delaware Hotel.

On November 4, 1889, Mary Coffey entered her room at the hotel to find her estranged husband waiting with the same loaded gun he had used on the police officer. With words to the effect that he had been waiting to do this, he shot his wife in the back—twice! The Leadville police managed to grab Mr. Coffey before he got out of the hotel. Paralyzed and with two bullets in her spine, Mary Coffey died three days later. Her spirit is said to roam the hotel to this day, although guests and staff report she is seen only from the waist up.

Fun Facts

- During the construction of the Delaware Hotel, the Callaway brothers contributed to the $9,000 state-of-the-art sewer system for Leadville that began at the manhole on the corner of 7th Street and Harrison Avenue.

- Leadville is the highest incorporated city in America at 10,200 feet. The city is so cold in the winter that in 1895 the town built a structure made entirely of eight-foot-thick ice blocks. The Ice Palace covered five acres, contained huge ice statues, and was the scene of balls and special events. The Ice Palace melted with the next spring thaw.

- With his new wealth and popularity, Horace Tabor grew bored with Augusta, eventually leaving her for the stunning young divorcée, Elizabeth Bonduel McCourt Doe. Following the death of Horace Tabor, his widow, known by then as Baby Doe Tabor, became something of a tragic figure. Living alone and in seclusion at the Matchless Mine above Leadville, Baby Doe would occasionally walk to town, with her feet wrapped in gunnysacks for warmth. She often visited the Delaware Hotel and sat at the desk in Mr. Callaway's office, where she would write letters.

- The guest rooms are always changing at the Delaware Hotel since guests and antique enthusiasts can purchase pieces of the hotel furnishings for their own collections.

Contact Information: Delaware Hotel
700 Harrison Avenue,
Leadville, Colorado 80461
www.delawarehotel.com   719.486.1418 or 800.748.2004

BEAUMONT HOTEL – 1886
FLAGSHIP OF THE SAN JUANS

With the discovery of gold in the San Juan Mountains in the 1870s, prospectors clambered up, over, and around these mountains, digging for ore. Not to be left out was the beautiful basin below the red-cliff canyons of the Uncompahgre Mountain Range. Near where Canyon Creek flows into the Uncompahgre River, the first recorded gold strike occurred in July 1875. A. G. "Gus" Begole and Jack Eckles filed their claim and left for Silverton to get supplies and more men. In the meantime, two men on a fishing trip along the Uncompahgre River, A. J. Stanley and Logan Whitlock, each discovered a rich ore lode in the Box Canyon area. In keeping with the nature of their original outing, they named their lodes Trout and Fisherman.

Built in 1886, the Beaumont Hotel is still the pride of Ouray. Landmark Register: NR5OR.62

A month later, Begole and Eckles returned and soon struck ore again, this time near the radium hot springs east of Silverton. Their mining claims, which they named Cedar and Clipper, were rich ore veins, running west, under the town, to the canyon wall. This remarkable find was followed with another rich thread of gold veins they called the Mineral Farm Mine.

Denver Public Library, Western History Collection, GB-7744

In 1906 the streets of Ouray were unpaved, and saddle horses often brought guests to the Beaumont or customers to the Miners and Merchants Bank on the first floor.

Before the summer was over, a stampede of miners had converged on the mountain basin, setting up tents—men such as Captain Cline and Judge Long. These men drew up a town site, laid stakes, and marked off streets. They called the town Uncompahgre City. By 1876 an occasional wagonload of lumber arrived in town, and businesses were soon operating in buildings rather than out of tents. The first frame building, built by W. J. Benton, was a saloon but it was also where miners met to formulate the area's mining laws. These laws differed from one mining district to another in the early days. In Ouray, they were known as the "gulch laws."

While the small mining camp never experienced an Indian raid, the Ute Indians were a constant threat after the Brunot Treaty of 1873. The treaty allowed the white men access to the San Juan Mountains, but not the valleys. As tensions rose just prior to the Meeker Massacre in 1879, Ute Chief Ouray and his wife, Chipeta, paid an unexpected visit to the mining town. Ouray's reputation as a fair man and peace negotiator had preceded him. The town's residents were impressed with his manner and his English as he expressed willingness to seek peace with them.

Chief Ouray proved true to his word and to be a remarkable friend to the white man. In his honor, the town was later renamed Ouray.

The Beginning

Nearly five hundred residents called Ouray home by 1879. The mines were producing so well that the governor's office in faraway Denver took notice. In July of that year, Lieutenant Governor Horace Tabor paid a visit to Ouray, where he inspected the mines

and made a few speeches. During this trip, he stayed at the Dixon House, a cabin offering rooms where guests provided their own bedding. It was the finest accommodations in town.

Although a rich mining settlement, Ouray was isolated and lacked the cultural refinement afforded to more accessible mining communities. What the town needed was a respectable hotel to lure travelers and investors.

Colonel Charles Nix visited Ouray and came away impressed with the town and the economic wealth. He sold his Albany Hotel in Denver and, with the profit, moved to Ouray intent on building a fine mountain resort in the center of the San Juan Mountains.

Nix hired Otto Bulow to design the mountain hotel and broke ground early in 1886. The architectural design was a masterful blend of Italianate, Romanesque, and French architectural elements. The three-story hotel, built on the corner of 5th Avenue and 3rd Street (today's Main Street), was constructed with brick from Frances Carney's local brickyard, which had been established specifically for the hotel project.

Beautiful locally quarried stone trimmed the facade perfectly. The impressive Chateauesque tower, the centerpiece of the design, rose four stories and was capped with the name of the hotel spelled out and facing both streets. A weathervane with the date 1886 crowned the tower.

Construction was completed within the year at a cost of $75,000. The hotel opened in the quiet of winter, December 1886, to local guests and businesses.

The first floor storefront spaces were occupied by the three banks in Ouray: Merchant's Bank in the corner space, First National Bank, and, later, the Thatcher Brothers Miner's Bank. The local Western Union office as well as gentlemen's clothing stores also operated out of the Beaumont's first floor.

Glory Days

Taking advantage of the summer tourist season, the Beaumont held a gala Grand Opening event on July 29, 1887. For residents attending the event, it must have been an extraordinary experience. The event was widely advertised, drawing guests from Durango, Montrose, Silverton, and Telluride. Nix called in a favor from his old friend Potter Palmer, owner of the Palmer House Hotel in Chicago, who graciously sent several of his top hotel staff to help Nix throughout the opening festivities. It was *the* social event of the year in the San Juan area.

```
Altogether, the formal opening of the
Beaumont was a most propitious one and
augured well for the future of this
already widely known house.
```
— *The Solid Muldoon*

There were two entrances to the hotel. The ladies entered from the 5th Avenue entryway, while the gents entered through the 3rd Street doors. Inside, the most remarkable feature was the rotunda in the foyer. Rising all the way to the third floor, separate balconies formed an open square around the rotunda. The impressive grand stairway, made of solid oak, led to the second floor, then split into two arms reaching toward either end of the third floor. The lobby glowed with the gold velour wallpaper.

Twenty-nine guest rooms on the second floor and twenty-four suites on the third floor were furnished with the finest furniture shipped from Marshall Field's in Chicago. Several mahogany pieces were used throughout the hotel, also from Marshall Field's. The ballroom and hotel dining room were on the second floor. The ballroom was elegant. Hardwood walls were graced with French windows. A skylight laced with cathedral glass allowed in natural light in the daytime, while fifty chandeliers, each illuminated by sixteen electric lamps, glowed with light for the evening dancing, with music provided by musicians in the orchestra gallery. The dining room, with walls and ceilings of paneled wood and rosewood finish, offered the finest cuisine from a state-of-

the-art kitchen. Guests were afforded entertainment in the game room and saloon, or could find quiet time in the parlor.

From the media accolades and visitor recommendations, the Beaumont enjoyed great success. Travelers from all across the country experienced joyous extended stays at the hotel. Entertainers in the grand ballroom included Sarah Bernhardt and Lillie Langtry. President Theodore Roosevelt stayed at the hotel, as did a young engineer named Herbert Hoover, years before he became president of the United States.

The Rest Is History

It seemed the Beaumont Hotel's grand opening in 1887 occurred in the right place at the right time, as fortune came to Ouray that same year. With the arrival of the Denver & Rio Grande Railroad, hauling ore shipments suddenly became much cheaper and faster than using Otto Mears's toll road through Uncompahgre Canyon. The arrival of the railroad was a cause for grand celebration in this isolated mountain town.

An added benefit to the guests of the Beaumont Hotel was the uniquely designed carriages that provided free transportation to and from the train depot. Meanwhile, the Circle Route Stage left daily from the front of the hotel.

The beautiful grand staircase is one of the many features that make a stay at the Beaumont Hotel an occasion to remember.

Business boomed at the hotel as well as in and around Ouray for several years.

When the country slumped into an economic depression as the result of the silver panic of 1893, Ouray mines simply turned to mining gold rather than silver. An article in the 1894 issue of the *Mineral Resources of Ouray County*, read: "No greater diversity of natural resources did the Almighty ever plan on an equal area. Ouray is peerless. She will be famous as a mountain resort when many of the now celebrated places are abandoned and forgotten."

Those words proved to be very true. A year later, Thomas F. Walsh, who operated the Silverton smelter with his partner, Andrew Richardson, purchased two claims for $10,000 each in the Imogene Basin above Ouray. The claim was named for Richardson's wife. Walsh struck gold and filed his claim, calling it the Camp Bird Mine. It became the second-largest producing gold mine in Colorado and brought hundreds of miners to Ouray for work, boosting the local economy. Ouray barely noticed the economic problems other mining towns experienced.

King Leopold of Belgium was once a guest at the Beaumont. The King Leopold Suite is named in his honor and indicative of the Victorian opulence offered at the historic hotel.

The Beaumont Hotel proved to be the "flagship of the San Juans," as one newspaper called the hotel, well into the turn of the century. As would be expected, the hotel suffered economically during both world wars. During World War II, the hotel managed to stay open, but several guest rooms were closed off. Later, some pieces of the original Marshall Field's furniture were lost when the warehouse where they were stored was destroyed by fire.

Following World War II, Americans were eager to get out and about, see the country, and enjoy life. The Beaumont Hotel enjoyed a resurgence as a new wave of tourists came to town. The hotel interior was refurbished in a style true to its Victorian origins. The exterior, on the other hand, with its unique pinkish brick, was painted white. Neon signs, the fad of the day, were hung over exterior windows and doorways.

The Hotel Today

The Beaumont Hotel benefited from new ownership, a major renovation, and updated electrical wiring and plumbing.

Today, the three-story historic hotel again captures the Victorian era of the time it was built and the atmosphere of days gone by. Twelve guest rooms are individually decorated in period décor, with several pieces of the original historic furniture still in use. There are three categories of guest rooms to choose from: the Luxury Rooms, Junior Suites, and Deluxe Suites. All guest rooms provide queen beds, private bathrooms, televisions with DVD players, telephone, and free wireless Internet.

The hotel features meals in either the dining room, the bistro cafe, or the heated outdoor dining room. The third-floor spa offers guests a relaxing afternoon or evening of enjoying the hot tub or a massage. There are elegant accommodations for weddings and other special occasions, as well as rooms for business conferences and seminars. And, of course, shopping the many boutiques located on the first floor is always a treat.

The Beaumont Hotel, in the center of historic Ouray, is a testament to the history of this mountain mining town and a symbol of its endurance.

FUN FACTS

- The entire hotel was one of the first in the country to be wired in the newfangled alternating current by George Westinghouse himself!

- Several employees of the Palmer House, loaned to Charles Nix for the hotel's grand opening, chose to stay with the Beaumont rather than return to Chicago. One of the maids who chose to stay was found dead shortly after the opening festivities. Her throat had been slashed by a jealous lover. It is said that her ghost appears on the third-floor balcony the first hour of every Monday.

- Otto Mears built a toll road in 1883 through Uncompahgre Canyon, connecting the Ironton and Red Mountain mining areas with Ouray. It was a major engineering accomplishment. Later, Mears carved out an incredible cliff-hanging toll road from Silverton to Red Mountain Pass. Today, this route along US Highway 550 is known as the Million Dollar Highway. Some say the name comes from the cost; others say it is because the scenic drive is worth a million dollars.

- Frances Carney's brick company, located on 5th Street, sat near an unknown hot spring. While digging clay for brick making, Carney discovered the hot spring, which was later developed into the hot spring resort it is today.

- In 2003 the Beaumont Hotel received the Governor's Award for Historic Preservation, followed in 2004 by the first of four Preserve America Presidential Awards for historic preservation.

Contact Information: Beaumont Hotel, 505 Main Street , Ouray, Colorado 81427
www.beaumonthotel.com   970.325.7000 or 888.447.3255

STRATER HOTEL – 1887
DURANGO'S DIAMOND

The Silvery San Juans. With the wealth of silver discoveries in Colorado's southern mountain range and the booming railroad industry in full force a decade following the Civil War, it wasn't a matter of *if* the railroads could cross the mountain range, it was a matter of *when* and which railroad would be the first.

The Strater Hotel has been a striking presence on Durango's Main Avenue for 125 years. Landmark Register: NR5LP.304

The Beginning

Former Civil War general William Jackson Palmer and his right-hand man, Dr. William A. Bell, had successfully built their Denver & Rio Grande Railroad enterprise through the area of the Royal Gorge canyon. Palmer's construction of the railroad through this scenic canyon included a bridge over the canyon, a marvel that survives to this day. By using the newest technology, narrow gauge rails, Palmer was able to beat his competitors to the San Juan Mountains area with a new line from Alamosa to

39

Durango. Surveying and explorations revealed that the curving valley of the Animas River was lower by several thousand feet and nearer to the silver mines of Silverton than any other route. That made it the best course for the railroad. The valley also held other resources advantageous to the railroad: an abundance of coal reserves, water, and a spot in the flat brush for a railroad town and for future expansion in all directions. Railroad construction began in 1879.

As vice president of the Denver & Rio Grande Railroad, Bell arrived in the Animas River valley—which is surrounded by the San Juan Mountains—during construction to promote the railroad and establish a depot site. The town of Animas City had high aspirations of becoming the railroad center for the San Juan area. During negotiations, Bell's powerful company asked for certain land rights and other concessions, in return for a nearly guaranteed economic boom to the city. Certain that Animas City was the only choice available to the railroad company, the city fathers brazenly refused all offers and concessions from the railroad. Bell urged reconsideration, or the railroad would be forced to find land and build the railroad town elsewhere. Unfortunately for Animas City, they held firm in their demands, and Bell found excellent flat land along the river two miles south of Animas City for the new town.

On September 13, 1880, the railroad town of Durango came into being. Palmer, in addition to being a railroad builder, was also a town promoter. He would become known throughout the state for developing communities along his railroad lines, the first being Colorado Springs. He perfected the idea in Durango, where his careful planning is evident throughout the town today.

Palmer set up a town company called the Durango Trust, which included prominent businessmen such as Alexander C. Hunt, the former territorial state governor. This group was entrusted with planning the long-term future of Durango. The first plat of the town, dated September 1880, shows a grand boulevard with designations for churches and residential communities. The trust company donated lots for the first church, the first school, and the city hall building. The "main" street was the street of commerce and enterprise.

Even before the railroad arrived, Palmer and the Durango Trust built an ore smelter on the outskirts of town and developed the nearby coal region for mining. Palmer instinctively knew all of these assets would bring growth to his railroad town as well as business for his railroad.

> The iron horse arrived in Durango about five
> o'clock yesterday afternoon. A large crowd
> gathered soon after at the corner of G and
> Railroad streets to witness the driving
> of the silver spike. With a well directed
> blow by Mayor Taylor, the silver spike

```
was driven home. "This symbolizes the
completion of the city and the Rio Grande
brings enterprise and prosperity for all."
The silver used in the spike came from the
well-known mines up Junction Creek, and is
of the best quality.
```
— *Durango Herald*, July 28, 1881

By September, sales of town lots skyrocketed, in spite of inflated prices. Durango's first Christmas was celebrated by its more than two thousand residents. The following spring, according to the *Durango Record,* Main Avenue had five lumber companies, four hardware stores, twenty saloons, and ten real estate firms.

Durango's proximity to the lucrative coal mines provided employment for many of its citizens and the fuel needed for businesses and homes. Local coal mining companies provided the power for generating electricity, which in 1887, made Durango one of the first cities in Colorado to go electric.

```
The electric light is becoming popular and
should be used in every business house and
residence in the city.
```
— *Durango Herald*, January 12, 1888

One eager Durango businessman embraced the energy technology in all aspects of his newest enterprise. He was Henry Strater, from Cleveland, Ohio, and his landmark hotel would change and mold the character of downtown Durango in legendary proportions.

Glory Days

Although a few hotels existed in Durango, young Strater wanted to build a first-class hotel that would set the bar for Durango and the entire Western Slope. He purchased a lot at the south end of Main Avenue, just two blocks from the train station. With the land purchased, and his vision for a grand hotel complete, Strater lacked the funds to move forward.

What to do? Young Henry went to his father and older brothers, who pooled together the necessary $70,000 for his dream hotel. With cash in hand, Strater received the building permit. Construction began in the summer of 1887 on the four-story hotel, which took up the entire block of Main Avenue and 7th Street.

Built of local red brick, the hotel featured two oriel windows expanding two stories tall and capped with white carved sandstone arches. The north end completed the

symmetry of the structure with an ornate cornice. Flanking the Main Avenue entrance were two large display windows for the businesses that occupied those spaces. Inside, the guests walked on inlaid tile throughout the lobby, which was furnished with the finest Victorian furniture of the era. Crystal chandeliers cast a lovely shine on the ornate woodwork throughout the main floor, along with splendid carved columns, all topped with a coffered ceiling. Fifty guest rooms occupied the second and third floors, all furnished in grand style, except for one important amenity.

Due to either cost-saving measures or Strater's lack of knowledge about modern hotel design, the building was constructed without modern plumbing. The guests' private needs, then, were accommodated by a fancy three-story privy located behind the hotel. All guest rooms contained washstands, complete with water pitcher and basin for personal grooming, and a few of the rooms also contained chamber pots located in the cabinet of the washstand. They were convenient, added privacy for the guest, and were emptied daily by the hotel staff.

"A decided metropolitan appearance to the eye," announced the *Durango Herald* newspaper on August 29, 1888, shortly after the official opening of the Strater Hotel.

The brass letterbox for guests is one of many original fixtures at the Strater Hotel.

Indeed, the hotel brought a glorious Victorian charm to Durango's Main Avenue. Businesses occupying the main floor brought services to the community such as a barbershop, a popular drinking establishment, the now legendary Diamond Belle Saloon, and a pharmacy.

Henry Strater, a pharmacist by trade, placed his pharmacy in the most prominent corner of the main floor of the hotel. He promptly leased the hotel to H. L. Rice. The hotel enjoyed success under Rice's management. It became the site of local social gatherings, from women's afternoon teas or card games to children's events. During the harsh winter months, the hotel was a reprieve of sorts for many residents of Durango who did not have sufficient heat in their homes.

For personal as well as professional reasons, a management dispute ensued between Rice and Strater in 1882. Unable to remove Rice because of the lease obligations, Strater boldly built a competing hotel next door to his beloved namesake hotel. Also built of brick, the Columbian Hotel was two stories tall. Business was apparently so successful that shortly after opening the new hotel, Strater added a third floor. The Columbian had a few good years, even surpassing the Strater Hotel

in the number of guests for a time.

The repeal of the Sherman Silver Purchase Act in 1893 changed everything for mining communities across the country. Economic panic hit Colorado, the center of America's richest mines, especially hard. Henry Strater lost everything in the economic crash. The Bank of Cleveland repossessed both the Strater and the Columbian.

Denver Public Library, Western History Collection, Z-4853

The opulent Strater Hotel occupied most of a block on Durango's Main Avenue and dominated the landscape in this photograph made late in the 1890s.

Despite the financial hardships, the Strater Hotel anaged to keep its doors open. That Christmas of 1893, the hotel advertised its then-famous holiday dinner, featuring a choice of prime roast beef, Yorkshire pudding, turkey and dressing, or boiled white fish. During the harsh winter, many Durango families again stayed at the hotel for the warmth.

In 1895, business partners Charles Stillwell and Hattie Mashburn purchased both hotel properties. In time, the two hotels merged into one with a total of ninety guest rooms. Great improvements were made, including a restaurant with fine dining and a carriage service that provided transportation for hotel guests to and from the train station. By the turn of the century, melodrama productions were part of the hotel offerings. These would become a favorite of locals and the new tourist trade.

The Rest Is History

The Strater Hotel's fine reputation gained prominence with Durango society, which attended gala balls or elegant dinners hosted by the hotel. The *Durango Herald*'s society writer often wrote about events there. "The cheery voices and din of carriage wheels told that all enjoyed the evening" is a typical entry.

Meanwhile, the back story, a few stories up on the fourth floor, was largely left out of the newspapers. By and large, the female employees of the hotel were good women. However, a few were known to offer personal services on the side. The fourth floor, which was reserved for living quarters for the hotel employees, became known as the "Monkey Hall," so dubbed by the traveling salesmen who hired such services.

Most employees and managers turned a blind eye on these extracurricular activities. That is, until tragedy struck on the fourth floor. A fragile young soiled dove by the name of Stella Dempsey lived there and plied her trade as a prostitute. Her lonely life ended in suicide in 1910. Stella, however, was the sister of famed prizefighter Jack Dempsey. Following her death, Dempsey arrived in Durango in a black limousine. He chose the casket and the small granite tombstone that marks Stella's grave in Durango's Greenmount Cemetery.

Several people with notable or celebrity status have stayed at the Strater Hotel over the years: Otto Mears, Will Rogers, Tom Thumb, Audie Murphy, Lowell Thomas, and General William Jackson Palmer. Perhaps the most famous hotel guest was the legendary writer Louis L'Amour. When staying there, L'Amour always requested Room 222. This particular room, located directly above the Diamond Belle Saloon, reverberated with the vibrant honky-tonk melodies from the piano below. L'Amour later said it helped set the mood for his many western novels. In fact, much of the research and writing of his epic Sackett novels were written in Room 222 of the Strater Hotel.

Restoring, updating, and refurbishing this historic hotel began in 1926 and has become an ongoing tradition of sorts ever since. That was the year the hotel came up for sale. A group of Durango businessmen, including banker Earl A. Barker Sr., organized to buy the historic hotel. With Barker's direction and interest in the history, the Strater Hotel was updated with modern conveniences, all the while retaining its Victorian elegance. Earl Barker Jr. and his wife, Jentra, continued the tradition when they took ownership of the hotel. Particular attention was paid to plumbing and adding bathrooms, air-conditioning, television, and telephones for their guests.

When it came to the décor, the Barkers elected to restore the hotel in authentic and refurbished Victorian-era furniture. The lobby was brought back to its former splendor. The lighting itself is historic. It came from the original La Plata County Courthouse.

With the new renovations, the hotel experienced a resurgence in business and clientele. Over the years, the hotel has hosted noted guests such as Robert Kennedy, President Gerald R. Ford, astronaut Buzz Aldren, and Hollywood film stars Robert Redford, Chevy Chase, and Michael Keaton, to name a few.

The Hotel Today

The Strater Hotel's Victorian charm and tradition of renovation and historic restoration continues today with the third generation of family ownership: Roderick E. Barker and his wife. As their own improvements to the hotel have evolved through the years, the Barker couple has showcased antiques, laying claim to one of the largest collections of American Victorian antique walnut furniture in the country.

Barker has given his personal attention to the renovation of the guest rooms. Each room contains flocked wallpaper and window draperies, reflecting nineteenth-century designs, including the famed Room 222, today known as the Louis L'Amour Room.

His attention to detail is also evident in the remodeling and current design of the hotel lobby, which has stunning woodwork and elegant marble and granite bathrooms. The hotel's three restaurants—the Mahogany Grille, the Office Spiritorium, and the Diamond Belle Saloon—offer some of the finest dining in Durango and have all benefited from Barker's detailed improvements.

Beyond the modern amenities of cable television and high-speed Internet, the hotel also hosts Durango's oldest continuing theater, the Henry Strater Theatre, in existence for over forty years and seating up to two hundred guests, featuring a variety of live performances.

Fun Facts

- Reportedly, 376,000 native red bricks were used to build the Strater Hotel. Who counted the bricks? During the year of the hotel construction, 1887, the cost of bricks was $4.50 for one thousand.

- Of the thirty Colorado hotels with historic landmark status, the Strater Hotel is the only one that once provided pianos in some guest rooms.

- Despite all the meticulous renovations the Barker family conducted throughout the years, they left the bullet hole in the bar of Diamond Belle Saloon untouched. It's a reminder of the wild days of the West.

- Durango was named after a city in Spain. The word *Durango* comes from the Basque word *Urango* meaning "water town."

- On the wall of the Fiorini Family Craft Memorial office—which sold Jack Dempsey the tombstone marking his sister's death in 1910—the handwritten check by Dempsey, which was never cashed, is displayed.

Contact Information: Strater Hotel
699 Main Avenue, Durango, Colorado 81301
www.strater.com   970.247.4431 or 800.247.4431

Hotel Jerome – 1889
Colorado's Golden Glitter and Glitz

For more than 120 years, Hotel Jerome has offered Aspen visitors gracious and comfortable lodging and a touch of glitz and glamour.

The beautiful mountain attraction that is Aspen, basks in the white powder of winter's glory, is the only ski resort with a rich cultural past that dates back to the beginning of the Colorado Territory.

For centuries this area was home to the Ute Indians. A few trappers began passing through the area, and for the most part, the Utes were friendly to the scouting parties that came through the Roaring Fork River Valley. When the policy of Manifest Destiny brought settlement of the West and an onslaught of westward migration, it was only a matter of time before the federal government would force the removal of the Utes. That occurred in 1879.

About that same time, the discovery of silver caused a frantic, mad dash to the hills of Leadville. It wasn't long before men began poking around the hills of the future town of Aspen. A small camp settlement named Ute City was created where the miners laid over that winter to guard their claims. The following spring, new miners arrived, boosting the population to some three hundred tough miners, and in 1880, the camp was renamed Aspen, after the colorful trees.

The gold rush of 1859 was replaced by the "silver dash" of the 1870s. If Leadville was the King of Silver, Aspen was about to become the Queen. Some Leadville mining engineers laid a few dozen claims near Aspen, then returned to Leadville to discuss the prospects. Predictions of a silver bonanza proved to be correct, and soon Aspen boomed like nothing ever seen in Colorado silver mining. During the next few years, more silver would be mined in the hills surrounding Aspen than anywhere else in the United States.

Almost from the beginning, the men who helped create Aspen had visions of a great town, not just another mountain mining camp. Few men had this sort of vision. Aspen had three of them: Henry B. Gillespie, a college graduate and accountant; B. Clark Wheeler, who came over Independence Pass on snowshoes and elicited business contracts; and H. P. Cowenhoven, a merchant from Black Hawk, who crossed the Continental Divide with two wagonloads of goods.

Within a decade of discovery, Aspen became the richest silver camp in the world and overtook Leadville as the leading commercial center between Denver and Salt Lake City. A population of more than 11,000 enjoyed employment, entertainment, first-class commerce, and community pride. Miners were producing $10 million a year, and railroad companies fought each other in court for the right-of-way to Aspen's silver lodes.

When Jerome B. Wheeler came to town, he saw the need for culture and built an opera house and a grand hotel complete with a ballroom, a greenhouse, and a gourmet chef from Paris. He called it the Hotel Jerome. Thus began Aspen's glittering era.

Courtesy of Hotel Jerome

The lobby of the Hotel Jerome is especially inviting on cold Rocky Mountain nights.

The Beginning

Jerome B. Wheeler first arrived in the ambitious mining camp of Aspen by stage in the spring of 1883. From his very arrival, Aspen's future was set on a course of commerce and prosperity. Historians say Wheeler's contributions to Aspen were the most important in the history of the camp's transformation to town status. In fact, if there was ever an example of one individual changing and shaping the future of a community, Wheeler was that man.

One of the luxurious suites offered at the Hotel Jerome.

A native of New York, twenty-year-old Wheeler enlisted in the Sixth New York Cavalry at the outbreak of the Civil War. By the end of the brutal war, he had served well and was brevetted to colonel of the cavalry. Colonel Wheeler then began his career in business, eventually entering into full partnership in Holt & Company, a leading flour manufacturer. In 1870, he married Harriet Macy Valentine, the niece of Randolph H. Macy, founder of Macy's Department Store, the largest department store in New York state and eventually the country. Following a series of family deaths—including the store's founder and Harriet's brother, Robert Macy Valentine—Wheeler became a partner in the family firm. Macy's flourished, and Wheeler made his fortune.

Looking to invest his income, Wheeler set his sights on the ore mining bonanza in the mountains of Colorado. In Aspen, he saw opportunities not only to invest in mining, but also to use his talents and capital in developing a real town. He accomplished both. He bought controlling interests in several mines and took on the completion of a much-needed ore smelter. With the completion of the new Aspen Mining and Smelting Company in the fall of 1884, Wheeler had invested more than half a million dollars in Aspen and its future. Yet he wasn't done. Next, Wheeler would bring a touch of European culture to Aspen with an opera house and a world-class hotel, which he would name the Hotel Jerome.

Wheeler purchased a corner lot at Aspen's Main and Mill Streets, which was the town's most favored business location (then and now). Construction began in May 1889 on the three-story hotel for $60,000. Another $40,000 would go for furnishings before completion. In the end, the Hotel Jerome would cost more than $100,000. The

somewhat box-shaped exterior, built of sandstone and a locally quarried pinkish brick, extended nearly half a block. The many windows, set within recessed rounded arches on the upper two floors on both sides of the hotel, are distinct.

The hotel was quite an accomplishment of architectural design, construction, and technology, given the logistics of getting materials to the remote mountain area at that time. The Hotel Jerome was one of the first buildings in the West to be fully lit by electricity. The lobby shone with bright lighting and polished oak and marbled floors. The Main Street entrance opened to a lovely twenty-foot-wide vestibule underneath a colorful cathedral glass rotunda with a lighted shaft. Steam heat throughout the hotel, and hot and cold running water in the fifteen bathrooms, were plumbing marvels of the era.

On the west end of the main floor was the elegant dining room, with sparkling china, crisp linen tablecloths, and—beyond the double doors—a serving room and a large, fully equipped kitchen. At the east end of the vestibule was an elegant and quite comfortable ladies reception room, and next to that was a large library, both of which had Victorian carpets and frescoed walls. The main floor also included a barroom and a billiard room, with tables delivered by famed billiard and bowling manufacturer, Brunswick and Balke.

From the rotunda area, two broad flights of finished hardwood stairs led to the second story and a fourteen-foot-wide main hallway. Two parlor rooms with mantled fireplaces and connected by sliding doors, invited guests to relax and visit, or to enjoy music from the pianist at the grand piano. On either side of the parlors, and along the Main and Mill Street sides, guests were treated to relaxed luxury in the ninety guest rooms and suites, complete with washstands, stationary bowls, and water closets. A small hall led to the single sleeping rooms. Nearby was a landing where the elevator, operated by hand-pulled ropes, brought guests to the second floor. More sleeping rooms were on the third floor, as was a smaller parlor.

The hotel's inner workings were located in the basement. Here was the boiler room with a 75-horsepower Haxton Steam Heating Company boiler, large enough to heat the entire hotel. Kitchen storage and laundry facilities were also located in the basement. *The Aspen Times* reviewed the new hotel on September 1, 1889, prior to its opening:

```
The sewerage system connected with the
building is perfect, as are the systems
of lighting, heating and ventilation, the
latter especially. Situated as the hotel
is, away from the stables and markets of
the city, it gets full, pure air off the
mountain all untainted. The Jerome Hotel,
all in all, is one of the finest hotel
structures in the West.
```

Glory Days

The Hotel Jerome opened in November 1889 with a grand ball. It was *the* social event of the season. The banquet was an extraordinary affair, the likes of which Aspenites had never experienced. Chef M. Fonseca of Paris, the first hotel employee hired by Wheeler, presented dishes that many in Aspen had never tasted. Everyone attending dressed in their finest. The men wore black-tie apparel complete with top hat, while the women were dressed in long flowing gowns adorned with diamond necklaces, earrings, and broaches. This was the first of the glitz-and-glamour affairs that would become customary and a way of life in Aspen.

The Hotel Jerome enjoyed great prosperity as Aspen's finest hotel, especially after the Denver & Rio Grande Railroad extended its tracks and relocated the depot within the Aspen city limits. Jerome B. Wheeler's namesake hotel was firmly established as the cultural center of Aspen and continued to grow in patronage, in spite of hard times to come. During the economic depression of 1893, when Congress repealed the Sherman Silver Purchase Act, ending silver's backing of the money supply, Aspen was hit particularly hard. Nearly overnight, mines shut down and jobs were lost throughout the community. Businesses failed, and loans were called in. In fact, the Wheeler Bank (owned by B. Clark Wheeler) closed its doors. Through the economic downturn, the Hotel Jerome stayed open and solvent, due to Jerome Wheeler's business practices. The local townsfolk were a loyal bunch and routinely patronized the hotel's J-Bar, a combination bar and soda fountain.

The Rest Is History

The economic turmoil of the silver crash finally reached Wheeler, and he had to file for bankruptcy in 1901. He had already lost most of his mining interests and liquidated what he could, given market conditions. In the end, he was able to hold on to the Hotel Jerome, but just barely. A few years later, Wheeler leased his hotel to his bartender, Mansor S. Elisha, who in turn later purchased the hotel for back taxes. During the Great Depression of the 1930s, the hotel offered discount rates and fifty-cent meals. On Sundays, there was entertainment, including live music. As the depression years rolled on, the hotel stayed open but cut back on the extras. The greenhouse was removed, and the hand-pulled elevator was taken out.

Even with the population down to seven hundred, the town never gave up. A group of men began plans for a ski resort in Aspen. Snowshoeing and skiing had come with the miners in the 1860s as a necessity for getting around on foot in the winter. In the late 1930s, skiing had emerged in Europe as a new winter sport. The Winter Olympics of 1932, at Lake Placid, New York, sparked interest in Olympic winner Billy Fiske, and Aspen's Thomas Flynn, later joined by Billy Tagert and other European experts like André Roch. In 1937 the Aspen Ski Club was formed, and plans were made to develop ski trails and lifts on Mount Hayden. By 1938, a few runs existed, and a rough "boat tow"

constructed from discarded mining equipment served as a ski lift.

It all came to a grinding halt when Pearl Harbor was attacked in 1941, and America entered World War II. The Tenth Mountain Division, which included a number of skilled skiers, was sent to Camp Hale above Leadville for training. Several members visited Aspen, saw the majestic mountains and deep powder snow, and vowed to return after the war.

Meanwhile, a wealthy, philanthropic couple from Chicago came to Aspen in 1945. Mr. and Mrs. Walter Paepcke saw the beautiful mountain town as the ideal place to fulfill Walter Paepcke's dream of bringing together great thinkers and leaders to engage in intellectual and philosophical discourse. The Aspen Institute first met in 1949 and is ongoing today. Mr. Paepcke also supported the growing ski industry. He worked with ski pioneers such as Friedl Pfeifer to establish the Aspen Skiing Company and installed the longest single-seat chairlift in the world at the time.

Paepcke took a twenty-five year lease on the Hotel Jerome, formed the Aspen Company, and undertook refurbishing the historic hotel. Construction included modern updates to the plumbing in the bathrooms and kitchens, and improving the appearance of many of the parlors and guest rooms by adding antique pieces from the historic Palmer House in Chicago. Fresh paint was applied to the hotel's exterior, and the hotel was ready to greet a throng of visitors in January 1947.

In 1986, a new owner, Dick Butera, refurbished the grand hotel again. The $10 million construction project included removing, rearranging, or replacing much of the interior of the hotel. The ninety original guest rooms evolved into twenty-three rooms including six suites. Eastlake furniture, rustic antler chandeliers, sixteen different wallpapers, and Carrara marble bathrooms added final touches to the remodeling. A fourth-story addition in 1988 added seventy guest rooms. From pioneer beginnings to a rich silver boom and bust, the Hotel Jerome survived, because she never lost her glitter.

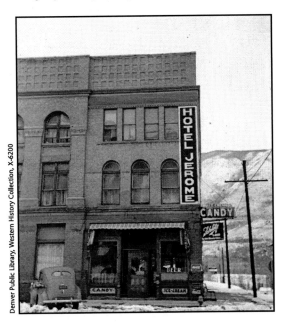

Denver Public Library, Western History Collection, X-6200

Aspen's Hotel Jerome was little changed from its 1889 construction in this circa 1940 photo.

The Hotel Today

For more than 120 years, the Hotel Jerome has remained the crown jewel of Aspen. Today, the grand lobby still welcomes guests with all the splendor and luxury of yesteryear. The ninety-three guest rooms and suites offer first-class accommodations, with modern amenities such as flat-panel televisions, high-speed wireless Internet, and twenty-four-hour room service.

The elegant historic dining room offers both casual and fine dining, or guests can enjoy an alfresco meal on the outdoor patio. The heated pool and two Jacuzzis are always inviting, particularly after a full day on the ski slopes.

Transportation to and from the Hotel Jerome is provided by a continuous shuttle service. A chauffeur-driven luxury SUV also transports guests to and from the ski slopes.

The hotel bar is always available for refreshments, relaxation, and entertainment. Top hats and ball gowns may be a thing of the past, but the diamonds and glamour still sparkle. One might even catch a glimpse of Aspen's current celebrities such as Kevin Costner or Goldie Hawn and Kurt Russell. The Hotel Jerome, an experience like no other.

FUN FACTS

- H. P. Cowenhoven's great wealth began as a grubstake to a typical miner, a common practice at the time. The transaction turned into the Aspen Mine Holdings, creating a cool $100,000 monthly income for him. Within two years, Cowenhoven's mine was the richest silver mine in the world. In fact, and this is indeed incredible, one block of silver ore from his mine weighed five pounds!

- In 1879, an ore prospector got sidetracked when he saw a bull elk. Taking aim, he shot at the animal and then gave chase up Smuggler Mountain. He lost sight of the elk but did find traces of silver in the hard ground. He staked out his claim and began his return trip to camp, when a stranger happened by. After a conversation, the stranger offered the prospector $50,000 in cash and a mule for his claim. The prospector took the deal. The Smuggler Mine became one of Aspen's richest mines and the most celebrated mine in the world when it produced the largest silver nugget ever. Weighing more than 2,300 pounds, the silver nugget had to be cut into three pieces just to extract it from the mine!

- When the Jerome Bar opened in 1889, the mining crowd flocked to the cherrywood bar to celebrate silver strikes. Although the mining boom lasted a mere ten years, the "J-Bar" has been a central gathering spot since 1889. Men would rush to enjoy a refreshing and lethal drink called the Aspen Crud, a tall milkshake with four shots of 90-proof bourbon. The J-Bar has recently reintroduced the historic beverage for those who dare.

- Several reports from hotel personnel recount service calls from guests staying in room 310. The guests always report seeing a despondent, shivering, and soaking-wet boy. When a member of the Jerome staff investigates, the boy has disappeared leaving behind wet footprints.

Contact Information: Hotel Jerome, 330 East Main Street, Aspen, Colorado 81611
www.hoteljerome.com   970.920.1000 or 800.331.7213

New Sheridan Hotel – 1891
A Golden Glory

Courtesy of New Sheridan Hotel

Today as in the past, the New Sheridan Hotel is an inviting stop for visitors to Telluride.
Landmark Register: NHL5SM.752

Rich gold strikes along the streams and rivers of the Colorado Rockies brought thousands of miners to the mountains, including the silvery San Juan Mountains. During the gold rush period of the late 1850s, a few prospectors found ore in the mountains that surround today's Telluride, but most attention was focused on the headline-grabbing gold diggings elsewhere. The majestic, isolated San Juans would have to wait their turn at glory.

It happened in 1875 when a fellow by the name of John Fallon discovered a rich deposit of silver, gold, copper, zinc, and iron near the headwaters of the San Miguel River in the Marshal Basin of those glorious mountains. When he filed the claim, Fallon named it the Sheridan Mine.

The Beginning

A mining camp called Columbia, with a population of one hundred, developed five miles below the Sheridan Mine. On October 1, 1878, the town site was laid out and

incorporated at 8,700 feet above sea level. The first mayor was G. N. Hyde. Amid the hustle and bustle of mining life, daily commerce took place on the main street called Colorado Avenue. The street was wide enough for mule trains to turn around. The long trains full of men and supplies left daily for the trip to the mines high above timberline. The local stable had one thousand pack animals available.

In 1887 US postal officials requested that the mining town change its name because it was being confused with a California town of the same name. With rich ores seemingly pouring forth from the surrounding mountains, the name Telluride seemed appropriate as tellurium is commonly found with precious metals. (Ironically, there has never been any evidence of tellurium in the mountains above Telluride.)

Telluride grew slowly but surely during the 1880s. The town became the county seat when San Miguel County was formed in 1883. By 1890 there were nearly a thousand residents. Businesses along Colorado Avenue included two grocery stores, a bank, a livery stable, a mercantile, a dozen saloons, the *Daily Journal* newspaper office, and the stage office, which had a telephone. The community took pride in its local school system, several churches, and large county courthouse built of brick.

When Otto Mears, known as the "Pathfinder of the San Juans," built the rails carrying the Rio Grande Southern Railroad from nearby Ridgway to Telluride in 1890, the isolated town was more accessible and visitors began coming to Telluride. What the town sorely lacked, however, was a fine hotel. The Sheridan Hotel filled that need. The three-story wooden building was built next to a corner lot on Colorado Avenue in 1891. Named for the mine that had brought about the fortune and the founding of the town, the hotel benefited from the travelers that the train brought to town and enjoyed success. Unfortunately, fire destroyed the hotel in 1894.

The Chop House Restaurant at the New Sheridan Hotel offers fine dining in a cozy mountain setting.

Glory Days

A German immigrant named Max Hippler and Swedish-born Gustaf Brickson wasted no time rebuilding the hotel. The New Sheridan Hotel was built in brick. The two-story hotel, enhanced with ornate metal cornices extending to the top floor, included large storefront windows facing Colorado Avenue. One entrance led to the main hotel

lobby, while another opened to the Sheridan Saloon—which featured calf-skin-covered walls and a thirty-foot-long cherrywood bar, capped on each end with hand-carved lion's heads. Behind the bar was a framed mirror extending the length of the bar. Both the bar and mirror were shipped to Telluride from Austria.

The Continental Room adjoined the saloon. The cherry-paneled room served as a billiard and gaming room. It had sixteen velvet-lined, curtained booths, each with a service button to summon a waiter when needed. Adjoining the Continental Room was the hotel dining room called the American Room, which also adjoined the main hotel lobby. The American Room also served as a ballroom. It was stunning with its mirrored walls and corner balcony where the musicians played. Built-in doors near the ceiling of both the Continental and American Rooms allowed a small trio or quartet of musicians to play for one or both rooms.

Entering the hotel lobby, guests were greeted with fine furnishings against paneled walls, including a large sofa built into the wall. From the lobby, a staircase led to second and third floor rooms that boasted electricity and central heating.

The New Sheridan Hotel, opened in 1895, soon became the premier hotel of Telluride and attracted celebrity guests and entertainers such as Sarah Bernhardt, Lillian Gish, and a young *Denver Post* writer named Damon Runyon. Bulkeley Wells, the wealthy and flamboyant manager of the incredible Smuggler Mine, threw lavish private parties at the hotel. He would often host costume balls for his not-so-secret love interest, Mrs. Crawford Hill of Denver. Wells would provide the costumes for his guests, ordering them tailor-made from Chicago. The hotel enjoyed such success that a third story was added in 1899.

The Rest Is History

As in all mining towns across Colorado, labor issues eventually became a source of contention between mine owners and the miners in Telluride. However, here it reached murderous proportions.

When the Western Federation of Miners (WFM), a labor union, was formed in 1896, the mine owners countered, organizing the Mine Owners Association (MOA). Local members of the WFM sought to gain the support of people such as Mayor C. F. "Fred" Hilgenhaus, county physician Dr. Anna Brown, and Gustaf Brickson, the owner of the New Sheridan Hotel. The local MOA members—including Arthur L. Collins, general manager of the Smuggler Mine—garnered their own supporters, chief among them Francis E. Curry, editor of Telluride's *Daily Journal* newspaper.

Members of the WFM often met at the New Sheridan Hotel, as did MOA members. On July 5, 1902, Collins requested a meeting of the union officers for the following day, a Saturday at 11:00 at the New Sheridan Hotel. Everyone but Collins showed up for the meeting. He later reported to the *Daily Journal* that his life had been threatened.

Nervous unrest gripped Telluride. Hostility sometimes led to mob violence. Following an unruly incident at the hotel, Curry wrote in his *Daily Journal*, "Such men deserve a good beating."

The streets of Telluride were filled with revelers on the afternoon of October 27, 1902. William Jennings Bryan had arrived by special railcar. From the train depot, a carriage took him to the front entrance of the New Sheridan Hotel. The large crowd greeted Bryan, and the Telluride band struck up a patriotic tune as he made his way to the platform in front of the hotel. With the backdrop of American flags and red, white, and blue banners, Bryan delivered a version of his famous "Cross of Gold" speech, which he had used during his presidential campaigns against William McKinley in 1896 and 1900. Bryan, who was an ardent backer of silver, declared, "You shall not press down upon the brow of labor this crown of thorns, you shall not crucify mankind upon a cross of gold." While his remarks were heartfelt, they had little effect on the labor wars of Telluride.

Less than a month later, the threat against Arthur Collins turned to action. On the night of November 19, 1902, thirty-five year-old Collins was shot in his office at the Smuggler Mine and died two days later. Bulkeley Wells, who detested the WFM, succeeded Collins as general manager of the mine, a position he held for the next twenty-three years.

When members of the WFM protested against hiring nonunion workers by walking off their jobs at the Smuggler and Tomboy Mines in September 1903, Colorado governor James Peabody sent in the National Guard. Heading the state's militia was none other than Bulkeley Wells. For the next year, labor warfare raged in Telluride. Saloons and parlor houses were closed, curfews were strictly enforced, and yet there were murders and severe beatings with no one held accountable. As tempers boiled over, members of the newly formed San Miguel County Citizens' Alliance arrested Charles Moyer, president of the WFM, on a trumped-up charge of desecrating an American flag. He was confined to a guest room at the hotel for six months. The town of Telluride was under siege.

Finally, on March 25, 1904, General Sherman Bell of the National Guard arrived in Telluride with nearly three hundred additional soldiers. He set up his quarters at the New Sheridan Hotel and wasted no time defusing the situation. Military troops patrolled the town, and soldiers protected the mines and the power and water supplies. The threat and presence of additional militia worked, and the labor war in Telluride soon ended. Governor Peabody sent a telegram to Bell with these instructions, "You will permit unarmed law abiding citizens to return to Telluride unmolested."

Bulkeley Wells' involvement and leadership through the labor wars earned him many enemies. When the Smuggler Mine reopened, Wells hired nonunion miners. A few years later, a bomb exploded in his bunkhouse at the mine. Wells was thrown

through the window, landing on the ground. Miraculously, he survived.

Gustaf Brickson had played a more than minor role in the labor wars. Aside from his hotel being the site of meetings, confrontations, and even the headquarters of the state militia, Brickson, in the end, supported the mine owners, even posting bail for a few who were arrested during the height of contentions.

Telluride and the New Sheridan Hotel survived the labor war and enjoyed continued prosperity.

The hotel changed ownership over the years. In 1914 an opera house was built next door, complete with a special entrance from the hotel dining room to the opera house. Upstairs, one guest room was converted into a hallway connecting to the opera house. Lovely evenings of operas and costume balls lasted until the years of the Great Depression and World War II.

Denver Public Library, Western History Collection, X-94

Telluride residents line the boardwalk in front of the New Sheridan Hotel near the turn of the century. The occasion seems to be a funeral procession.

The Hotel Today

Historic Victorian charm is still the order of the day at the New Sheridan Hotel. In 1995, more than one hundred years after its opening, the hotel was renovated. Today, the hotel offers twenty-six guest rooms with antique furniture and all modern conveniences.

The hotel is also home to Telluride's oldest bar—literally. The original Austrian cherrywood bar and thirty-foot-long mirror are still in use at what is known today as the Historic New Sheridan Bar. A first-rate menu and wonderful atmosphere await guests at the hotel's Sheridan Chop House restaurant, or guests can enjoy a lighter fare in the charming café. Evenings can be topped off by relaxing in one of the rooftop hot tubs.

The New Sheridan Hotel in downtown Telluride is a convenient place to stay for the wonderful adventures available in this historic mining town.

FUN FACTS

- The New Sheridan Hotel carries on a longtime tradition of providing free chocolate chip cookies and a copy of the newspaper to its guests daily.

- The American Room once proudly boasted of a varied menu ranging from vichyssoise to possum!

- It is most unfortunate that during a downturn in the hotel's prosperity, several of the original Victorian furnishings were sold to Knott's Berry Farm, a Southern California amusement park.

- The fabulously wealthy Smuggler Mine and the mining history of Telluride are featured in the song "Smugglers Blues" by Glenn Frey of The Eagles.

- The hills above Telluride are the site of the highest electrical power transmission line in North America. Constructed in 1891 by L. L. Nunn with help from the genius of Nikola Tesla and George Westinghouse, an electric generator and an eight-mile-long transmission line over Imogene Pass provided electricity from Telluride to the Camp Bird Mine above Ouray.

- Telluride has gone through a few cultural changes throughout its history. From hippies to Hollywood, Telluride now is home to part-time residents such as Tom Cruise, Oliver Stone, and Oprah Winfrey.

- There is an apocryphal story that lingers regarding the town's name. Some say it was inspired by Otto Mears's cliff-climbing road built on hanging shelves against the mountainside. They said the journey to the mining town was "to hell you ride."

- Telluride's claim to western history fame happened in June 1889, when an unknown outlaw and two cohorts robbed the San Miguel Valley Bank of nearly $25,000. It would later be learned that the bank robbers were Butch Cassidy (Robert Leroy Parker), Tom McCarty, and possibly the Sundance Kid (Harry Alonzo Longabaugh). Incidentally, Cassidy's brother, Arthur Parker, is buried in Telluride's Lone Tree Cemetery.

Contact Information: New Sheridan Hotel
   231 West Colorado Avenue, Telluride, Colorado 81435
   www.newsheridan.com   970.728.4351 or 800.200.1891

THE OXFORD HOTEL – 1891
THE REAL HUB OF DENVER

Filter Press Image Collection

Located just through the Welcome Arch. The Real Hub of Denver. Fire Proof, European Plan, Absolutely Modern. Rooms $1.00, $1.50 and $2.00 a day.

The Oxford Hotel, a block from Union Station in the heart of Denver's lower downtown (LoDo), has been a part of the cityscape for more than 120 years.
Landmark Register: NR5DV.47.62

So proclaimed a Denver newspaper ad extolling the amenities of Denver's grand Oxford Hotel, located in the heart of the city's business district.

The Beginning

From the dusty, busy, and often rowdy mining supply camp known as Denver City in 1859, a western metropolis slowly emerged at the base of the Rocky Mountains. Larimer Street was the central business area in the formative early years. Lining both sides of the street were shops, saloons, banks, restaurants, and hotels, including Denver's crown jewel at the time, the Windsor Hotel. Following the arrival of the Denver Pacific Railroad in June 1871, the population grew by thirty-five thousand new residents by the end of the decade. More railroads built tracks to the city. In 1881, to accommodate the more than one hundred trains arriving daily, the stately Union Station was built at the north end of 17th Street. As the new decade dawned, commerce slowly shifted away from Larimer Street.

Banks, retail stores, office buildings and theaters were built along 15th, 16th, and 17th Streets. The first commercial development was the Tabor Block, built by H. A. W. Tabor fronting 16th Street. It was not coincidental, as Tabor owned most of the real estate along 16th and 17th Streets. As a final indicator that this area had become downtown's commercial district, three major department stores: Daniel's & Fisher, Joslin's, and McNamara's all moved from Larimer Street to 16th Street.

Business boomed in this new area soon to be known as Denver's "Wall Street of the West." The need for an elegant hotel soon became a priority among Denver's business leaders including Adolph Zang, owner of Denver's largest brewery. In 1890, Zang along with other investors purchased land on 17th Street, a short block away from Union Station. Construction began the following year. Denver's celebrated architect Frank E. Edbrooke designed what is believed to be the city's first steel-skeleton building two years before he would build The Brown Palace Hotel at the opposite end of 17th Street.

Constructed in 1891, The Oxford Hotel was a short walk to and from the Union Station train depot making it the hub of Denver.

Glory Days

Zang's red brick Oxford Hotel, completed in an astonishing ten months, contained all the latest technology including its own private power plant and steam heating for

all five floors. It was built in a *U* shape and was nearly half a block long. To guests entering through the inviting doors, elegance was evident in all aspects. Guests walked across marble floors and imported European carpets graced with beautiful oak furniture and accented by frescoed walls. Silver chandeliers lit the interior, powered by gas lighting with the latest in electric wiring throughout the new hotel. Part of Edbrooke's unique design was an electric light well built in the center of the hotel, casting light in every room from floor to ceiling. Stained glass windows accented the streaming light.

On opening day, October 3, 1891, guests were treated to all the amenities the hotel had to offer. The *Rocky Mountain News* later reported, "This luxury hotel with all the latest in gadgets and technology is Gilded Age opulence."

The paper went on to describe the revolutionary kitchen area, which was located, the writer explained, "so that none of the odor can possibly permeate through the house, and is provided with a series of ranges, broilers and all the utensils known to the culinary art."

Courtesy of Amy Stansbery, The Oxford Hotel

The Cruise Room is decorated in vintage art deco style.

The spacious dining room with its inviting tables covered in the finest linen, glistened with engraved cut glassware, Haviland china, and silverware inscribed "Oxford." A separate dining room, provided for gentlemen only, came to be known as the Lobby of the West. It was here that wealthy merchants, bankers, and politicians gathered in privacy to eat fine food, drink the best libations, and relax with cigars, all the while wheeling and dealing in various business or political ventures.

Vertical railways, the term used at the time for elevators, were installed in the Oxford Hotel, the first in Denver. These strange, speedy cages took hotel guests to the four floors above where their private rooms or suites were nothing short of luxurious. Every floor included bathrooms, and many of the rooms had separate "water closets" with the latest in sanitary conveniences. From the windows of the upper floors, one could gaze out over the city, watch the sun setting over the mountain range, or look down at the daily hustle and bustle of 17th Street. Imagine watching travelers flowing out of Union Station making their way to the hotel amid the horse-drawn carriages and noisy streetcars, or spotting influential businessmen such as Adolph Zang or Colorado

governor Job A. Cooper, who frequently visited the hotel, or even Colorado's "Silver King," H. A. W. Tabor.

The Rest Is History

Built during the height of Colorado's silver bonanza, The Oxford Hotel survived the severe economic downturn when the government repealed the Sherman Silver Purchase Act, which had provided for a certain percentage of silver to back the US monetary supply. The entire country went into a depression known as the Silver Panic of 1893. Overnight, the silver mines in Colorado and across the country closed. Businesses failed, and thousands were without jobs. Due in no small part to Zang's business management skills, The Oxford Hotel survived this depression. In fact, when Governor Cooper completed his term, he bought the third interest in the hotel from a man named Mygatt, who had not fared well in the hard times. The ex-governor worked side by side with Zang, and their persistence paid off—for while banks, railroads, and mines collapsed, The Oxford Hotel persevered.

By the turn of the century, The Oxford enjoyed great gains in business as economic prosperity returned to Denver. Under the leadership of Adolph Zang, the hotel provided outstanding accommodations, two dining rooms, a barbershop, a library, a pharmacy, a Western Union office, and a first-class saloon serving the Zang Brewery signature brew.

With the close proximity to Union Station and fully equipped horse stables, The Oxford was Denver's finest hotel and its own city within a city.

In 1902, Edbrooke was again hired to design a two-story addition to the hotel along Wazee Street. It blended perfectly with the details of the main hotel. Also that year, Zang bought the corner property at 709 Clarkson Street, in Denver's fashionable Quality Hill area, just south of Capitol Hill. The three-story Zang mansion built on the property is a historic treasure to this day.

Twelve years later, a third addition to the hotel, built by Fallis & Willison, extended the property to 1628 17th Street. While this annex is the same height as the hotel, the facade is white terra-cotta.

In celebration of the repeal of Prohibition in 1933, the hotel was again remodeled. A Streamline Moderne cocktail lounge, designed in the art deco style in fashion at the time, contains a bar, booths, and the suave atmosphere of the 1930s. Architect Charles Jaka created the Cruise Room with flowing lines, shaping the bar's continuity. The walls are paneled beaverboard with bas-relief portraits of notable characters from several nations created by Denver artist Alley Henson.

The Hotel Today

The Oxford Hotel remains in the heart of downtown Denver. Throughout the five floors, first-class luxury is evident. The eighty guest rooms and suites provide

In 1894, when this photograph was made, travelers stopping at
The Oxford Hotel often arrived by streetcar from Union Station.

contemporary comfort and convenience amid Victorian elegance. Extraordinary attention is given to the comfort and convenience of guests through services including twenty-four-hour room service, high-speed wireless Internet in each room, access to the Oxford Health Club, Cadillac car service to downtown locations, and evening sherry served in the lobby. In the guest rooms, amenities include a comfy robe and slippers and nightly turn-down service of the soft, high-thread-count cotton sheets. In the morning, coffee is served on each floor and in the lobby, along with the daily newspaper. And guests can have their shoes shined before starting the day. Simple, sweet, and all complimentary!

Other services include an in-room CD player, same-day laundry or dry cleaning services, and valet parking. Several hotel packages are offered throughout the year, such as "New Year's in Style," "Romance at the Oxford," "Book Lovers' Package," and "Urban Escape Package."

Fun Facts

- Since 1991, The Oxford Hotel has had a tradition known as the Dolls' Tea Party, which is one of the most anticipated events of the Denver holiday season. Parents and their children, who bring their favorite doll, come to the hotel, where they are served formal tea with sandwiches, scones, and crumpets.

- During World War II, The Oxford Hotel was the meeting point for military personnel both departing and arriving from busy Union Station. The hotel filled with soldiers, and mothers of local servicemen voluntarily came to the hotel to serve coffee, doughnuts, and hot turkey sandwiches around the clock.

- Adolph Zang was also instrumental in buying the land and providing the funding for the White City Amusement Park, later renamed Lakeside Amusement Park. A one hundred-foot-high casino tower greeted visitors.

Contact Information: The Oxford Hotel
1600 17th Street, Denver, Colorado, 80202
www.theoxfordhotel.com   303.628.5400 or 800.228.5838

THE BROWN PALACE HOTEL – 1892
WHERE THE WORLD REGISTERS

Courtesy of Stephanie Panico, The Brown Palace Hotel

A sculpture of a cowboy outside The Brown Palace Hotel in Denver was commissioned in 2006, the 100th anniversary of the National Western Stock Show, and symbolizes the long-standing relationship between the hotel and the stock show.

The Beginning

When Henry Cordes Brown, a carpenter by trade, arrived in Denver in July 1860, he had already made and lost fortunes from California to Washington, and from Nebraska to South America. While working in St. Louis, Missouri,

he learned of the gold riches of the West and again set out to seek his fortune. Brown journeyed by covered wagon as far as the Colorado Territory with his second wife, Jane, and their infant son, James. Jane refused to travel farther, and Brown agreed to stop. In the new, bustling area that would become Denver, he easily found work as a carpenter and builder. His experience would serve him well when he sized up the opportunities the city had to offer.

In 1863 Brown took advantage of the new Homestead Act, claiming 160 acres just southeast of the city, an area that detractors called Brown's Bluff. However, a portion of this land would soon become the site of the Colorado state capitol, and a triangular piece of land, west at Broadway, would become home to the now world-famous H. C. Brown Palace Hotel.

When the Union Pacific Railroad chose to run its east-west tracks through Cheyenne, Wyoming, rather than Denver, Colorado Territory's efforts to obtain statehood were jeopardized. Brown did his part to help the statehood effort by donating ten acres of his land—bordered by Lincoln Street, Grant Street, Colfax Avenue, and 14th Avenue—to the territorial government in hopes that the state capitol would be built there. Brown, hoping to generate growth and prosperity in his city, envisioned an exclusive residential community on the property as well. The legislature accepted the gift, but nothing happened.

Several landowners in the vicinity—including former territorial governor John Evans and the current territorial governor, Alexander Cameron Hunt—donated portions of their land for the capitol site. While the territorial legislature fought over the location for the capitol, the landowners, including Brown, fought each other in lawsuits. Even after Colorado gained statehood in 1876, the location of the capitol remained unresolved. Miffed, Brown sued the state of Colorado to get his land back, resulting in years of legal battles.

In 1872, Brown bought the *Denver Daily Tribune* newspaper and served on the editorial board for three years. He was one of the charter members of the first business organization in Denver, the Denver Board of Trade, which later became the Denver Metro Chamber of Commerce. It was through Brown's influence and the Board of Trade that the Denver Pacific Railroad ran a rail route from Denver to Cheyenne, finally achieving for Denver the transportation access it greatly needed. On January 1, 1873, Brown and his partner, C. D. Gurley, opened the Bank of Denver, which operated in a ground floor space of the *Tribune* newspaper building, at the corner of 16th and Market Streets.

In the ensuing years, Brown developed the area around Sherman and 12th Avenue. His three-story brownstone residence at 17th and Broadway, built in 1875, was his finest accomplishment to date. In time, as more residences were built on both Grant and Sherman Streets, families moved into the area, now called the Capitol Hill

neighborhood. Settlement had reached Brown's Bluff, and Brown's belief that Denver would grow eastward had proven to be correct.

The economic panic of 1877 hurt many businesses and hit Henry C. Brown particularly hard. In an effort to save what he could, he sold much of his residential holdings, including his brownstone residence, to Horace Tabor for $50,000. The sale proved to be worthwhile. By 1880, Brown had successfully invested his liquidations into a personal portfolio worth more than $5 million and had become one of the wealthiest men in Colorado.

Now past the age of retirement, the energetic Brown took on the project of building a grand hotel for Denver. A colorful story is often told about his reason for wanting to do this. It is said that when Denver's finest hotel, the Windsor, turned Brown away because he was wearing cowboy boots, he resolved to build his own hotel—a hotel that would be a western palace.

Glory Days

Brown began forming his hotel plan in 1888. Because water was scarce, he first hired a team of workers to locate water and develop an artesian well on the property. The land, at the corner of Brown's Capitol Hill subdivision, was a triangular piece of property bounded by the corners of Broadway, Tremont, and 17th Streets.

Three artesian wells provided water for the hotel. A *Denver Times* article dated September 30, 1900, stated, "The deepest well still in use in the city, belongs to Henry C. Brown, and is over 1,000 feet deep." Frank Edbrooke, Denver's leading architect responsible for many fine Denver landmark buildings, was hired to design the building to fit the odd piece of land. From hotel concept to opening day would take four years.

Edbrooke's design of a triangular stone structure

Denver Public Library, Western History Collection, X-18432

When completed in 1892, The Brown Palace Hotel was the showplace of downtown Denver. This view of the hotel is from the corner of Broadway and Tremont Place.

nine stories tall began in 1890 with a solid steel framework. According to *Scientific American* magazine of May 21, 1892, it was one of the first in America to be fireproof. Geddes & Seerie, a stone contracting firm, was hired to do the exterior construction of the hotel. Colorado red granite and Arizona sandstone were used on the facade, with the three corners of the building curving, rather than being cut off diagonally, preserving the continuity of the stonework.

Famed sculptor James Whitehouse was hired to create several sculptures within the stonework facade, including a stone engraving of H. C. Brown, detailed engravings over the doors, the inlaid stone garland gracing the three corners of the building, and the marvelous stone medallions. Positioned symmetrically below the seventh-floor windows, the carvings depict twenty-six different animals native to the Rocky Mountains.

The three entrances to the hotel, one on each street, were fashioned with electro copper plated iron and enhanced with leaf designs in the grillwork.

Once guests stepped through any of the three street entrances, their eyes would immediately go to the eight-story open atrium in the center of the hotel lobby, the first such architectural design built in America. From the expansive skylight eight floors above, sunshine and light filtered down through the stained glass, which is maintained today by the great-grandson of the original designer. A beautiful, oversize stone fireplace graced the wall along the 17th Street side. Intricately designed cast-iron balcony railings on each of the seven guest floors surrounded the atrium lobby. The four-passenger Hale elevator cars were designed to complement those railings. The stairways, grand staircase, and the ladies' staircase were all built of copper-plated iron and pink Tennessee marble. Eleven open arches in the second-floor balcony—each with seven incandescent electric lights—led to meeting rooms, offices, parlors, restaurants, and bars. The lobby flooring, encaustic tile with Greek border designs, glowed light and bright from the sunshine above. The walls were stunning in their golden onyx (a semiprecious

Denver Public Library, Western History Collection, X-22067

This 1898 photograph of The Brown Palace shows the lobby, which featured an eight-story-high open atrium, the first such architectural design in America.

variety of quartz imported from Mexico) and trimmed with supporting classical pilasters. In fact, several thousand feet of the luxurious onyx graced the hotel counters, desks, tables, and the grand admission desk—more than had been used in any other building to that date.

The second floor contained the grand drawing room and separate reception parlors for ladies and gentlemen as well as several luxurious guest suites, including the popular bridal suite. The upper floors were devoted exclusively to guest

Courtesy of Stephanie Panico, The Brown Palace Hotel

The Palace Arms, one of three restaurants in The Brown Palace, offers a fine contemporary dining experience.

rooms. Each room could be occupied as a single or, by opening adjoining doors, could be a double room or even a suite. In all, the new hotel contained 400 guest rooms and nearly 130 private bathrooms. Room prices were divided into 100 rooms for $3.00 per night, 100 rooms for $4.00 per night, 100 rooms for $4.50 per night, and 100 rooms went for $5.00 per night. Because of the triangle shape of the hotel and the open atrium lobby, all guest rooms had a view of the city, the plains, or the Rocky Mountains.

An additional elevator, specially constructed for transportation of goods from the basement to the eighth-floor kitchen, in addition to a freight elevator added to the modern conveniences. In the basement, a billiard room with tables from the Brunswick Balke Collender Company, provided a private relaxation space for the gentlemen.

From the beginning, Brown had financial backers from the East as well as the influence and encouragement of local businessmen such as James Duff and Henry Wolcott. By the time the artesian wells were dug, the foundation set, and steelwork placed on the first three floors, the funds promised by the backers had not materialize and work stopped. It was at this point that Brown's brought on board as advisors a team of experts in hotel management. In a hotel coup of sorts, Brown managed to acquire the services of William H. Bush, the manager of the Windsor Hotel. Bush had successfully operated the Teller House in Central City and later built the Clarendon Hotel in Leadville, where he met Colorado's wealthiest man, Horace A. W. Tabor, eventually becoming Tabor's closest adviser. Bush became close friends with Tabor's son, Nathaniel Maxcy Tabor,

who held the lease on the Windsor Hotel (his father being a major stockholder). Both Bush and Maxcy Tabor severed their lease with the Windsor to join Henry C. Brown in the greatest hotel venture Denver had ever seen. With their talents in hotel management, the H. C. Brown Hotel would build a reputation of excellence unsurpassed to this day. The finest hotel in Denver opened its doors on August 6, 1892.

> The Henry C. Brown Palace hotel, conceded to be the finest hotel in the world, was opened last evening with a week long convention of the Masonic Order of the Knights of Templar. All business rooms on the ground floor have been engaged by various state comanderies. Every room has been furnished in the most perfect taste, the furniture and fresco work blending harmoniously in colors.
> — *Rocky Mountain News*, August 7, 1892

A formal seven-course banquet, costing ten dollars per plate, opened the hotel on August 12, 1892.

The Rest Is History

The H. C. Brown Palace Hotel, unquestionably the most luxurious hotel in the West, became known throughout the country and has secured its place in the history of Denver and America. The Brown Palace has been a favorite of dignitaries and celebrities from around the world. The hotel's slogan, "Where the world registers," which is featured prominently on menus, brochures, and advertising, grows truer with time.

This grand hotel has hosted U.S. presidents, visiting royalty, foreign ambassadors, Colorado's politicians, the rich and famous, world-famous celebrities, and rock stars. Denver's legendary con man Jefferson Randolph "Soapy" Smith stayed at the hotel on several occasions, although it is unlikely he practiced his swindling arts on the guests. Evalyn Walsh McLean, daughter of silver millionaire Tom Walsh and a frequent hotel guest, brought her jewelry, which included the Hope Diamond, when she stayed. William F. "Buffalo Bill" Cody stayed at the hotel frequently during his years with the Wild West show.

Margaret Tobin Brown often stayed at the hotel following her separation from her husband, Leadville mining engineer J. J. Brown. Hotel historian Corinne Hunt recounts a particular stay during the Christmas season when Mrs. Brown personally placed small Christmas trees in the lobby and at the registration desk. One evening, she gathered the cooks, bellhops, waiters, and maids together and presented each with a gift. Mrs. Brown

was again a guest at the hotel in April 1912, just a week after the sinking of the *Titanic*; this time, she was known as the "Unsinkable" Molly Brown.

Hollywood film stars such as Lionel Barrymore, Jack Benny, Jimmy Durante, Helen Hayes, Red Skelton, Robert Taylor, and John Wayne all stayed at the hotel. When Lillian Russell stayed, she always requested a bridal suite.

In 1905 President Theodore Roosevelt became the first president to visit the hotel. Since his historic visit, the hotel has hosted every sitting president with the exception of Calvin Coolidge. Roosevelt arrived in Denver by train after a successful hunting trip near Glenwood Springs. Following a flag-lined parade route to 17th Street, Roosevelt spoke to a group of local businessmen during a lavish banquet at the hotel.

An orchestra provided the entertainment following the meal, playing merry tunes such as "There'll Be a Hot Time in the Old Town Tonight." Caught up in the music and merriment, President Roosevelt banged the tables in rhythm and jovially sang along. His room on the eighth floor became forever known as the Presidential Suite. By the time of Franklin D. Roosevelt's stay, the Presidential Suite had taken on a new elegance with imported furniture and carpets. No president stayed at the Brown more than Dwight D. Eisenhower. His wife, the former Mamie Doud, had lived in Denver since childhood, and the couple were married at her parents' home on Lafayette Street. The Brown Palace Club, located on the second floor, served as the campaign headquarters for Eisenhower during his bid for the White House in 1952. As hectic as it must have been, the hotel staff managed all of the phone calls, letters, foreign correspondence, and the media—to the great satisfaction of the World War II general. His personal suite, now called the Eisenhower Suite, has a bit of presidential history. It seems the future president enjoyed practicing his golf swing in the suite and once hit a golf ball into the fireplace mantel. The resulting dent remained until the room was remodeled in 2000, when a chunk of the mantel with the dent was preserved in a display case in the suite.

William Jennings Bryan, who ran for president in 1896 on the silver standard—so important to Colorado's mining industry—later gave a speech at the hotel. One of the American flags from his banquet table was used for years whenever a president sat at a banquet event. Today the flag is framed and on display in the hotel.

Queen Marie of Romania, who stayed at the hotel in 1926, was given the proverbial royal treatment. A separate entrance from the hotel elevator corridor to the outside was constructed so that the queen could exit her limousine and enter the elevator in complete privacy. Other royal guests of the Brown have included the Crown Prince and Princess of Finland and the Crown Prince of Sweden. Dr. Sun Yat-Sen stayed prior to becoming president of the newly created Republic of China. President Bill Clinton stayed at the hotel during the 1997 GE Summit held in Denver, as did several heads of state.

With all the royalty and pageantry The Brown Palace Hotel has hosted over the years, nothing compares to the arrival of the 1960s rock icons—the Beatles. In town for their historic concert at Red Rocks in August 1964, the four band members insisted on staying at The Brown Palace. The hotel management, on the other hand, was not very interested in hosting the most popular rock group in the world. After negotiations, the management relented. As feared, pandemonium ensued the day the Beatles arrived. An additional police detail was sent to control the estimated five thousand fans who had gathered at the hotel hours before the rock band was to arrive. By midday, people had been trampled, young girls had fainted, and several people had been injured, including two police officers. When the Beatles finally arrived, very few in the crowd saw them. Their security detail craftily whisked them into the hotel through a service entrance near the lobby and onto a service elevator.

Rosemary Fetter, historian and author, was one of the many young teenage girls who vied for a job at the hotel that summer just to see the Beatles. She got the job, and on the day the famous rock band arrived, she was working at the front desk, waiting for a glimpse of them. Fetter relates, "Just as a commotion in the crowded lobby began, the phone rang. I never saw them." Neither did anyone else in the lobby, as the Fab Four had bypassed the lobby.

Mystery, mystique, and murder are part of The Brown Palace's history. A love triangle ended in murder at the hotel's "gentlemen's bar" on May 24, 1911. Isabel "Sassy" Springer, the wife of wealthy cattleman and former Denver mayoral candidate, John W. Springer, was conducting love affairs with two different men. Mrs. Springer began an affair with her husband's business partner, Harold Francis "Frank" Henwood. Meanwhile, she had been carrying on an affair with a traveling salesman, Sylvester Louis "Tony" von Phul. When the two men learned of each other, a bitter rivalry ensued, egged on by the goading of Mrs. Springer. As happens, jealousy reared its ugly head, and this time jealousy led to rage and murder. Following an evening at the Broadway Theater, von Phul and his friends went across the street to The Brown Palace for drinks. In the bar with a drink of his own was Frank Henwood. Words were exchanged between the two, and von Phul threw a punch, which landed on Henwood's jaw. Henwood drew a gun and fired three shots. Von Phul died that night. Two shots had gone astray, hitting two bystanders. One of those stray shots ended the life of George Copeland. In shock, Henwood yielded himself up to a hotel employee who grabbed his gun. After a lengthy and sensational trial, Henwood was sent to prison for life. The Springers later divorced.

Over the years, rooms and even entire floors were changed or adapted to the era—only to be changed and adapted again. During the booming economy of the Roaring Twenties, the hotel added a second restaurant, the Casanova Room. Created to attract the party crowds of the era, it was wrapped in glorious silk window coverings, bathed in bright lights, and featured fabulous china dinnerware, sterling silver utensils, and

white-gloved waiters. In 1934, in the midst of the Great Depression, the Casanova Room offered a New Year's Eve package with dinner, dancing, and souvenirs for $12.50 per couple. The following year, disaster struck when fire destroyed the interior of the restaurant. When reconstruction was completed, and the rooms redecorated in the art deco style, it retained the Casanova name and had a new musical stage. By 1941 it had been renamed the Emerald Room and had emerged as a meeting place for Denver society. Reinvented again in 1958, and redecorated in an Italian style, it became the San Marco Room, with weekend entertainment that included dancing to big band music and performances by the strolling San Marco Strings.

In a celebration of better times to come, the Ship Tavern opened in 1934, following the repeal of Prohibition. The décor theme was, obviously, nautical and featured antique lithographs on the walls, an old ship's clock, Jamaican rum barrels, and a mock crow's nest in the center of the tavern. Several shelves of Cape Cod sailing ship models were displayed along the walls. This collection, which is still on display, belonged to then-owner Charles Boettcher. While many restaurants and bars closed during the Great Depression, the Ship Tavern stayed open, and stayed true to the quality of product and service.

Another historic hotel restaurant, the Palace Arms, has remained nearly unchanged since it opened in 1950. Hotel co-owner Claude K. Boettcher, son of Charles Boettcher, wanted a new restaurant decorated in Napoleonic style. After considerable research and acquisition of historical artifacts, the now world-famous Palace Arms opened in great splendor. Antiques dating to 1670 decorate the walls, including a pair of dueling pistols believed to have belonged to Napoleon and his second wife, Louisa. Display cases were built at the entrance of the restaurant to showcase other artifacts, including an ornate silver centerpiece commissioned by the British royal family that dates to the 1700s. Inside, the curved walls of the private dining area are decorated with wallpaper depicting scenes from colonial America.

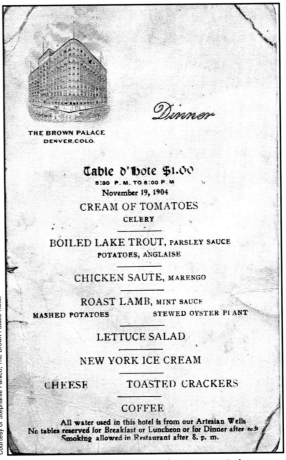

A 1904 dinner menu from The Brown Palace featured cuisine of the era at the most reasonable price of $1.00.

Other improvements under the Boettcher ownership included the addition of The Brown Palace West Tower. Built in 1959 at a cost of $4 million, the twenty-two-story annex was connected to the main hotel by a second-story walkway across Tremont Street. A natural complement to the original hotel, the addition was constructed in a stone comparable to the sandstone of the original building. Inside, the décor in the addition made use of marble whereas the original hotel made extensive use of onyx.

One room that has remained a favorite since the hotel's opening—and the only room that does not have windows—is the Grand Ballroom. This room has hosted many notable events, including the Inaugural Ball for Colorado Governor John Love in 1968, the arrival of Sir Humphrey's Hereford yearling at the Junior League Ball in 1962, a dinner for French president Valéry Giscard d'Estaing in 2001, and the filming of scenes for the movie *Lady Bugs* starring Rodney Dangerfield. The ballroom also has been the scene of more than three thousand weddings and many charity events.

The Hotel Today

The history, tradition, and elegance that made The Brown Palace Hotel famous across the globe is the same today. For more than 120 years, this hotel has been a major attraction in downtown Denver and continues to draw visitors, national celebrities, presidents, and foreign dignitaries.

Afternoon tea in the hotel lobby is a long-standing tradition with pleasant music provided either by a pianist or harpist. Extraordinary commissioned Royal Doulton bone china graces each tea table, complemented by engraved tableware and silver teapots. High tea fare of scones and Devonshire cream, pastries, and finger sandwiches is served.

The Churchill Bar, which opened in 1996, complements the Palace Arms perfectly. The bar is located in the spot once occupied by founder Henry C. Brown's office and offers a retreat to the luxury of premium spirits and rare, but popular, cigars.

Soft lighting in the second-floor archways sparkles like jewels over the historical photographs of the hotel that decorate the walls. The large hanging lamps as well as the lights in the arches are the original light fixtures stemming from the time when the hotel generated its own electricity (until the 1930s). Guest rooms have replaced the hotel's ballroom and separate clubrooms for men and women on the eighth floor.

Convention rooms, meeting areas, suites, restaurants, and bars, while all modern in décor and technology, still convey the history and pride of this grand hotel. All of the meeting rooms feature windows overlooking downtown Denver and high-speed Internet access. The Onyx Room has original white onyx walls with wainscoting and columns. Next door, the Gold Room features walnut paneling and a beautiful gold sunburst wall clock hanging above the marble fireplace. In 1997 President Clinton used the Gold Room as his headquarters during the G8 Summit held in Denver. Clinton conducted several high-profile meetings with world leaders in this room.

Two rooms with storied pasts are the Tabor and the Stratton Rooms. The Tabor Room was originally the Executive Chamber, used primarily for regional sales conferences. After renovation and redecorating in 1955, it was renamed the Tabor Room in honor of Maxcy Tabor, the hotel's first manager who operated the hotel until 1909. This room can be opened to adjoin with the Stratton Room, creating the Onyx Suite. The Stratton Room is named for the hotel's second owner, Cripple Creek mining millionaire Winfield Scott Stratton, who in the summer of 1900 bought the hotel for Brown's outstanding mortgage of more than $600,000, and gave H. C. Brown a suite in the hotel for life. The Boettcher Board Room, located on the eighth floor, conveniently adjoins a one-bedroom executive suite. It is named in honor of three generations of the Boettcher family, who owned The Brown Palace from 1922 until 1980 and were the last owners with Colorado ties.

The hotel includes three exceptional restaurants, from fine dining to champagne buffets to casual dining. Ellyngton's is the newest restaurant, updated from the San Marco Room in 1988. The menu features a wide variety of courses for lunch and dinner. The Dom Perignon Sunday brunch is a fabulous affair, with a decadent chocolate fountain as the centerpiece.

It all speaks to the elegance that is The Brown Palace Hotel. Henry Cordes Brown would be very pleased.

FUN FACTS

- With the exception of bread and crackers, the hotel prepares all of its baked items in a unique, sixty-year-old carousel oven. This oven, which is used daily, is one of only three known to be in existence.

- After the Beatles' historic stay, fans besieged the hotel with offers to buy the dishes they ate from and the sheets on which they slept. The Fab Four stayed in an eighth-floor corner suite now known as the Beatles Suite.

- The hotel's inaugural booklet, boasted that among the many self-sufficient technologies, a basement furnace that "could burn hot enough to serve as a crematory." At 3:00 a.m. on December 14, 1903, a hotel employee working in the basement boiler room observed two well-dressed men throwing a large box into one of the fireboxes of the boilers. When they left, the employee peered into the inferno and was horrified to see an infant's body in the blaze. "The Most Awful Crime Ever Committed in the City," the *Denver Times* declared. Three weeks later, after some excellent detective work, it was discovered Dr. W. S. Holmquist had delivered a stillborn child to parents with no means to pay for a burial. They asked the doctor what could be done, and the doctor took care of the matter.

- Famed African explorer Paul L. Hoefler, his wife, Maudie, and their daughter, Jacqueline, stayed at The Brown Palace Hotel during the planning stages of Paul's Colorado African Expedition of 1928–1929. Financing for the expedition came from the hotel owners, Charles Boettcher and Horace Bennett, as well as from Denver Post owner Frederick Bonfils. During Hoefler's African trip (July 16, 1928 to September 16, 1929), his wife and daughter continued their stay at the hotel. Hoefler returned to the hotel and his family, following his successful trip that had resulted in the first trans-Africa journey and the first film footage of African Bushmen. The family stayed at the hotel three years while he worked on his book about the adventure. During that time, Jacqueline was stricken with scarlet fever. The hotel management was forced to quarantine the floor where the Hoeflers stayed. For an entire month, only medical personal were allowed on the floor, even the young girl's parents were kept away.

- Until recently, a long-standing tradition of The Brown Palace Hotel coincided with Denver's National Western Stock Show. The hotel would purchase the Grand Champion steer to be exhibited in the atrium before eventually being served to hotel diners. The Brown Palace no longer buys the champion, but the tradition of displaying the steer in the hotel atrium for the viewing public during the final days of the stock show continues.

- In 1937, the hotel remodeled the top two floors into private residences complete with kitchenettes. The small apartments were known as the Skyline Apartments. Several wealthy and influential people stayed in the apartments, including Evalyn Walsh McLean of Hope Diamond fame, and Denver socialite Mrs. Crawford (Louise B. Sneed) Hill. The widowed Mrs. Hill moved into Suite #904 in 1944, claiming she could not get quality servants at her twenty-two-room mansion near Capitol Hill. She spent her last years there in near seclusion. At the age of ninety-four, Mrs. Hill died alone at midnight on May 28–29, 1955. Years later, the hotel began conducting "Affairs of the Heart" tours, which included Mrs. Hill's scandalous romances. Around the time the tours were started, phone calls from Mrs. Hill's former suite began coming in to the hotel's front desk, but there was never anyone at the other end. Hotel historian Julia Kanellos conducted the tours and deduced that Mrs. Hill did not appreciate her dirty laundry being aired in front of the general public. The historian dropped the story from her tour, and the phone calls immediately ceased. But even more curious, there were no telephones on either the eighth or ninth floor. The calls were coming from a room with no phone!

Contact Information: The Brown Palace Hotel
321 17th Street, Denver, Colorado 80202
www.brownpalace.com, 303.297.3111 or 800.321.2599

Rochester Hotel – 1892
An Accidental Tourist Destination

Courtesy of Carley Felton, Rochester Hotel

The vintage neon sign above the entrance welcomes guests to the historic Rochester Hotel in Durango. Landmark Register: NR5LP.1210

No other Colorado mountain town, with the exception of Leadville, had such an economic boom from mining as Durango. With the first mining smelter on the Western Slope and the arrival of the Denver & Rio Grande Railroad in 1881—not to mention the majestic mountain beauty surrounding it—Durango was destined to become a mecca for newcomers. Within ten years, the town had a booming business district, a residential area, schools, and churches. However, as with many early mountain towns, fire was a constant threat, and in July 1889, a fire nearly leveled the town.

View of the Peeples Hotel later named the Rochester Hotel. The two-story brick structure is shown circa 1895.

"Durango Wiped Out" screamed the headline of the *Rocky Mountain News* on July 2, 1889. The article went on to say that despite the "superhuman efforts of the firemen," the "incredible rapidity of the terrific west winds" spread the fire through the town. When the smoke cleared the following morning, the significant losses could be seen. Twenty-one businesses had been destroyed along Main Avenue as well as the city hall, courthouse, and three churches. The *Durango Herald* reported in the July 26, 1889, issue that business had resumed and proprietors were rebuilding with brick. One resident said, "Citizens are not disheartened by the disaster. The burnt district will soon be rebuilt." Such was the attitude of many in Durango. The fire seemed, in time, to be a blessing in disguise. With the new, bigger and better buildings came a resurgence of progress and growth.

The Beginning

Construction of Durango's newest hotel began in 1890 on 2nd Avenue in the heart of the rebuilding area. The land was purchased from Alexander C. Hunt, former territorial governor and one of the founders of the Denver & Rio Grande Railroad. E. T. Peeples, an accountant by trade and former county commissioner, laid the foundation for the two-story brick building, originally known as the Peeples Hotel. The enterprise suffered several setbacks, not the least of which was financial backing. This caused a series of ownership changes before completion in 1892. When it finally opened, the owners were J. E. Schutt, owner of the local mercantile company, and W. C. Chapman, Colorado State Bank director.

The grand vernacular-style red brick building, with a large front balcony, invited guests in to enjoy fine accommodations. Inside, the lobby and restaurant often overflowed with cheery guests who occupied the thirty-three guest rooms on the upper floor. The *Durango Herald* announced:

```
The  Peeple's  Hotel  offers  the  best
accommodations to the public.
```

The hotel enjoyed great success for a little over a year, until the silver panic of 1893 crippled the economy in the San Juan Mountain area. The local smelter, run by Ernest Amy, closed down for six long months, throwing hundreds out of work. In addition, local miners were out of work and railroad employees, lacking business, were laid off. Durango businesses suffered as well, and several closed their doors.

The Peeples Hotel suffered a severe decline in business, but Jerry Sullivan purchased it for $6,000 and managed it successfully through the economic downturn. He would own the hotel for the next thirteen years.

By 1895 Durango's smelter was again in business, the train was experiencing several daily connections, and a new tourist trade sprouted up, bringing guests to the hotel.

In 1905 Mary Francis Finn bought the hotel and renamed it the Rochester Hotel. She made many improvements during her fifteen years of ownership. She extended the front of the building to the sidewalk, adding more space inside the hotel and bathrooms in the back of the hotel.

Glory Days

When the current owners, Diane Wildfang, and her son, Kirk Komick, bought the Rochester Hotel in 1992, they embarked on an extensive remodeling effort. They brought their experience renovating the nearby Leland House and a zeal for western history to the Rochester, keeping much of the original furnishings and woodwork. They updated the entire hotel with all the modern conveniences and converted the original thirty-three rooms into fifteen individual, uniquely decorated guest rooms, all with private bathrooms. The original trim, transom windows above the doors, and the doors themselves were retained, but particular attention was given to other details of the building. The work was completed in 1994.

The exterior of the Rochester remained architecturally true to the Victorian era and is graced by a beautifully landscaped area, including a large, flower-filled courtyard. This exquisite area has been the scene of many Durango weddings over the years as well as myriad social functions.

Courtesy of Carley Felton, Rochester Hotel

Guest rooms at the Rochester Hotel are a blend Old West décor and modern conveniences such flat-panel TVs.

The Rest Is History

Hollywood came to the San Juan basin in the 1950s. *The Naked Spur*, a western film starring James Stewart and Janet Leigh, was filmed just north of Durango in 1952 (not far from the intersection of Highways 160 and 550) and released in 1953. The beautiful mountain area, including Engineer Mountain, is visible in several shots. Other Hollywood movies filmed in the area include *She Wore a Yellow Ribbon*, starring John Wayne; *Butch Cassidy and the Sundance Kid*, with several scenes utilizing the Durango & Silverton Railroad; *Around the World in Eighty Days*; and *City Slickers* capitalized on the many ranches in the area.

The Rochester's owners enthusiastically embraced the history of film making in the Durango area. So inspired, the owners decorated the guest rooms in the Old West style. Movie posters, complete with marquee lights, line the upper hallway. Each room is decorated in a particular Hollywood western theme or as a tribute to a western actor, featuring movie related displays, filming tidbits, and locations in the Durango area.

The Hotel Today

The Rochester Hotel offers luxurious accommodations in the heart of Durango. Within one block of Main Avenue and the historic Durango & Silverton Narrow Gauge Railroad, this landmark hotel is a must on any itinerary that takes travelers to the area.

Guests enjoy many amenities, including whirlpool tubs with showers. The complimentary gourmet breakfast, served each morning in the spacious lobby, features a hot entrée as well as an abundance of fresh fruit and homemade baked goods such as muffins, scones, and coffeecake. Homemade cookies and tea are served every afternoon. The hotel offers three pet-friendly rooms, free parking, wireless Internet, and complimentary computer use for guests.

FUN FACTS

- Hotel guests can check out Rochester Cruiser bikes without charge for riding throughout downtown Durango.

- The Rochester Hotel has undergone many changes over the past century and had no fewer than five owners between 1890 and 1902.

- During the renovation of 1993, some of the contractors quit working because they "just didn't feel comfortable there." Several times a year, guests report seeing a woman in room 204, the hotel's John Wayne Room. It is said that she appears wearing sophisticated Victorian clothing or stylish lingerie.

Contact Information: Rochester Hotel, 721 E. 2nd Avenue, Durango, Colorado 81301
www.rochesterhotel.com   970.385.1920 or 800.664.1920

THE CREEDE HOTEL – 1892
A "HOLY MOSES" MINING TOWN

Courtesy of Creede Hotel proprietor David Toole

The historic Creede Hotel
maintains charm of Creede.
Landmark Register: MCHL.34

The Beginning

Silver was discovered, and in unbelievable quantities, in Colorado's San Juan Mountains in 1889. The narrow Willow Creek Canyon yielded silver by the ore lode, and in no time, a slew of tiny mining camps sprang up along the canyon with colorful names such as Willow, Jimtown, and String Town. In less than a year, more than ten thousand people were crammed into the small canyon, searching for

their great chance at riches. In 1890, with winter coming, the tiny camps merged and hastily constructed slab lumber dwellings, causing some to leave the tents that had been erected all over the canyon for marginally better housing.

It was about this time that a wandering prospector by the name of Nicholas C. Creede picked through a rock outcropping along Willow Creek, a couple of miles above its junction with the mighty Rio Grande River. Realizing the streak embedded in the rock was indeed silver, he hollered to his partner, "Holy Moses!"

Creede filed his claim—which had a yield of nearly $5,000 a ton—as the Holy Moses Mine.

With the word out, a second wave of prospectors, fortune seekers, and the like arrived in the camp following the spring thaw. A building frenzy occurred and a town committee was formed. The mining camps became the town of Creede, named in honor of the man who discovered the Holy Moses Mine. By 1891, nearly $2 million a month was being produced from the mines in the Creede area, surpassing silver production in both Aspen and Leadville. Mines such as the Amethyst and the Ethel, also discovered by Nicholas Creede, as well as the Kentucky Belle, Last Chance, Champion, and Yankee Girl brought in more than $1 million a year—each! The Commodore Mine, which literally hung off the side of Bachelor Hill, became one of the largest silver-producing mines in the world.

In 1891 General William Jackson Palmer, the railroad magnate from Colorado Springs, along with David H. Moffat extended the original narrow gauge rail line from Wagon Wheel Gap into Willow Creek Canyon, bringing the Denver & Rio Grande Railroad into Creede. With so much ore shipping out, Palmer's railroad paid for itself in just four months. The following year, there were two trains arriving and departing daily. The *Denver Republican* reported the train service to Creede with the headline, "It looks like everybody is heading for Creede!"

It seemed to be true, for by 1892 more than three hundred people were arriving daily in Creede. Nearly half of those eager arrivals were bunco artists, pickpockets, thieves, gamblers, prostitutes, and mining sharks. One writer wrote, "Creede was a community born in violence." Creede was indeed a wild, unsettled town. Saloons, gambling dens, and dance halls were the thriving businesses. It's no surprise that the mountain mining community attracted the likes of Bob Ford (the killer of Jesse James), who opened a tented dance hall and saloon called The Exchange. Denver con man Jefferson Randolph "Soapy" Smith came to town in early 1892, bringing with him his bunco cronies and John Light, Smith's handpicked chief of police. In this way, Smith ran the underworld of Creede from his Orleans Club.

Creede was an "equal opportunity" town as well. There were three female gamblers, Poker Alice, Calamity Jane, and Killarny Kate, all of whom were fond of smoking stogy cigars.

Given the criminal culture, it was courageous of the *Creede Candle* newspaper to write, "Creede is unfortunate in getting more of the flotsam of the state than usually falls

to the lot of a mining camp." However, the owner and editor of the newspaper, Cyrus "Cy" Warman—who left Denver and his position at the *Rocky Mountain News* to launch the *Candle* in 1892—wrote a poem that immortalized his new hometown with the lines: "It's day all day in the daytime, And there is no night in Creede."

Parson Tom Uzzell came to town and preached a sermon so fine that Soapy Smith himself was moved to donate seventy-five dollars to help build Creede's first church. The first school was opened that same spring.

Philip Zang, owner of Denver's largest brewery (Philip Zang & Company), opened the P. H. Zang Brewing Company in Creede. With so many people in the crowded mining town, not to mention thirsty miners, the brewery soon became the most popular business in Creede. In an effort to expand his business holdings, Zang bought prime real estate on the northern end of Creede Avenue, where he built the Zang Hotel.

Glory Days

When completed in 1892, the two-story wooden frame hotel was considered Creede's finest hotel. Three sets of large twin windows graced the upper floor. A balcony overlooked the main street of Creede's commerce district. Fancy wooden rocking chairs on the balcony invited guests to relax. There were five guest rooms on the upper floor and five guest rooms on the ground floor, which were rented primarily by miners and businessmen. Past the hotel lobby was the dining room with an adjoining saloon. The high ceiling of the dining room included a ceiling heater and an elaborate chandelier. The kitchen was at the back of the hotel.

A separate building in the back of the hotel expanded business opportunities, as it were. The smaller building was constructed from local stone, known by the locals as moss rock, and housed a brothel. It employed local prostitutes with colorful names such as Lulu Swain, the Mormon Queen, Slanting Annie, Timberline Rose Vastine, Marie Contassot, and the leading madam, "Creede Lil." Her real name was Lillis Lovell, and she went on to own her own brothel on Denver's fancy Market Street.

The Zang Hotel became so popular that Creede's self-

The hills surrounding Creede are shown in this 1892 photograph of the Zang's Hotel and Zang's Hotel Annex. Brewmaster Philip Zang built the hotel.

proclaimed town boss, Soapy Smith, had his own suite in the hotel. When Bob Ford first arrived in town, he too stayed at the Zang Hotel. It wasn't long before Zang built an annex to the hotel, which advertised a barber shop and baths for twenty-five cents. The annex building later became the saloon.

Culture and refinement were making inroads in the mining camp when disaster struck in June 1892. Fire! It started in the early morning hours of June 5. Fire horns roared throughout the town, but the fire, fanned by canyon winds, jumped from one wooden building to the next. Most of Creede was a smoldering ruin by nightfall. Within two days, as cleanup continued, tents were once again set up and businesses resumed. Before the summer was out, Creede was rebuilding, this time with brick.

The Zang Hotel was one of the few buildings that survived the fire. During the town's restoration, the hotel improved the dining room and added several more rooms, to keep up with the popularity of the establishment.

The Rest Is History

Creede was a wild, lawless town during the summer of 1892. The "Louisiana Kid" held a gun to Soapy Smith when he lost money in the Orleans Club. Fortunately for Smith, the "Kid" was clubbed over the head with the butt of a six-shooter. The four murders in town that summer included the killing of "the dirty little coward that shot Mr. Howard," Bob Ford, by Ed O. Kelly.

All this lawlessness brought frontier lawman Bat Masterson in to tame the town. While Masterson set about his duties in Creede, he stayed at the Zang Hotel. As many lawmen did, Masterson supplemented his income with a second job. In his case, Masterson was manager at the Watrous Saloon. With his reputation well known, it is said that the shout, "Here comes Masterson," was generally all it took to calm any disturbance. Interestingly enough, it was about this time that the con artist Soapy Smith left Creede.

By 1893, more silver ore was being shipped by rail from Creede than anywhere else in the country. Between Creede's silver production and Cripple Creek's gold production, it is fair to say that Colorado's economy brought the country out of the depression it had been experiencing.

Following the death of Philip Zang in 1899, Mr. and Mrs. John Zang took ownership of the hotel. They continued the fine service, and the hotel remained popular. Then, in the summer of 1911, murder and scandal changed the hotel forever.

Murder! John Zang Shot and Instantly Killed!

This was the headline of the *Creede Candle* on June 17, 1911. The article described the event: "Mrs. Michael Lefevere, wife of a prominent lessor of this district, shot and instantly killed John Zang, proprietor of the Zang hotel here, at the Lefevere home in

South Creede yesterday. Zang was 55 years old and his slayer 25 years old. Mrs. Lefevere was placed in the county jail here charged with murder." At her murder trial, Mrs. Lefevere pleaded self-defense and was acquitted. In the aftermath, Mrs. Zang struggled both emotionally and professionally. She ran the hotel by herself the best she could but always kept a pistol nearby. Then in the fall of 1919, she remarried, sold the hotel, and left Creede.

Over the next several years, the hotel had a series of owners, and in an effort to shirk the past and move forward, it was renamed the Creede Hotel and has retained that name ever since.

The Hotel Today

Through two world wars and the Great Depression, hard rock mining continued to be the economic driving force in Creede. Then in 1985, the price of silver dropped again, causing the last operating mine in the area, the Homestake, to close. Yet Creede has always held on to its history. That history is evident at the Creede Hotel, which remains the most popular place to stay in Creede. Although small, with just four guest rooms all on the second floor, the hotel prides itself in the simplicity of yesteryear. Each room has a private bathroom, but there are no televisions, telephones, or Internet access. Hotel owner David Toole says, "Stepping into the Creede Hotel is stepping back in time."

The guest rooms are named for the infamous folks who once stayed there, including the Bat Masterson and the Calamity Jane Rooms, each of which has a queen-size bed and access to the balcony overlooking Creede Avenue; the Soapy Smith Room, located on the hotel's east side, which has a full-size bed and gets the sunrise; and the Poker Alice Room, which has a queen-size bed, private bath, and the morning sun as well (Toole says this is the quietest room in the hotel).

Guests receive a complimentary breakfast in the hotel dining room. The menu varies daily, and Toole, who does double duty as the hotel chef, says most guests return for the great food and quiet atmosphere. The dining room also serves lunch and dinner with seating for fifty guests. A second dining room and adjoining bar can seat another fifty. The outdoor rock patio is a delight on a sunny day in the mountains.

FUN FACTS

- The hotel provides a journal for guests to comment on their stay. From the many entries in the journal in the Calamity Jane Room, it seems that some sort of presence is felt there. Several guests have reported hearing bells in the room.

- A few years ago, a hotel employee took pictures of the dining room. When they were developed, the staff was stunned to see a female apparition, dressed in black Victorian clothes, reflected in the glass of an original hotel mirror that still hangs in the dining room.

- Today, the original Zang Annex is the Creede Hotel Bar and is as popular as it was back in the day. The original Decker Brothers' 1887 grand piano, which no doubt provided many nights of musical entertainment, is now on display at the Creede Museum.

- As disliked as Bob Ford was, it seems he occasionally did a good deed. In June 1892, Ford hired young Nellie Russell as one of his "ladies of the evening." A day later, she was found dead, the result of alcohol poisoning and morphine overdose. Ford paid for her burial, signing the note with this epitaph: "Charity covereth a multitude of sins." This was a profound epitaph with double meaning, for minutes after Ford signed to pay for Miss Russell's funeral expenses, he was murdered by Ed O. Kelly.

- The town of Creede became the second mining town, after Telluride, to install electricity throughout the community—ironically, that was one week before Cy Warman penned his poem that included the line, "there is no night in Creede." The Creede miners helped to build the electric system in a remarkable five days.

- Nicholas C. Creede, discoverer of the Holy Moses Mine and for whom the town was named, died an unhappy man in Los Angeles, California, in 1897. Separated from his wife, who was asking to be reconciled at the time, Creede committed suicide by morphine. The local newspaper, the *Apex Pine Cone*, reported, "His wife wanted to live with him again and he preferred death."

Contact Information: The Creede Hotel and Restaurant
  120 North Main Street, Creede, Colorado 81130
  www.creedehotel.com   719.658.2608

Western Hotel – 1892
A Fire Survivor

Courtesy of Western Hotel proprietor Gregg Pieper

Fire was a constant threat in the mining towns of the Colorado Rocky Mountains. While many towns were nearly burned to the ground—and some never rebuilt—Ouray managed to survive three fires in the early days of the mining boom.

By the 1890s, most business blocks were being built with brick rather than the wooden frames susceptible to fire. The exception to that rule was the Western Hotel and its remarkable history of survival.

Of the many wooden frame hotels built in the 1890s in Colorado, only the Western Hotel in Ouray remains today. Landmark Register: MCHL.34

The Beginning

The only wooden frame hotel in Ouray with historic landmark status, the Western Hotel, was built at the time the town was getting noticed across the country for the rich ore deposits discovered there.

The lobby of the Western Hotel contains original woodwork and flooring.

Construction began in 1891 when the stone foundation was built by Francis Carney, who also built the county courthouse and the Ouray Miners Hospital. The firm of John Johnstone and Frederick Mayol were hired by Denver hotel owners William Holt and H. P. Foster for the rest of the construction. Facing 7th Avenue, the three-story hotel, with its attractive false facade, was greatly enhanced by a full-length second-floor balcony supported by four handsome four-by-four posts. The ground floor, with elongated transoms, included large plate glass storefronts.

When the hotel opened to the public in 1892, it was known as the Holt and Foster Hotel, the name still ensconced on the hotel's pediment. The inviting hotel lobby contained the finest Victorian-era furnishings, surrounded by beautiful wood paneling and exquisite stained glass windows, all below an ornate tin ceiling. After registering at the beautiful lobby desk, guests took the grand stairway to one of forty-three rooms on the second and third floors. There were three bathrooms in the hotel, one of which included a bathtub. Room rates were $1.25; for another twenty-five cents, a meal was included.

Just off the lobby area, several businesses serving Ouray customers occupied hotel space, and there was a sample room for traveling salesmen to demonstrate their wares. A splendid dining room served the hotel guests, and a saloon provided a place of relaxation for the local miners. Relaxation of another sort was provided by a rear exit from the saloon that led to the town's red-light district.

Glory Days

The Holt and Foster soon became known as one of the finer hotels in Ouray. Business was boosted by the hotel's complimentary carriage service that provided free transportation to and from the Denver & Rio Grande Railroad depot. There was fierce competition between this hotel and the elegant Beaumont Hotel, which also offered carriage service. Still, the Holt and Foster maintained

its popularity with travelers and seasonal miners, who could afford the rates.

An 1896 issue of the *Ouray Plaindealer* advertised the hotel as "'The Hotel Western,' an authentic hotel of the old west." By the time Clifford Rogers purchased the hotel in 1899, it was officially known as the Western Hotel. The hotel was updated with modern conveniences, including electricity.

```
The Western Hotel. A favorite stopping place
for the miners.
— Ouray Times, August 27, 1903
```

In 1916 Floro and Marie Flor purchased the hotel. They had previously owned the Geneva Hotel, located a block to the east. The Flors, particularly Marie, catered to the mining clientele. The miners would leave their laundry in their room as they went off to the mines, only to return to see clean clothes folded on their beds. The miners affectionately called her "Mother Flor." So trusting were they of Mother Flor that when they left the hotel for the winter season, they would leave their personal trunks at the hotel until they returned in the spring. Mother Flor cared for the miners when they were sick and never let any of her guests go hungry.

The Rest Is History

The Flors called the Western Hotel home and raised their seven children there. Floro died in 1931, leaving the hotel management to Marie. Despite the poor economic conditions of the Great Depression, Mother Flor kept her hotel open.

The hotel continued to operate during World War II, offering cigars for a nickel and beers for a dime in the historic saloon. Even so, the hotel struggled financially. Following the war, the tourism trade began to grow, and the hotel offered jeep tours of the historic gold mines. Slow to start, the tours gained in popularity as tourism increased.

By 1946, Mother Flor was getting on in years. She retained ownership of the hotel but chose to lease it to others for management. Then in 1961, she sold the hotel.

Denver Public Library, Western History Collection, X-12800

The bar of the Western Hotel, shown in 1937, was a popular gathering place for hotel guests as well as the town of Ouray.

In 1942 Mother Flor served six percent beer for a dime at The Western Hotel according to the sign that is barely visible on the far wall in the photograph.

The Hotel Today

The Western Hotel is the largest historic wooden structure in Ouray. Little has changed in landmark hotel. The second-floor veranda still exists, extending over the modern sidewalk along 7th Avenue. Guests relax on the veranda and enjoy the view of Ouray's street scenes from the comfort of ice cream chairs.

Inside, fine meals and beverages are offered in the historic saloon restaurant, where the original bar still stands.

The hotel has two large suites with windows that overlook the veranda on the second floor. The Honeymoon Suite, ironically enough, has two double beds! Victorian décor dominates, incorporating original furnishings and the original blue flowered wallpaper. The second suite contains a queen-size bed and a Victorian-era claw-foot bathtub in the bathroom. There are twelve additional guest rooms, the original boarding rooms of the hotel.

The hotel is available for weddings, reunions, and party gatherings. The jeep tours to the mines, which began in 1946, follow the original stage routes of the nineteenth century.

Fun Facts

- Of the many wooden frame hotels built in the 1890s in Colorado, only the Western remains today.

- With the discovery of high-grade ore in the mountains near Ouray, miners rushed to the area. Christmas of 1875 was celebrated at the base of a hill, near the site that would become the town of Ouray. Following a dinner of roasted local game, the group toasted the holiday with vinegar, as there was no liquor to be had. Thus the hill is known as Vinegar Hill.

Contact Information: Western Hotel
210 7th Avenue, Ouray, Colorado 81427
www.historicwesternhotel.com   970.325.4645 or 888.624.8403

Rio Grande Southern Hotel – 1893
A Railroad Reprieve

Courtesy of Rio Grande Southern Hotel proprietor, Sheila Trevett

The remote area of southwestern Colorado lays claim to some of the oldest evidence of human habitation in the state, dating as far back as AD 900. Archaeologists estimate the Anasazi population was nearly ten thousand, and that they left the area following a severe drought sometime during the fourteenth century.

By the time of the Spanish explorations, particularly the Dominguez-Escalante Expedition of 1776, the Ute Indian tribes called this area home, often warring with the Navajo Indian tribe for control.

During the 1776 expedition, Father Silvestre Vélez de Escalante named both the river and the canyon through which it flows from the San Juan Mountains "Dolores." The complete Spanish name, El Rio de Nuestra Senora de los Dolores, translates to "River of Our Lady of Sorrows."

The Rio Grande Southern Hotel in Dolores has changed little since its construction in 1893. Landmark Register: NR5MT.10460

91

Rumors of gold in the area were whispered in the wind for years, however, trappers and traders in the area as early as 1832, counted on the beaver and trade with the Indians for their financial payout. When the first significant gold claim was filed in 1866, pioneers headed west and established small settlements in the area, including Big Bend and eventually Dolores, named for the river that flowed nearby.

The Beginning

Delores was an agricultural and ranching community and was not incorporated as a town until after the arrival of the railroad. Prospects for the future of Dolores brightened when Otto Mears built a leg of his Rio Grande Southern Railroad to Dolores. Mears began his 172-mile narrow gauge rail line at Ridgway, in the heart of the silvery San Juan Mountains in March 1890. Serving the many gold and silver mines along its route, the line connected the towns of Mancos and Dolores, ending at Durango. Along the way, Mears decided that a secondary function of the railroad would be connecting Rico, Ophir, and Telluride with the Denver & Rio Grande Western Railroad. This would form a "narrow gauge circle" within the San Juan region.

When the railroad reached the town of Dolores in 1891, almost overnight, Dolores became an important railroad stop for shipping goods and natural resources to points north and south.

An early settler in Dolores, E. L. Wilber, saw the opportunity the new railroad provided. With a bit of renovation and pioneer grit, Wilber transformed his family's home, built in 1873, into the first hotel in Dolores.

Glory Days

The two-story frame building with a German colonial architectural design, opened to railroad travelers in 1893. The Rio Grande Southern Hotel enjoyed great success. It offered clean guest rooms and the only railroad eatery along the rails between Ridgway and Durango. The hotel served home-cooked meals prepared by Mrs. Wilber.

The production of coal, timber, and livestock also increased with the arrival of the railroad. These businesses shipped their goods by rail, which benefited them and helped the town to prosper.

The Rio Grande Southern Railroad accommodated these shipments by adding special cars for the livestock and container cars known as freight cars. With such a good working relationship between the railroad company and the town of Dolores, everyone prospered.

The Rest Is History

When the Rio Grande Southern Railroad added passenger service to Dolores, the Wilber family constructed a small addition to their hotel in 1902, increasing the guest rooms to fifteen. Business at the hotel and throughout the town continued with growing success.

The McPhee Lumber Company was one of the more prosperous businesses. Working from the timber mesas above town, the company was able to transport the cut timber affordably by railroad flat cars to places such as Durango and Rico.

By the 1920s, oil and shale were booming enterprises, bringing two national companies to Dolores: Conoco and Texaco, both of which operated oil depots in the area.

It was about this time that the Rio Grande Southern Hotel began to serve double duty as a boardinghouse. Work in the oil companies was seasonal, so workers needed a temporary place to stay. They found the hotel more than hospitable.

A horrific fire in 1913 claimed several Dolores businesses. While the hotel itself was untouched, its icehouse and livestock stables were destroyed. Eventually the city of Dolores passed an ordinance requiring all business structures to be as fireproof as possible. For this reason, the original 1873 hotel building received a face-lift under the ownership of Mabel Williams. The facade was covered in stucco, although the original gables along the roof remained, as did the wooden shingles.

By 1931, with the negative economic repercussions of the Great Depression, the Rio Grande Southern Railroad's passenger services declined. The hotel suffered a loss of business because of this, but nevertheless continued operations. In 1940, B. C. Benham, a new owner, attempted to attract a larger clientele by renaming the hotel Benny's Hogan.

During World War II, the railroad carried only freight after 1942, and the hotel was used primarily as a boardinghouse.

The Hotel Today

In 1962 owners Adare and Mary Ann Hill renamed the historic landmark, the Rio Grande Southern Hotel. Today, this fine hotel is the oldest building in Dolores. Eight beautifully

Courtesy of Rio Grande Southern Hotel proprietor, Sheila Trevett

This vintage photograph of the Rio Grande Southern Hotel hangs in the lobby of the hotel.

decorated guest rooms bring back Victorian charm. The hotel restaurant, under current owners Sheila Trevett and Don King, carries on the tradition of home-cooked meals, serving breakfast, lunch, and dinner daily.

FUN FACTS

- The Dolores River is the only river in America that runs south and then turns north, running eighty miles toward the Colorado River near Moab, Utah.

- When Dolores was established as a station stop for the Rio Grande Southern Railroad, it replaced an earlier town, Big Bend. The site of Big Bend is now covered by McPhee Reservoir, named for the local logging company.

- The Rio Grande Southern Railroad served the eastern half of Montezuma County until December 1951, when it was abandoned. Interestingly enough, the western portion of the county never had railroad service. Even more interesting, the town of Dolores isn't even in Dolores County! It is actually in Montezuma County.

- During the severe decline in passenger and cargo traffic in the Great Depression, the Rio Grande Southern developed an unusual form of carrier cars known as the "Galloping Geese." Their design was a kind of hybrid gasoline-powered railcar that combined the engine a Pierce-Arrow or Buick car or a Wayne Corporation bus with a boxcar body mounted on the chassis. Named for the way they "waddled" down the track, the Geese handled mail contracts and merchandise that would have filled less than a typical train car. The original Galloping Goose #5 is on display at the railroad depot in Dolores.

Contact Information: The Rio Grande Southern Hotel
101 South Fifth Street, Dolores, Colorado
81323, 866.882.3026

Hotel Colorado – 1893
It's in the Water

The Beginning

The world-famous hot springs that bubble up from deep in the earth's crust, both at Siloam Springs and today's popular Yampah Hot Springs, pour hot mineral waters into the Colorado River. It's a debate for the geologists rather than historians as to which came first, the rivers or the vapored waters. Scientists have estimated that the bubbling springs of today originally fell as rain more than twenty thousand years ago.

The waters were a spiritual as well as natural healing source for the Ute Indians. The largest spring, the Yampah, meaning "big medicine" in their language, was the most sacred to the Utes. They had also discovered limestone caves nearby, near the great Colorado River. These caves were filled with warm vapors, creating steam that brought spiritual benefits. For hundreds of years, the Utes fought to retain their sacred waters, but they could not fight the force of the white

Hotel Colorado, "Grande Dame of the Rockies," is a legend in Glenwood Springs and across the state.

Landmark Register: NR5GF.767

man. By 1879, the Utes had been forced onto an Indian reservation called the White River Ute Indian Agency.

The splendor of the bubbling springs, vapor caves, and roaring rivers was virtually unknown to anyone except the Utes—that is, until a wandering explorer by the name of Isaac Cooper traveled over the pass and through the canyon. The Civil War veteran found that the mineral waters offered great relief to his injured body. Realizing the waters held a potential healing bonanza, in 1881 he managed the purchase of the springs and surrounding land for a little over $1,000. Cooper improved the land and did his best at marketing, yet few people came to enjoy his dream spa. It was his wife, Sarah, who changed everything when she simply changed the name of the tiny community from Defiance to Glenwood Springs. This new name had vision and imagery.

Courtesy of Janet Koelling and Kerry Koepping, Creative Dimensions

Guest rooms at the Hotel Colorado are quaint and cozy.

In 1883, a visitor named Walter Devereux took great interest in the waters surrounding Glenwood Springs. A mining engineer, he had the same vision as Isaac Cooper had. But Devereux had the financial means to make the dream a reality. He bought the property and, in 1889, began building a large red sandstone bathhouse on the north side of the Colorado River, encompassing the Yampah hot spring pools. The project took more than a year to complete. In the meantime, Devereux transformed the new town into a mountain hot springs spa mecca. The spa nearly surrounded a four hundred-foot-long pool that was built in 1888. Promoted as the world's largest natural outdoor springs, the complex drew the rich and famous from all over the world. However, Devereux wasn't finished. He also had visions of a matching hotel. While still working on his spa complex, he hired the New York architectural firm of Boring, Tilton, & Mellon and—incorporating the work of Theodore von Rosenburg, who designed the spa—began designing an elegant hotel in the Rockies.

Construction on the Hotel Colorado began in August 1892. The grand hotel was erected in a perfect spot atop a bluff of rich, red soil overlooking the majestic Colorado River and conveniently situated near what was arguably the finest natural hot springs in the state. The towering sandstone hotel was modeled after the sixteenth-century Villa de Medici in Italy. Constructed from the same sandstone from Wilson's Peach Blow

sandstone quarry (on the Frying Pan River) that was used on the hot springs spa, the hotel mirrored the appearance of the revered spa.

Ten thousand tons of brick and sandstone were used in the construction. Tall, square corner towers with Palladian belvederes brace the structure. The hotel's six-story *U* shape loomed large over the center of the hotel. Graced by twin towers of red sandstone and Roman cream-colored brick, the hotel extended 260 feet long, and more than 200 feet wide. The center opened to a massive foyer lit by high arched windows. Beautiful terraced gardens and an outdoor cafe gave way to the center attraction: a large, Italian-style fountain in the center of the courtyard which spewed a stream of water 185 feet into the air, creating an iridescent rainbow when the sun was right. Amazingly, this jet stream of water was powered electronically in the nineteenth century.

Vintage dinnerware from the Hotel Colorado with the hotel's logo, which contains elements from the State Seal of Colorado.

The east and west wings were joined by an open lobby. The east wing contained elaborate suites, a dining room, nursery, and a lady's room. In the west wing, a large music room and a ballroom entertained guests well into the night. Across this area, through the lobby to the south courtyard, was yet another open area dining room, the most stunning of all. The highlight was a magnificent waterfall in the center of the room flowing from the ceiling into a large pool filled with swimming trout. It was, and still is, a very special part of the Hotel Colorado. It is said that in the past guests could sit beside the pool and catch the trout for their morning or evening meal.

The full basement contained a separate area for the gentlemen, with a barber shop and billiard room. The enormous kitchen was also located in the basement, with a separate cooling area that could hold up to three hundred tons of ice. A tunnel led to the servants' living quarters.

Two grand wooden staircases with stone stairs led from the lobby to the upper floors, where two hundred guest rooms and nearly thirty bathrooms provided comfortable accommodations. The rooms, which rented for as much as three dollars a night, had European carpets, Victorian brass beds, and open fireplaces. The hotel had a state-of-the-art electrical wiring system, making it the first hotel with electricity on Colorado's Western Slope. Even with electricity, the hotel operated only in the warm months of May to October, as it did not have central heat.

Glory Days

The new Hotel Colorado opened its doors to the growing community of Glenwood Springs, and all of Colorado, on June 10, 1893. It was a splendid affair, with a full-course formal dinner followed by dancing on the smooth maple floors in the ballroom. The local newspapers acclaimed the Hotel Colorado "The Grande Dame" of Colorado.

An invitation from proprietor A. W. Raymond to the Grand Opening Ball of The Colorado on June 10, 1893.

Courtesy of Janet Koelling and Kerry Koepping, Creative Dimensions

From that opening day forward, the great hotel proved its grandeur. It soon became the most popular hotel not only in Colorado, but in the entire West. Rivaling even the posh hotels in the East, it attracted the wealthy, the famous, and the adventurous from all over the country. Wealthy New York families such as the Astors and the Goulds, Margaret "Molly" Tobin Brown, and Colorado railroad tycoon David H. Moffat were present for the grand opening and continued to return as guests over the years. It is quite possible that Molly Brown first met the Astors and Goulds at this hotel. She would later stay in their homes in New York, and she was with them on the ill-fated *Titanic* ocean liner in 1912.

Another Colorado icon who stayed at the hotel was William F. "Buffalo Bill" Cody. He actually came strictly for his health. During what would be his final visit, in December 1916, the last photo of the Wild West celebrity was taken on the porch of the hot springs spa.

Theodore Roosevelt, Colorado governor James H. Peabody, and Hollywood star Tom Mix, were among the many who came to Glenwood Springs for relaxation and to enjoy the many benefits of the medicinal hot springs.

The hotel became so popular with politicians and presidents that it earned the moniker "Summer White House." The first U.S. president to stay at the hotel was Theodore Roosevelt, who spent three weeks at the hotel in April 1905. The occasion was one of his legendary hunting trips. The hotel set up separate suites and increased security for him, his assistants, and staff so that the country's business continued uninterrupted. It was during this trip that Roosevelt's hunting expedition was so successful that he posed for photographers on the lawn of the Hotel Colorado with his hunting trophies that included several bears and three lynx. Later that evening, a celebratory dinner was

held at the hotel, with much fanfare and backslapping.

However, on another day of hunting, the president came back empty-handed. As legend has it, the hotel maids gathered scraps of cloth and stitched together a cuddly bear, presenting it to Roosevelt in an effort to lift his spirits. The local papers carried the story, dubbing the cloth stuffed bear the "Teddy bear," and thus the legend was born. Toy manufacturer Benjamin Michtom wrote to Roosevelt, requesting permission to use the name Teddy Bear for the little bear. The Ideal Novelty and Toy Company began distribution of their trademarked teddy bear in 1903.

Roosevelt returned to the Glenwood Canyon area many times to enjoy hunting and fishing, and he always stayed at the Hotel Colorado.

A few years later, President William Howard Taft visited the hotel. Arriving in Glenwood Springs via the hotel's special train car on September 23, 1909, Taft only stayed a few hours at the hotel. He did manage to have a fine lunch of grilled trout, after which he addressed a large crowd from the second-floor President's Balcony. Declining an invitation for a dip in the Hot Springs Pool, Taft remarked, "I've found it's much better for a man of my size not to bathe in public."

The Rest Is History

The Hotel Colorado managed to withstand economic downturns over the years and remained open through the years of World War I. As America rejoiced and rebounded following the war, the Roaring Twenties brought a whole new clientele to the hotel. For whatever reason, it became a favorite destination for a number of Chicago gangsters during the 1920s and early 1930s, including Al Capone and "Diamond Jack" Alterie.

Stories are often told of Capone arriving at the hotel in a large, black Lincoln convertible. He entered the hotel flanked by bodyguards and was rarely seen until his departure. Another story tells that Capone used the supply lift system from the basement as an escape route on more than one occasion when the hotel was raided in search of him. There are several photos of Diamond Jack Alterie dressed in flashy western wear, a wide-brimmed cowboy hat, and sporting large diamond rings. Alterie liked the area so much that he leased land on the shore of Sweetwater Lake, where he lived comfortably in a log cabin with his wife, Erwina, the daughter of Leadville bootlegger Mike Rossi. Later, he built a large structure on the north side of the lake, which he called The Dude Ranch-Club House. In reality, it was a secret refuge for his Chicago crime buddies.

Tom Mix stayed at the hotel in 1926 while filming the movie *The K & A Train Robbery*. While in town, he participated in local events, including a parade.

During World War II, the war effort affected the Hotel Colorado as it did thousands of businesses all over the country. In 1943, the hotel was used as a naval hospital, and the basement area was converted into a morgue. The Hot Springs Pool was closed to the public and used exclusively by recuperating military patients. The U.S. Navy did a great deal of repairing and updating the plumbing and electrical wiring throughout the hotel

as well as installing a fire alarm system. By 1944 six thousand patients had received care at this military hospital. Following the war, the hotel returned to public use in 1946.

The Hotel Today

Modern updates and renovations occurred over the years, particularly in the 1990s. The original Palm Room, with its eighteen-foot-tall windows, was fashionably restored as was the barrel-vaulted, five thousand-square-foot Devereux Room. The Colorado Room was refurbished to include a new dance floor, classic Italian drapes and valences, and elaborate Italian chandeliers. Extensive remodeling reduced the number of guest rooms to 130 but provided spacious luxury. The basement is used as a storage area, with a few small tourist businesses accessed from the street level. Today, the charm and elegance are once again first rate at the grand hotel, and the rich and famous can be seen here occasionally. For example, the late Patrick Swayze stayed at the Hotel Colorado while filming the Disney production of *Tall Tales*.

Modern conveniences include room service, cable television, and Internet connections. There are group meeting rooms and dining options to please any appetite. Relaxation as well as recreation can be found at the Hot Springs pool, and there is a twenty-four-hour fitness area.

Hotel Colorado was completed in 1893 and offered a commanding view of the Colorado River.

Denver Public Library, Western History Collection, X-8778

FUN FACTS

- There are two pools in the Hot Springs Pool. Here are a few facts about them.

  The average daily flow from the springs into the pool is 3.5 million gallons.

  More than one million gallons of water are contained in the large pool.

  The small pool holds 91,000 gallons of water. The average temperature of the spring water is 122 degrees, but it cools rapidly when it enters the pools.

  The small pool maintains a temperature of 104 degrees.

  The large pool maintains a temperature of 90 degrees.

  The large pool is 405 feet by 100 feet.

  The small pool is 100 feet in length.

- Today, one of the hotel's tower suites has been transformed into the Molly Brown Suite as a tribute to one of the most dynamic women in Colorado's history. The suite is decorated in Victorian-era style and displays Brown's family photos and memorabilia.

- Employees of the hotel and business owners at the street level of the basement have reported strange creaking noises, sudden drafts of cold air, and, on occasion, distant sounds of human moaning. Tales are told of locked doors opening mysteriously and electric lights turning on or off on their own. On the main floor just above the basement, the first room along the basement stairs is said to be so haunted that it has been closed to the public. This area of the hotel was, after all, the morgue during World War II when the hotel was used as a naval hospital.

- Apparently, during the time the hotel served as a naval hospital, a chambermaid was caught in a lover's triangle and murdered by a jealous lover. It is said her screams can still be heard in the corridor and in the room where she was murdered.

Contact Information: The Hotel Colorado
  526 Pine Street, Glenwood Springs, Colorado 81601
  www.hotelcolorado.com   970.945.6511 or 800.544.3998

THE TELLER HOUSE HOTEL – 1896
A SAN JUAN SENTINEL

The Teller House Hotel in Silverton is always inviting, and particularly so on snowy winter nights.
Landmark Register: NR5SA.59

The Beginning

The arrival of the Denver & Rio Grande Railroad in July 1882 opened this part of the San Juan Mountain area to greater prominence. The railroad brought commerce, investors, travelers, and much-needed affordable supplies to the otherwise isolated mining town of Silverton. The *San Juan Herald* reported, "The difficult problem of our prosperity will then be solved, and we will then have to thank the enterprise and pluck of the much maligned narrow gauge railroad."

With the Denver & Rio Grande, our miners would no longer seek to induce capitalists to purchase prospects. The miners will make

Silverton a mining town second to none in
the state.
—*La Plata Miner*, December 24, 1881

By the 1890s, mines such as the Gold King and the Silver Lake were producing enough high-grade ore to eventually surpass the mighty Camp Bird Mine of Ouray. Silverton benefited from the mining prosperity, and new businesses opened throughout the town. The business district included grocery stores and meat markets, doctors' and lawyers' offices, hotels and saloons.

Charles Fischer, an early entrepreneur in Silverton, saw a need that he could fill. With all the saloons in town, Fischer decided to cut out the middle-man supplier and open a brewery. By offering discounted prices to the saloons, Fischer soon became a well-respected and financially successful businessman.

Glory Days

Fischer expanded his Silverton enterprises by building a fine hotel in 1896. He named it the Teller House, in honor of his friend Henry M. Teller, Colorado's US senator who served from 1876 to 1909.

The three-story red brick building facing Greene Street featured large arched windows on either side of the entrance. Local businesses occupied the first floor, including a grocery store, a saloon, and a bakery. Upstairs guest rooms were large and offered all the modern conveniences of the era.

The hotel attracted visitors and travelers as well as businessmen to Silverton. One of those business-

An ornate stairway leads to the second floor guest rooms in the Teller House.

men was Guy Emerson. So impressed was he with the local economy and the town's population (nearly three thousand counted in the 1900 census) that he opened the Silverton National Bank in 1905. Unfortunately, Emerson didn't care for drinking, and he circulated a petition to shut down the saloons. The miners and several businessmen, including hotel owner Charles Fischer, in turn, did not care for Emerson's actions and took their banking business elsewhere. Silverton and all of Colorado would face the

prohibition movement head-on in the next decade.

The Rest Is History

Colorado was the first state in the country to pass a law banning the sale of alcoholic beverages. On New Year's Eve of 1915, nearly three years before the Eighteenth Amendment to the US Constitution made Prohibition the law of the land, the end of an era came about in Colorado when alcohol was outlawed. The repercussions of the new state law rippled throughout Colorado businesses, causing a tidal wave of business closures in the industry. Breweries such as Charles Fischer's closed overnight, and business at his Teller House Hotel declined.

By 1916, most of the businesses on Silverton's notorious Blair Street, the town's red-light district, had either closed or gone underground, as it were. Perhaps the one legitimate business on Blair Street was the French Bakery, which had been in business since 1900. With the economic downturn, the bakery moved into the Teller House, which proved to be a winning proposition for both parties.

The Teller House Hotel survived the Prohibition years, endured the Great Depression, and was revitalized following World War II by the increase in tourism trade.

The Hotel Today

With only four owners in its entire history, the Teller House Hotel continues to provide the charm of Victorian days gone by but with all the modern conveniences. In 1997 new owners Tiffany and Kevin deKay refurbished the hotel to its former glory. The ten guest rooms, decorated in the Victorian-era style, have the original woodwork and high ceilings. While there are no televisions in the guest rooms, there are plenty of board games stocked in the common parlor room.

The hotel offers the choice of a private or European shared bathroom and amenities such as complimentary wireless Internet, on-site meeting rooms, and a restaurant.

Courtesy of Teller House Collections

Guest rooms at the Teller House feature Victorian décor and antiques as well as views of the San Juan Mountains that surround the hotel.

FUN FACTS

- Although the French Bakery relocated to the fashionable Teller House Hotel, it retained its strongest customer base: the working girls of Blair Street.

- The miners of the San Juan mining district introduced the use of trams to overcome elevation and rugged mountain ledges. Buckets of ore, supplies, and even miners could be carried along the tram line—up, down, and across the mountainsides. "The invention revolutionizes mining in this section," David Day reported in the *Solid Muldoon.*

Contact Information: The Teller House Hotel
1250 Greene Street, Silverton, Colorado 81433
www.tellerhouse.com   970.387.5423 or 800.342.4338

THE IMPERIAL HOTEL & CASINO – 1896
A MOUNTAIN MELODRAMA

Courtesy of Maria Cunningham

The three-story Imperial Hotel in Cripple Creek was among many brick structures constructed in the aftermath of the disastrous fires of April 1896.

Landmark Register: NR5TL.2

When roaming cowpoke Bob Womack, who had been peddling his gold theory for years, (at least from as early as 1878) finally discovered an abundant gold float in the low-flowing waters of Cripple Creek, the reaction was slow, to say the least. In October 1890, an ore sample assayed in Colorado Springs at $250 a ton, proved Womack right, and the Cripple Creek Mining District was formed on

April 1, 1891. Miners flocked to the south side of Pikes Peak to file mining claims, while local businessmen Horace Bennett and Julius Myers laid out a new town soon to be called Cripple Creek.

Cripple Creek Mines Set Off Rush — Pikes Peak Gold at Last

This was the headline of the February 28, 1892, issue of the *Rocky Mountain News.* The last great gold rush of Colorado was on. Within three years of Womack's strike, gold production had exploded, and millionaires by the ore lode would be made from Cripple Creek gold. By this time, the tiny mountain town boasted a population of ten thousand. Bennett Avenue, the main street in the town, had an astonishing forty brokers, seventy lawyers, thirty-nine mining agents, fifteen newspapers, ninety doctors, seven hotels, more than forty saloons and gambling establishments as well as clothing stores, grocery stores, bakeries, meat markets, and livery and blacksmith shops. Cripple Creek was the classic mining boomtown of Colorado. In fact, during the economic depression of 1893, it was Cripple Creek gold that helped pull the nation through the crisis. The rich mining turned Cripple Creek into the "Greatest Gold Camp on Earth."

Disaster struck the very heart of Cripple Creek on April 25, 1896, when fire broke out in a Myers Street bordello and soon engulfed the entire town. The town's fire hoses couldn't keep up with the fire, and the high winds quickly spread the fire north. In three hours, the fire was out, but much of Cripple Creek was gone. Because of the strong economy of the mining town, businesses were quick to rebuild: this time in brick. From the ashes, new businesses emerged, one of which was today's Imperial Hotel & Casino.

Guests at the Imperial Hotel can leave comfortable rooms to take chances at limited stakes gaming at the casino located inside the hotel.

The Beginning

Following the fire, J. M. Roseberry financed much of the construction in the rebuilding of businesses in Cripple Creek. One of the brick buildings he financed was a hotel with office space available. Located on a steep sloping lot at the northeast corner of Carr and 3rd Streets just off Bennett Avenue, the three-story brick building was completed in late 1896 and had twelve large arched windows, six on each of the upper two floors. The windows and doors were finished with natural sandstone.

In January 1897, the building was leased by a widow named Mrs. E. F. Collins. She named her establishment the Collins Hotel and rented furnished rooms to professional men, assayers, mining engineers, stockbrokers, and foreign investors. A hotel advertisement boasted, "...everything first class, with meals included." Rates ranged from two dollars to three dollars per day. In 1906 Mrs. M. E. Shoot bought the hotel, making major changes and additions and renaming it the New Collins Hotel. Among the changes was the annex of the three-story Roseberry Block building next door. An elevated passageway connected the two buildings.

The New Collins Hotel offered electric lights, steam heat, porcelain bathrooms, and a dining room that could seat 150 guests. The hotel had seventy guest rooms on the upper floors of both buildings, furnished in the finest of furniture and draperies. The open lobby was decorated with imported Victorian floral wallpaper.

While considered one of the finest hotels in Cripple Creek, Mrs. Shoot nevertheless faced financial difficulties. She was unable to meet her mortgage payments, and the holder of the note, an Englishman named George E. Long, foreclosed in 1910. Subsequently, Long and his wife, Ursula, moved to Cripple Creek intending to operate the hotel for a time, but they stayed for forty years.

Long was a descendant of British nobility and received a handsome yearly sum from the British Crown. With his wealth, he turned the hotel into a formal Victorian hotel. His first act was to change the name to the Imperial Hotel. Next, he ordered the finest furniture from the Daniels & Fisher department store in Denver, which was shipped by railroad to Cripple Creek. Then he sold the corner building to the YMCA and limited the hotel operation to the Roseberry Block building. The Longs continued the respectable service and amenities of the previous owners and added tourist services as well.

The narrow gauge Short Line Railroad arrived daily at noon. The hotel heavily advertised its location, which was just two blocks from the train depot. Pierce Arrow limousines bearing the hotel's logo waited at the depot. Sharply-dressed drivers often brought three hundred guests a day to the hotel, where a fine luncheon was served in the large dining room. For thirty years, the Longs kept the hotel operating, through the mining downturn and the Depression years. In 1940 George Long fell (some say under mysterious circumstances) down the narrow basement stairs to his death, and his widow struggled to manage the hotel for four more years. In 1944 Ursula Long padlocked the doors and walked away forever.

Glory Days

The hotel sat empty and decaying until Wayne and Dorothy Mackin purchased the building in 1946. With intense cleaning, remodeling, refurnishing, and updating, the couple turned the Imperial into Cripple Creek's premiere hotel. "We set our tables with crisp white linen, nice china and silver, and even candles in the evening," Dorothy Mackin wrote in *Cripple Creek Centennial 1892-1992*.

Yet the couple faced an unforeseen challenge. The hotel was located just around the corner from Bennett Avenue, the city's main street, but the locals and the tourists were largely remaining on Bennett Avenue. So the Mackins asked around and became friendly with the local tour drivers, who informed them of a little money racket going on. It seems the restaurants and hotels along Bennett Avenue were paying the tour drivers a fee for delivering guests to their establishments. If the Mackins wished to increase their business, they would have to pay to play, as it were.

A deal was struck. The Mackins would furnish one full meal to each driver per day. Impressed with the excellent cuisine and service, the drivers delivered customers. Another local tradition among the restaurants was to offer two menus: one for the locals and a higher-priced one for the tourists. The Mackins took this idea head-on, and created one menu for all customers. Soon, the summer tourism business was booming, and local groups held parties and banquets at the Imperial.

Business in the winter months was quite another matter. Looking to draw people to Cripple Creek year-round, the Mackins had been in contact with the Piper Players,

Denver Public Library, Western History Collection, X-656

This view of the Imperial Hotel on steep slope of 3rd Street in Cripple Creek is from the mid-1970s.

a small theater group in Idaho Springs that was seeking a performance venue. By a stroke of luck, the Mackins were asked by the Colorado Springs Chamber of Commerce to

provide dinner and entertainment for a national meeting of the Chamber of Commerce. The Mackins invited the Piper Players to the Imperial Hotel to perform. With a bit of improvisation, the theater group performed for the convention in the fall of 1947. The following night, the group again performed at the Imperial, this time for the Sylvanite Club, Cripple Creek's most prestigious organization.

With good timing, good booking, and a warm response from audiences, the Mackins realized they had found their year-round attraction. They spent the rest of that season remodeling, planning, advertising, and recruiting entertainment for what was soon to be known as the Imperial Players.

The remodeled basement area became the Gold Bar Room Theater and was decorated with old mining stock certificates, photos from the gold rush era, and a piano with a stained-glass front that had been rescued from a former bordello. Nineteenth-century melodrama opened on July 3, 1948, and an estimated 45,000 patrons attended that first season. The popularity of the melodramas soon gained statewide attention.

The Rest Is History

In the years that followed, the hotel was updated, yet retained its tasteful Victorian style and elegance. Local history was brought into the hotel with the installation of two sets of leaded-glass doors from the old Glockner Hospital in Colorado Springs. One set was installed at the hotel entrance, and the other set was installed in the entrance to the dining room. The lobby, refurbished with wood flooring and Victorian carpet, received a registration desk and box office that had been original fixtures in First National Bank in Colorado Springs.

The infamous Red Rooster Room opened next to the lobby in 1953. The casual restaurant and bar attracted locals and tourists. From the stained-glass doors to the handmade buffet top and period paintings, the elegant dining experience in the quiet, spacious Victorian room allowed guests to step

Courtesy of Maria Cunningham

The walnut bar in Imperial Hotel came from the Red Rooster Saloon at Twin Lakes, Colorado. Roosters in all sizes now decorate the room, gifts from all over the world.

back in time. The walnut bar came from the Red Rooster Saloon in Twin Lakes, Colorado, hence the name. In subsequent years, the name has taken on an added dimension, as glass roosters, handmade roosters, and porcelain roosters in all sizes decorate the area—gifts from patrons around the world.

In 1958, the Carlton Room opened within the hotel. Named in honor of Mr. and Mrs. A. E. Carlton, who had done so much for Cripple Creek, the room had a unique oak bar assembled from sections of three different bars resurrected from the days of yesteryear. Carlton was responsible for bringing the transfer and trading business to the mining camp and later financing several underground mining tunnels. Mrs. Carlton handled her husband's financial affairs and was involved in philanthropic efforts. Among the many Victorian additions to this room is an antique grand piano imported from Germany and inlaid with mother-of-pearl.

With constant improvement, consistent quality, and great entertainment, the Imperial Hotel attracted thousands of guests from all over the world to the hotel every season to enjoy the Victorian hospitality, luxurious rooms, fabulous food, and great melodrama. Not only did the Mackins improve their hotel business venture, they brought a quality venue to Cripple Creek that improved and sustained the town's economy for nearly fifty years. The Mackins improved the community in other ways as well. In 1948, they spearheaded the Cripple Creek-Victor Tourist Bureau. Through their efforts, local mines—including the Elkton, the El Paso, and the Mollie Kathleen—were opened for tours. In 1953 the Mackins, along with newspaper owner Blevins Davis, opened the first museum in the area, showcasing the great mining district's history.

The Hotel Today

When the state's voters approved legalized gambling in 1991, the Imperial Hotel added limited-stakes gaming to its list of attractions and began operating as the Imperial Casino Hotel. With gaming on the main floor, and in-house hotel accommodations, guests can take their chances at their own stake of striking it rich.

In 2010 longtime area residents Gary and Wini Ledford bought the landmark hotel. Having restored the former high school into the Carr Manor, they were experienced in historic renovation, and now they went to work on the Imperial Hotel & Casino. It was remodeled to include fifteen guest rooms and suites.

The hotel basement, the site of the legendary melodrama performances, is now a splendid dinner theater. The walls are lined with memorabilia of yesteryear, including photographs of early performers such as Craig T. Nelson and musical groups such as the Mamas and the Papas, the Lovin' Spoonful, and the Grass Roots. Historic playbills and early posters also adorn the walls. The new Midland Depot restaurant, located inside the hotel, offers a fabulous Italian menu at affordable prices.

"Our intent," says owner Gary Ledford, "is to continue to embellish history, bring back the things the Mackins did for fifty years here in Cripple Creek before gaming, and add other dimensions." He's off to a great start.

FUN FACTS

- When George Long fell down the basement steps to his death in 1940, rumors abounded that his daughter Alice had either pushed him or hit him with a skillet. Regardless of the cause of the fall, the ghost of George Long is said to roam the stairs and the basement.

- The ghost of Alice is also known to roam the Imperial Hotel. A mentally challenged child, she was often locked in the room that is now a portion of the Red Rooster. Hotel employees have often reported the sounds of scratching on the door to the room.

- Since 1948, when the Mackins' Imperial Hotel introduced the Imperial Players and melodrama to Cripple Creek, the entertainment format has experienced nearly five decades of unprecedented success. The Imperial Hotel boasts the honor of hosting the longest-running melodrama theater in the nation.

Contact Information: The Imperial Hotel & Casino
123 North 3rd Street, Cripple Creek, Colorado 80813
http://imperialhotelrestaurant.com   719.689.2561 or 877.546.0925

GOLDMINER HOTEL – 1897
A HAPPY VALLEY FOCAL POINT

Courtesy of Silvia Pettem

Gold became the backbone of Colorado's early economy, and it was gold that saved the state and the nation from the depression of 1893. Successful gold mining enterprises could be found across Colorado's Rocky Mountains, including the area that would become Eldora.

As early as 1861, the Grand Island Mining District was formed, extending to the crest of the Continental Divide, where small discoveries of gold were found. The Civil War led to the temporary collapse of the mining industry, until a decade later, when in May 1875, C. C. Alvord discovered the large gold lode he called the Fourth of July. Just three months later, the Alvord Placer Mine was located, followed by the Clara Lode on Spencer Mountain.

It wasn't until the Happy Valley Placer gold mine was discovered in 1892 that the real boom materialized. It happened along a stream in a beautiful setting nestled in the

When built in 1897, the Goldminer Hotel in Eldora was the only such accommodation for miles around in the Happy Valley area. This gathering at the Hotel took place in 1900. Landmark Register: NR5BL.758.2

113

shadow of Spencer Mountain, causing a new rush of prospectors. Over the next few months, two square miles of Spencer Mountain were dotted with more than fifty mining claims, a veritable mecca for mining. The *Rocky Mountain News* would later call Eldora, the town that grew up here, "The youngest rival of Cripple Creek."

The Beginning

In the fall of 1891, John H. Kemp and several fellow miners from Central City panned for gold in Middle Boulder Creek, just a few miles upstream from Nederland. Finding a consistent amount of gold, the group staked a gold placer claim and named it the Happy Valley. Word spread, and soon prospectors swarmed into the area. Most folks were skeptical, but when the Enterprise and Clara mines proved to hold real promise, a viable mining community developed. A rival mining camp set up a town site within the Happy Valley land grant. Litigation followed, with an eventually ruling in John Kemp's favor.

Courtesy of Goldminer Hotel proprietor, Scott Bruntjen

The historic interior of the Goldminer Hotel has been preserved and maintained through dedication and hard work.

Kemp laid out a tract of land and divided it into lots for building. Within a few months, a semblance of order gave rise to a budding mining town. For whatever reason, a new name for the mining camp was chosen but soon faced obstacles in the choice of the name. The newly named Eldorado Camp had a post office that received no mail. California had a town of the same name, so in an effort to cooperate with the US Post Office, the mining town simply shortened its name to Eldora. That satisfied the government, and Eldora was incorporated on March 9, 1898.

Not so much as a single saloon existed in early 1898. But the town soon saw a building frenzy, and commerce emerged nearly overnight. Among those in the crowd looking to start a business were the Randall brothers. They happened to notice there was no hotel for the enterprising town's workers and future guests. The brothers found a partner in Alice Smith, who had connections in nearby Boulder real estate, and so, in December 1897, the group was able to purchase the corner block of 6th Street and Klondike Avenue for an astonishing sum of fifty dollars.

The Randalls had access to a sawmill where milled logs were skillfully placed together in the practical mountain architectural style of the day. Three months later, the new two-and-a-half story Goldminer Hotel was nearly complete with a fresh coat of white paint and was ready for business. The *Denver Republican* published this announcement in the February 1898 issue, "The Randall Brothers and their associates have a 30 room hotel nearly completed."

Business got off to a slow start, however, as the winter of 1897–1898 saw some fifteen feet of snow fall over the valley, leaving the new streets of Eldora under mountains of snow. Guests were finally able to arrive, and word soon spread that the Goldminer Hotel was the place to stay in Eldora. Lavish meals were served, followed by lavish entertainment. Dances were held in the large dining room, where the whole town gathered for the many festivities.

William N. Byers, a strong advocate for Colorado enterprise and the editor of the *Rocky Mountain News*, used his powerful newspaper to promote the Goldminer Hotel and the new mining camp:

> There is not a dance house in the town, nor will there be, the pioneers of the camp, experienced miners know the limitation of morality in a new and prosperous camp.

Glory Days

The Goldminer Hotel started out as a two-story bunkhouse for miners but quickly emerged as the social spot of Eldora. The overnight accommodations were said to be the finest for miles around, with very reasonable rates. Business was so brisk that the owners had to hire a general manager to handle the influx of guests.

Mena Given, the new general manager, had a great résumé and an interesting presence. She came from Boulder, where she had managed the Colorado House for twenty years. It is said that her personality and charity brought a following to the Goldminer. The residents of the small community whispered among themselves that Given was the wife of Charles Guiteau, who had assassinated President James Garfield in 1881. She wasn't; that was actually a Mrs. Giben, who owned a restaurant in Chicago. But as gossip goes, it made for a good story. In any case, at the direction and organization of Mena Given, town receptions, dances, and weddings were held at the Goldminer. There were also musicales, card game associations, and skiing and sledding parties.

Within a year, the Goldminer Hotel was the social hub of the town and was granted the first liquor license by the first city council. For the next two years, Eldora grew in population, with an average of forty miners arriving daily, most staying at the Goldminer Hotel. With over three hundred buildings, homes, and businesses in Eldora, the Goldminer remained the focal point in the town—so much so that even the local jail

was constructed behind the hotel.

In 1898 the hotel was sold to Charles W. Caryl, who bought it for $2,500. But scandal and bad investments clouded the hotel for quite some time. Changes in management were a part of the new sale, yet curiously, the new manager, Sarah Martin, mirrored the old manager. Described as a robust, no-nonsense woman, she ran the hotel starting in 1904 with an iron hand and had no time for freeloaders, be they employees or customers. Rumors about her surfaced as well. She was a woman of divorce at a time when divorce was extremely rare, and vicious gossip once again distorted the facts. In reality, cruel abuse had led Sarah Martin to file for divorce. Regardless of the gossips, Martin continued the tradition of hotel hospitality and entertainment, and personally saw to it that only the finest food available was on the hotel menu.

With the best accommodations and entertainment in town, the hotel managed to survive the downturn of the mining business following the turn of the century. The arrival of the Colorado & Northwestern Railroad, just after the Christmas holiday of 1904, brought a short-lived vitality to Eldora. When the first train rolled into the Happy Valley, the many dignitaries on board were treated to a hearty home-cooked turkey dinner at the Goldminer Hotel.

The Rest Is History

Shortly after the turn of the century, the rich surface ore played out, leaving only low-grade ore. The mining community took a big hit when the Mogul Tunnel project, designed to filter and advance the chlorination process of ore refinement, became a near disaster. Mines struggled, while others failed. When the management of the Bailey Mill missed a payroll, the employees staged a protest. Things got out of hand when the group set fire to Bailey's house, smoked him out, and then promptly shot him. When the Fourth of July Mine finally shut down, Eldora became a near ghost town. The 1910 census listed six hundred residents. Most businesses closed their doors, but not the Goldminer Hotel.

The availability of the automobile led to an explosion of tourism. At Eldora, a fleet of Stanley Steamers offered tours to the area in the summer of 1914. The Goldminer Hotel capitalized on the tourist trend with this advertisement:

```
Summer tourists are invited to spend their
vacation at this beautiful health-giving
resort. The best the market has will be
provided at this hotel. Come spend the summer
months here.
```

Tourists traveled to Eldora for weekend excursions, often staying at the Goldminer. The hotel's business was slow but steady in these lean years. During the Great Depression,

hotel owner Frank Anderson rented out rooms in an effort to keep the hotel in operation. In 1935, he built an addition on the north side of the hotel called the Club Room. After he added a piano, the club became the new local hangout. Anderson also made the room available for community events including weekly social meetings, ladies luncheons, and weddings. Once a week, Dr. Carrie Anderson of Nederland came to the Goldminer offering "needed medical services" to the townsfolk. With these events and services, the hotel sustained the Depression as well as the war years.

By the 1950s, outdoor adventure had come to Eldora, bringing with it a new customer base. People discovered nearby Lake Eldora and the wonders of the backcountry. In 1962, a new business boom hit the area in the form of white powder: skiing the Rockies had become the rage across the state. Eldora Mountain Ski Resort opened and was the closest ski area for people from the metropolitan areas of Denver and Boulder. The business generated from the folks skiing at Eldora brought new life to the town and the Goldminer Hotel once again thrived in the center of it all.

The two-story log-hewn hotel went through a few

Groups have gathered at the Goldminer for more than a century. This high scool reunion was in 2008.

changes of ownership in the following years and a few renovations as well. The Club Room and dining area had opened to the community for town meetings. In the late 1960s, the guest rooms were remodeled into five larger rooms, while the upper level remained largely unchanged. In 1979 the Bell family bought the property and returned it to the historic hotel era by implementing the modern bed and breakfast model.

The Hotel Today

The rugged two-story log hotel still brings visitors and travelers to the quiet community. The log structure has a clapboard front and finely trimmed original porch that have withstood the mountain weather for more than a century. Despite renovations

Courtesy of Goldminer Hotel proprietor, Scott Bruntjen

The "club room" addition to the hotel is shown in this 1940 photograph.

made over the years, the individual rooms have largely retained their turn-of-the-century feel. A cozy log cabin ambiance is prevalent in every room. Individual rooms contain either a four-post bed or an elegant iron bed, with comfy bedding, and each room is uniquely decorated. All rooms have bathrooms, and some include jet baths. The dining room and community room remain unchanged and offer guests impeccable service as well as breathtaking views of the Rocky Mountains.

FUN FACTS

• When the post office in Eldorado was established in February 1897, postmistress Lois Holzhauser soon realized the mail was going to Eldorado, California. When the payroll for the Terror Mine went to California, angry Colorado miners demanded action. Thus, the town shortened its name to Eldora. Today, the mail officially goes to the nearby town of Nederland.

• During its heyday, the town of Eldora boasted it had everything except a cemetery, claiming there was no need for one.

• The mining district in the Happy Valley area was sixteen miles long and four miles wide, ranging from Boulder Canyon west to the Continental Divide.

Contact Information: Goldminer Hotel
   601 Klondike Avenue, Nederland, Colorado 80466
   www.goldminerhotel.com 303.258.7770 or 800.422.4629

GENERAL PALMER HOTEL – 1898
THE RAILROAD TOWN THAT COULD—AND DID

Courtesy of Joyce B. Lohse

The Gay Nineties is the name of a period of prosperity during the late nineteenth century. For William Jackson Palmer's Denver & Rio Grande Railroad and his town of Durango, it was indeed a era of great prosperity. In the fall of 1881, Palmer and his partners, Dr. William Bell and former Colorado Territory governor Alexander Cameron Hunt, began construction of a forty-five mile extension of their railway, called the Silverton Branch.

The General Palmer Hotel in Durango is named for William Jackson Palmer, who built the hotel and whose Denver & Rio Grande Railroad opened the area to trade and tourism. Landmark Register: NR5LP.304

The advent of the railroad and the telegraph will rebound prosperity. All hail then to the Rio Grande. The railroad will be pushed on to Silverton as the company is desirous

of reaching the San Juan country, and the officers of the company are the owners of the smelter at Durango.... Durango will always be an important point on the D.&R.G. between Denver and Silverton.
— La Plata Miner, July 28, 1881

Completed in just eleven months, the rails reached Silverton on July 10, 1882. Known today as the Durango & Silverton Narrow Gauge Railroad, this line carried passengers, freight, and the mineral riches of the San Juan Mountains, bringing an economic boom to Durango.

A strategic economic move in 1882, this rail line today remains not only an historic relic of the past, but Durango's strongest tourist attraction.

The Beginning

Thanks to the railroad, Durango prospered at a phenomenal pace, as Palmer had envisioned. More than two hundred businesses opened. In an annual report to railroad stockholders, Palmer said, "Durango's progress is strong evidence of the faith of the people of Colorado in the immediate future output of the San Juan silver mines."

Built in 1898, the hotel was known as Hotel Savoy. This photograph is from the 1920s.

A series of failed attempts to extend his railroad south into New Mexico became the subject of conflicting right-of-way issues, lawsuits, and even a Supreme Court ruling against his railroad company. Yet an undaunted Palmer used his intellect and talents to move forward with other new enterprises.

In 1898 Palmer built a fine hotel, rivaling even the stately Strater Hotel for the patronage of the railroad travelers. Located just one block north of his Denver & Rio Grande Railroad depot, and closer to it than the Strater, the hotel would be his final legacy in the town he created.

Glory Days

Palmer chose a practical plan for his three-story brick hotel, which was first named the Savoy Hotel. The exterior was skillfully constructed in Georgian Revival architecture. The main floor displayed large windows providing for a fine street view, while the second- and third-floor windows were hooded with elaborate flattened arches. The street entrance was graced with a full-length front balustrade that supported a second-floor balcony.

Entering the hotel from the Main Street entrance brought guests into a large inviting lobby with several open as well as semi-private areas with comfortable chairs and sofas. Hotel carriages awaited travelers at the train station, providing them with free transportation to the hotel, where the gracious staff greeted the guests at the impressive open portico at the opposite end of the lobby.

Luxurious guest rooms with the most modern conveniences attracted people from all over the country. Palmer must have been pleased with the success of his hotel.

Noted Durango historian Duane Smith related a bit of the luxury found at the General Palmer in *Rocky Mountain Boom Town: A History of Durango*:

```
The Savoy's six o'clock Christmas dinner
featured soups, relishes, meats, fish, roasts,
vegetables, salads and desserts, homemade
mince and pumpkin pies, old English plum
pudding and other treats. All this costs
only $1.
```

The Rest Is History

With a steady increase in business, Palmer soon acquired the Palace Hotel, built in 1895. The annexed hotel increased the number of guest rooms and expanded amenities to include a first-class restaurant.

Improvements continued over the years as the hotel changed in ownership several times following the death of General Palmer in 1909. Renovations, improvements, and additions have occurred over the years, the most notable change being the new name: the General Palmer Hotel, which was fitting, as the historic integrity has always been a priority at the hotel.

As Durango prospered, so did the General Palmer Hotel. During the years of World War I, Durango smelters and coal mines contributed fuel for the war effort, producing nearly 150 tons of coal per year. At the same time, newly created roads commissioned by the Durango Board of Trade and the Chamber of Commerce, allowed for automobile travel to destinations such as Silverton, Mancos, Wolf Creek Pass, and the newly created Mesa Verde National Park.

As a result, the new tourist trade in the Durango area brought more business to the hotel.

The Hotel Today

Stepping into the lobby of the General Palmer Hotel today is like stepping into the elegance of the Victorian era. The spacious lobby offers the same inviting setting with Victorian furniture for visiting or just relaxing, as it did in 1898. Just off the lobby, the solarium is equally charming as well as open and inviting with plenty of windows. Fresh-baked cookies are offered daily in the lobby and solarium.

The hotel offers thirty-nine guest rooms, all decorated with furnishings of the Victorian period that blend quite nicely with the comforts of modern amenities. There is cable television in each room as well as climate-controlled heat and air conditioning. Complimentary turndown service includes bedside treats of Astor Chocolate. A continental breakfast is provided with an assortment of fruit, cereal, yogurt, and muffins.

It is the personal touch, added amenities, and outstanding hospitality that have garnered the General Palmer Hotel the prestigious status of being the only historical four-diamond hotel in southwestern Colorado. Noted celebrities such as Christie Brinkley, Michael J. Fox, Sam Shepard, and Tanya Tucker have enjoyed the charm of this fine hotel.

The staff and charming atmosphere make a stay at the General Palmer Hotel one to remember for a lifetime.

Fun Facts

- Guests of the General Palmer Hotel are greeted with a cuddly teddy bear on each bed as a personal welcome by the staff.

- Palmer's narrow gauge rail line from Durango to Silverton has run continuously since 1881 and is one of a very few rail lines in America that still uses the original steam locomotives.

- General William Jackson Palmer received the Medal of Honor for his leadership of the 15th Pennsylvania Cavalry during a skirmish at Red Hill, Alabama. On January 14, 1865, Palmer and just under two hundred men attacked and defeated a significant force of Confederates, capturing nearly one hundred prisoners—all without losing a man.

- The *Durango Record*, one of the first newspapers in town, was run by a fearless crusader, a woman named Caroline Romney. In her editorials, Romney championed Durango as "the new wonder of the Southwest." She also rallied for women's right to vote. When Colorado granted women the right to vote in 1893, however, Durango and La Plata County voted against the measure.

- During the years of the Great Depression, Durango's original smelter was forced out of business. However, during World War II, the US Vanadium Corporation bought the property. The company built a mill and processed uranium ore, which was used in the production of the atomic bomb.

- There was fierce competition between Durango's newspapers, *The Democrat* and *The Herald*, and it ended in murder. Rod Day took over editorial duties from his infamous father and the founder of the *Durango Democrat*, David Day. Rod shot and killed the editor of the *Durango Herald*, William Wood, on Main Street in broad daylight in April 1922. Amazingly, Rod Day was acquitted of the charge of murder. He sold his newspaper business and left town.

Contact Information: General Palmer Hotel
567 Main Avenue, Durango, Colorado 81301
www.generalpalmerhotel.com   970.247.4747 or 800.523.3358

THE HOTEL ST. NICHOLAS – 1898
THE GREATEST GOLD CAMP ON EARTH

Courtesy of Maria Cunningham

The Hotel St. Nicholas, overlooking downtown Cripple Creek, was originally The St. Nicholas Hospital. Landmark Register: NR5TL2

When Bob Womack found traces of gold in 1878 in the flowing waters of Cripple Creek, which meandered through scattered ranch lands, no one paid attention. Ranchers on the south side of Pikes Peak knew there was no gold in this area of lush green cow pasture! Bob was a stubborn old cuss, though, and he searched for gold for the next twelve years, often spending more time prospecting than he spent ranching—to the disapproval of his family. Bob's search finally paid off on October 20, 1890, when he filed his El Paso Lode claim in Poverty Gulch, the name given to the area where he built his cabin. The find assayed at $250 a ton! The following spring, Ed De La Vergne, a mining man, took some interest in Womack's find and formed the Cripple Creek Mining District on April 5, 1891. It seems that some folks did listen to Ol' Bob.

The Cripple Creek Mining District boomed, and the last great gold rush in Colorado was on. Cripple Creek became known as the "Greatest Gold Camp on Earth." Bob Womack was in his glory

124

and watched as the mining camp became a prosperous town and many men became rich from Cripple Creek's gold. By 1893 the town's population had grown to more than ten thousand.

The Beginning

Within three short years of Womack's gold discovery, Cripple Creek boasted nearly forty groceries and meat markets, fourteen bakeries, four department stores, and eight newspapers. Yet, with

Courtesy of hotel proprietor Susan Adelbush.

The St. Nicholas Hospital, built in 1898 and shown here in 1902, replaced an original wooden structure after the great fires of 1896.

eighty practicing doctors, there was no hospital. Cripple Creek citizens appealed to the Catholic Order of the Sisters of Mercy to help open a hospital. The Sisters of Mercy had introduced hospital care to several Colorado communities, including Denver, Conejos, Durango, and Ouray. To entice the Sisters to Cripple Creek, the citizens donated a wood frame house, located at 326 East Eaton Street, for the hospital.

In late 1893, Sister Mary Claver Coleman arrived in Cripple Creek to establish the town's first hospital, which opened to patients on January 4, 1894. St. Nicholas Hospital was dedicated by Colorado Bishop Nicholas Matz, for whom it was named. More than three hundred patients were treated that first year.

A devastating fire swept through the mining community on April 25, 1896. By nightfall, nearly the entire business district and the surrounding houses were destroyed. Most houses on the west end of town, although there were not many, were spared, including the new hospital. As the citizens began the cleanup process, four days later a second fire nearly finished off what the first had not. Again, the hospital survived. The Sisters were convinced the two fires were a sign and began plans for a larger, safer hospital. This hospital would be built of brick.

Financial arrangements were made, and the Sisters purchased land in 1896 at 235 East Eaton Street, a block from the original hospital location. (The wood frame house, which first housed the hospital still stands. Today, it is a private residence.) This new location was convenient to parishioners of St. Peter's Catholic Church located just across the street.

Renowned Denver architect John J. Huddart designed a state-of-the-art hospital. The three-story red brick building with stone trim was built in the traditional Victorian

style and included elements of Italian design. Two marble columns, rising two stories high, graced the extensive entry porch. Inside the hospital, the first and second floors were designed with rooms for patient care, while the third floor was living quarters for the sisters. It is said the hospital orderly lived in the attic.

Given the transportation obstacles of the day, the new brick hospital was quite an accomplishment. Construction of the St. Nicholas incorporated new technology and used the city's remarkable infrastructure to install hot and cold running water, steam heat, and electricity in the state-of-the-art operating room. The completed building project cost an estimated $12,000.

Although not officially open, the Sisters of Mercy received their first patient in the new location on March 12, 1898. A miner named Elijah Ayers was admitted with injuries suffered from a fall through the shaft of the Specimen Mine. It wasn't until May 15, 1898, that the formal dedication took place with great fanfare. The Cripple Creek business directory of 1902–1903 included an ad for the St. Nicholas Hospital:

```
Thoroughly    Equipped    with    all    Modern
Improvements.   Beautifully   located.   Best
Physicians  in  the  District  in  Attendance.
- Telephone  73  -  Corner  of  Third  and  Eaton
Streets.
```

Glory Days

The Sisters of Mercy ran a very efficient hospital, leaving no room for error. There were rules and regulations that were strictly followed, not only by doctors, nurses, and staff, but also by the patients. All personnel and patients were advised that "loud conversation, unseemly noise, all conduct violating the ordinary rules of propriety, and promenading in the halls, was forbidden."

The original "Hospital Regulations" are displayed today in the ground floor hallway of the hotel. Patients received the best of care at affordable rates. Private room rates started at twelve dollars a week. Use of the operating room cost extra. Cripple Creek mine owner Albert E. Carlton formally leased and elaborately furnished one of the twenty-six rooms for the exclusive use of his employees.

As the hospital grew, so did the medical community. Early on, local doctors formed the Teller County Physicians' Business League and joined with the local Retail Credit Men's Association to create a systematic ad campaign in the many local papers.

In January 1901, a severe health risk broke out in Cripple Creek. Local physicians reported twenty-five cases of smallpox to state officials, as required by law. The Colorado State Board of Health sent a consultant from Denver, and with the help of the excellent staff at St. Nicholas, hospital isolation was established and vaccination for the entire community began within twenty-four hours. Not all agreed to vaccination. Several

miners refused, believing it was another action by the mine owners to intrude on their lives. Fortunately, the local miner's union interceded. Additional measures were taken in the community, including fumigating infected houses and temporarily closing the town's many bars and dance halls, despite protest by the patrons.

By 1902 the hospital had been expanded to better serve the community and create additional living quarters for the sisters. In the continuing years, the hospital grew to include a school. Most of the citizens enjoyed and benefited from the hospital's success, fondly referring to the hospital as the "Sister's hospital." In an aggressive regimen of continued learning, the sisters often held symposiums, lectures, and educational retreats.

In 1905, for example, esteemed Colorado doctors J. N. Hall and Leonard Freeman were guest lecturers at the hospital. Nearly eighty

Turn-of-the-century photographs decorate the walls of the hallway leading to the Boiler Room Tavern.

physicians in the Cripple Creek area attended the event. According to Robert H. Shikes in his book, *Rocky Mountain Medicine*, "Both men's addresses were very practical and especially adapted for a company of general doctors as was present." At the following dinner, much was made of the banter between the two doctors as Dr. Freeman's "Christian disposition was severely taxed in trying to restrain Dr. Hall, who told some wonderful experiences of Cripple Creek, which, if repeated to his Denver friends, will dumbfound the wise."

Influenza, often referred to as "la grippe" in the Victorian era, was not a new disease, and occasional outbreaks were not uncommon. However, in the fall of 1918, just after the end of World War I, a severe outbreak grew into a worldwide pandemic. When it was over, influenza had taken more than twenty million lives across the world, more than were lost during the war. Across Colorado, influenza took more than six thousand lives between September 1918 and June 1919. Colorado's death rate was one of the highest in the nation, affecting primarily young, otherwise healthy, males. The St. Nicholas Hospital was overflowing with patients, and for as well as the facility was staffed, there were not enough doctors and nurses for such a catastrophic emergency. Doctors and nurses

worked around the clock, saving those they could, and caring for those they could not.

Undertaker Oscar Lampman's mortuary, down the hill on Bennett Avenue, became the depository of the deceased. At times, bodies were actually stacked outside the mortuary. Funerals were limited to only four mourners. The local ministers and priests often accompanied the doctors as they made their rounds to the residences, in an effort to save time.

Following the influenza epidemic and the subsequent mine closings and economic downturn, a slow but steady decline in Cripple Creek's population occurred. During those years, the hospital continued to serve the community while operating the school and opening a convent. In 1924, after thirty years of medical service, the Sisters of Mercy left Cripple Creek. A group of doctors, led by Dr. W. Hassenplug, bought the hospital. The facility was used as a private hospital until 1960, when it was sold to the county for one dollar. The City of Cripple Creek took over the administration of the hospital until the hospital closed in 1972.

Eventually The St. Nicholas became a semi-hotel and boarding house.

The Rest Is History

Then in 1995 the century-old hospital was bought and lovingly restored to the grand luster of yesteryear. After a year of top-to-bottom renovations, and an investment of nearly half a million dollars, the new Hotel St. Nicholas emerged, transformed into a wonderful blend of hotel and bed and breakfast inn complete with the Victorian atmosphere and relics of the bygone era. Fifteen rooms have all the expected features, and there are a few extras in the premium rooms, such as enclosed balconies, a sitting room, and panoramic mountain views. All rooms include a private bath and cable TV. Other amenities include a convenient shuttle to the Cripple Creek casinos, free wireless Internet, fax, copier, guest phones, and in-room coffeemakers.

From the original porch entry into the main lobby, the history of the building is evident. Turn-of-the-century photographs decorate many of the walls and hallways. On the main floor of the hotel is the Boiler Room Tavern, named for the hotel's original cast-iron coal-burning boiler on display behind the bar. The massive boiler, weighing in at well over a thousand pounds, heated the entire three floors of the hospital, using one hundred pounds of coal each day! In the office of the hotel is an enormous safe, believed to have been in continual use in the Cripple Creek district for more than one hundred years. The kind folks at the hotel will gladly show the visitor the elaborately painted designs on both sides of the door.

The Hotel Today

Relaxation is the key offering for guests of The Hotel St. Nicholas. They take in the spectacular panoramic view of the Sangre de Cristo Mountains or look down on the town of Cripple Creek. They settle in to the rooftop Jacuzzi, with 104-degree warm

waters, or use the indoor dry sauna, which hosts views of many of gold mines and tailings in the historic Cripple Creek Mining District. Guests can start their day with the elaborate continental breakfast buffet before taking the convenient shuttle to Cripple Creek for a day of sightseeing or gambling.

The hotel also has a large special events room ideal for conferences, parties, and weddings, and can be reserved to accommodate any special occasion.

Courtesy of Maria Cunningham

Some attribute creaking floor boards along the hallway to ghosts from the hotel's days as a hospital.

Fun Facts

- The Hotel St. Nicholas has a history of ghostly encounters. Unexplained events have been reported, including a couple of mischievous ghosts lurking around the old hospital. There are sightings and shenanigans of an apparition known as Little Petey, a child who was a patient at the hospital around the turn of the twentieth century. From time to time, Little Petey has been seen in the building, but his presence is usually known when small objects such as silverware, candles, or keys seem to be moved or hidden, with no explanation. Another ghost has been sighted in the form of a miner, who is seen at the back stairways of the building, and is associated with mysterious sounds of creaking floor boards along the hallway. By all accounts, these ghosts seem to be of a friendly sort. The hotel has even hosted several ghost-hunting groups.

- The massive Cripple Creek fires in April 1896, which destroyed much of the mining community, led to an ironic incident involving the Sisters of Mercy and their first hospital. While the sisters were evacuating patients to safer locations, a member of an anti-Catholic group stormed into the kitchen of the hospital. In an attempt to destroy the hospital, a man placed dynamite in the stove chimney. The dynamite quickly exploded, severing the man's leg. The good sisters took the injured man, along with others, to safety. Through the care of the sisters, he recovered, remorseful to say the least. His shoe, which had landed in the tea kettle, was kept by the sisters as a memento.

- Cripple Creek founder Bob Womack was the honorary marshall of the 1902 Fourth of July parade, where he remarked, "This is sure some Cripple Creek." He contracted pneumonia during the return train ride to Colorado Springs, and his health declined steadily thereafter. He died penniless in 1909.

- The mining district's first millionaire, Winfield Scott Stratton, sold his Independence Mine for a cool $10 million, the largest sale price of any mine in America to that date.

- Spencer Penrose, who would later open the opulent Broadmoor Hotel in Colorado Springs, got his millions from his investment in the C.O.D. Mine in the Cripple Creek Mining District.

Contact Information: The Hotel St. Nicholas
303 North Third Street, Cripple Creek, Colorado 80813
www.hotelstnicholas.com   719.689.0856 or 888.786.4257

ST. ELMO HOTEL – 1898
A WOMAN'S TOUCH

Courtesy of St. Elmo Hotel Collection

The Beginning

In the early days, Ouray was a rough-and-tumble mining town. It took a special breed of men to work the mines in the rugged San Juan Mountains. They worked hard, and they lived harder. The streets were lined with saloons, and, of course, there was the red-light district.

As more and more families settled in the area, the ladies' influence began to civilize the town somewhat. One of those ladies was an enterprising woman by the name of Mrs. Catherine "Kittie" O'Brien Porter Heit.

In 1886 Heit operated the Bon Ton Restaurant. A wooden frame structure with a false facade, the Bon Ton was a fine local restaurant. With the distinct hospitality Heit

The lovingly restored St. Elmo Hotel is located in the heart of the Ouray historic district. Landmark Register: NROR.585

131

offered—it was said she could not resist a miner down on his luck—and improvements in the cuisine, the Bon Ton soon became the most popular restaurant in town. By 1890, Heit was able to purchase the restaurant.

Kittie Heit did so well financially that she expanded her fortune by building a hotel next to her restaurant. She called it the St. Elmo Hotel.

The lobby of the St. Elmo Hotel lobby combines style and comfort.

Glory Days

In 1898 Heit hired architect Frances Carney to build the two-story brick hotel on the north side of the restaurant. When completed and opened for business in early 1899, the exterior was a neat square-shaped building, but the arched windows that graced the arched entranceway added a refined touch. Inside, the hotel lobby was open and spacious, bathed with sunlight from the roof's skylight. Just off the lobby, an elaborate parlor featured French doors opening to an outdoor deck. From the lobby, a wonderfully wide staircase led to the guest rooms on the second floor.

Catering to the miners and traveling businessmen, Heit rented her rooms for an affordable one dollar per night. Of course, meals were available next door at the Bon Ton.

The Rest Is History

A fire in the fall of 1909 destroyed many of the wooden frame buildings in Ouray's downtown commerce area, including The Dixon House hotel and the Delmonica Hotel. Fortunately, the St. Elmo Hotel was built of brick and survived the fire virtually unscathed.

Another disaster occurred that same year when a torrential rainstorm caused a massive flood. Without warning, water rushed from the mountainside bringing with it a gush of mud and rocks, filling the downtown area and many businesses with thick muddy debris. Among the businesses affected was the Bon Ton Restaurant. Yet next door, the St. Elmo Hotel escaped severe damage.

The restaurant building was finally torn down in 1924 and replaced by a wonderful outdoor patio on the north side of the St. Elmo Hotel, where the restaurant had stood. In 1977 a new restaurant in the spirit of the Bon Ton opened. Located in the hotel's lower level, the restaurant resurrected the continental cuisine of the original owner.

Denver Public Library, Western History Collection, X-12722

Kitty O'Brien Heit stands with others on the snow cleared boardwalk of her St. Elmo Hotel, next door to her Bon Ton Restaurant on Main Street in Ouray circa 1899.

The Hotel Today

Fully restored to the splendor of yesteryear, the St. Elmo Hotel offers nine guest rooms, each decorated with period antiques. Guests may enjoy a variety of activities at the hotel, including an afternoon wine and cheese social hour in the comfortable parlor. A relaxing late afternoon or evening spent in the outdoor hot tub, with the backdrop of the silvery San Juan Mountains, is a spectacular way to end the day.

A full buffet breakfast is served to guests in the sunny breakfast room. Delightful meals are also available in the Bon Ton Restaurant in the same tradition that Mrs. Kittie Heit established well over a hundred years ago...with a woman's touch.

FUN FACTS

- In 1879, high freight charges caused shortages in several commodities, including—of all things—butter. Guests at the Bon Ton Restaurant unfortunately had to eat their warm bread without a buttery spread.

- A horrific crime of child abuse, resulting in the death of the child in 1884, led to vigilantism. An angry group of citizens stormed the local jail where the parents of the child were being held and hanged them. This was the only documented lynching of a woman in the mining camps of Colorado.

- Ouray's mountain gold made a millionaire of Thomas Walsh and a legend of his daughter, Evalyn Walsh McLean. She bought the infamous Hope Diamond for $154,000. Today, on display at the Smithsonian in Washington, DC, the diamond is said to be priceless.

Contact Information: St. Elmo Hotel
426 Main Street, Ouray, Colorado 81427
www.stelmohotel.com   970.325.4951 or 866.243.1502

Victor Hotel – 1899
The City of Mines

Courtesy of Maria Cunningham

After major restorations, the Victor Hotel retains many original features and remains the pride of the City of Mines. Landmark Register: NROR.585

The Beginning

The quiet mountain community of Victor still holds the Victorian charm of the mining camp born in the volcanic bowl of gold-mining splendor. Sitting at an elevation of 10,000 feet on the side of Battle Mountain, and part of the Cripple Creek Mining District formed in 1891, Victor is rich in history. It is one of the best-preserved mining towns in the Rocky Mountains, retaining an abundance of Victorian buildings and gold-mining relics such as shafts, hoists, and other remnants of its mining

history. While Cripple Creek received the attention and benefits, the largest and richest gold mines were discovered and developed on Battle Mountain near Victor. Thus, "the City of Mines" became the common name for the congregation of tents and shanties, before the name Victor was officially adopted and the town platted in 1893.

That year, Denver businessman Warren Woods arrived in the mining district with his sons, Frank and Harry. They looked over the area at the foot of Battle Mountain, intending to develop a town site, and eventually bought out their competitor (the Mount Rosa Mining, Milling, and Land Company) for $1,000. After forming the Woods Investment Company, they laid out the new town site, and on November 6, 1893, the town of Victor—named for Victor C. Adams, a local homesteader—was officially platted. At twenty-five dollars a lot, land sold quickly, businesses were built, and a mining town was formed.

Marketing these lots as "gold mines" for the prospective merchants turned out to be quite prophetic. When the Woods brothers broke ground for a new hotel in early 1894 in the center of the town, they struck gold! Their future pay dirt would come not from the hotel, but rather the gold, which became an investment benefiting both the Woods and the town. And that's how Victor, literally, became the City of Mines.

When Frank Woods hit that twenty-inch vein of gold at the corner of Diamond Avenue and 4th Street while grading the land for the hotel, construction of the hotel immediately ceased. The Woods brothers traced the vein to the Gold Coin claim, which they quickly bought for a few thousand dollars. A shaft was sunk in the middle of the strike, and the Gold Coin Mine was erected on the main thoroughfare of Victor. Within a year, the Woods brothers' Gold Coin Mine was producing $50,000 a month, and by 1899 the returned dividend to their stockholders averaged $200,000.

For many years the Victor Hotel housed a bank on the first floor. The spacious hotel lobby still contains the original bank vault.

In the meantime, the Woods brothers bought another lot, downhill and a block south—at the southeast corner of Victor Avenue and 4th Street—and built their Victor Hotel. The opening of the hotel in July 1894 coincided perfectly with the first completed rail line into the mining district: the Florence & Cripple Creek Railroad. The three-story hotel was the tallest building in town and the showplace of Victor. Its wooden frame was topped by a cone-shaped tower, a technical marvel for Victor. The corner entrance was down slope of 4th Street and featured enclosed

balconies directly above it on both the second and third floors. Guests were accommodated in rooms on the upper floors. An added feature was electricity throughout the hotel. Town festivals and social gatherings were always held at the well-regarded Victor Hotel, and guests could watch as parades passed by.

> A grand ball will be given at the Hotel Victor, Victor, Colorado, to-night. A special train will leave Cripple Creek at 8:30 p.m. returning after the dance closes. The ball will be one of the most interesting of the season.
>
> — *The Cripple Creek Journal*, November 2, 1894

A raging fire on the hot afternoon of August 21, 1899, changed everything. It started in the red-light district known as Paradise Alley, between 3rd and 4th Streets, and swept through the entire town of Victor, burning nearly every structure, including the Victor Hotel, in less than five hours.

Glory Days

The Woods brothers, along with most folks in Victor, wasted no time rebuilding. The hotel was relocated across the street, at the corner of Victor Avenue and 4th Street, and the new structure was built of pale brick, making it nearly fireproof. The four-story, rectangular building commanded a large portion of the commercial block. The grand opening was held on Christmas Eve 1899, with a cheery crowd who very much needed something to be proud of in their newly built town.

Larger than the first hotel, this building accommodated businesses as well as hotel guests. The first floor provided private offices for lawyers, mining engineers, and bankers. In fact, an entire bank, the First National Bank of Victor, owned by Frank and Harry Woods, was located on the first floor and had two entrances: one from 4th Street and the other from Victor Avenue.

Dominated by Romanesque arches with intricate woodworking at the windows and doorways, the large and open lobby featured an elaborate elevator complete with wrought iron bars and a safe-locking door, the first in the district. The largest bank vault in the district securely held the majority of the local mining wealth in gold and currency.

The upper floors were decorated in wallpaper patterns of the era, and the ceilings were intricately designed metal. The second and third floors held more businesses. Guest rooms were on the fourth floor, with bathrooms conveniently located along the hallway. The comfortable rooms rented for $2.50 a night.

Considered "the most modern edifice in the Cripple Creek District," the new building

contained the offices of many prominent and influential businessmen and leaders in the district. The Woods Brothers Investment Company, the Colorado Telephone Company, and the Western Union Telegraph Company all ran their businesses from the second floor. Doctors, dentists, and surgeons had offices on the third floor, including osteopathic surgeon Dean M. Bodwell and general practitioner H. G. Thomas, father of national radio host, Lowell Thomas. Attorneys J. W. Huff and J. E. Ferguson had offices on the third floor. Mining engineers such as Davis & Byler, with the US deputy of mineral surveyors, also located their offices there.

The Rest Is History

By the turn of the century, Victor, once a small mining camp, had developed into a thriving mountain community. The largest producing mines in the district were on Battle Mountain. Refining ore mills were built in Victor, and area employment soared. In 1900 the population was near eighteen thousand, making it the fifth-largest city in Colorado. Three railroads and two electric streetcars ran in, out, and around the city limits of Victor. Monthly payroll just for Victor's mines was in excess of $600,000. Even the rival mining town of Cripple Creek could not deny the riches of Victor gold.

Much of the wealth and prosperity was due in no small part to the Woods brothers. In addition to their extensive real estate holdings—including the Victor Hotel, the First National Bank of Victor, and the Gold Coin Mine—the brothers also formed the Pikes Peak Power Company, the Teller County Mining Supply Company, and the United Mines Transportation Company, and had controlling interest in more than two dozen mining companies. Their mining empire spread from Victor east to Arequa Gulch, north for more than four miles including the Bull, Ironclad, Raven Hills, Wild Horse and Deadwood Mines.

Victor's prosperity and the Woods brothers' empire would be short-lived. In 1900, the Gold Coin Mine began to play out, and profits declined rapidly. This had a domino effect on the economy of Victor, which was based largely on the Woods empire. Because the local economy had shriveled greatly, there was a run on the First National Bank of Victor. Even the district's first millionaire, Winfield Scott Stratton, withdrew his money from the bank. By 1902, the struggling Woods brothers consolidated their various holdings into the United Gold Mines Company. The violent labor wars of 1903 and 1904, which brought in the National Guard and martial law, made national headlines. In the end, organized labor had been defeated, yet the mining town of Victor never fully recovered.

Despite all their property, investments, and wealth—in excess of $40 million— the Woods brothers had huge debts. Bank auditors declared their First National Bank insolvent and closed its doors on November 4, 1903. The hotel and investment company were the next victims in the fall of the Woods empire.

A. E. Carlton, a wealthy mine owner, brought the Cripple Creek Mining District, including the Victor-area mines, back into operation. The drainage tunnels he built ran several miles under and around the town, connecting with many mines and providing adequate water drainage. Carlton bought the Victor Hotel and established his own bank, the City Bank, on the first floor. Business offices remained on the second and third floors; the fourth floor was converted into a hospital.

Known for generations in Victor as The Bank Building, this photograph of the hotel was made in 1965. The bank itself closed during the Great Depression.

In 1917 Carlton sold his bank to J. R. Gardner, who incorporated and changed the bank name to the Citizen's Bank of Victor. Thus, for years the building has been known by generations of Victorites as The Bank Building. The bank itself, however, closed during the Great Depression.

The Hotel Today

In 1992 the Victor Hotel underwent a massive $1 million restoration. The most prominent building in Victor, the cream brick structure with peach-colored trim, still features the original twelve-foot-tall plate glass windows as well as the original pressed metal ceiling.

The spacious hotel lobby still displays the original bank vault, the original birdcage elevator (which is still operational), and the restored office suite of the Wood brothers. Surrounded by the grand Victorian era style, guests at the hotel enjoy a step back in time.

All guest rooms have a private bath as well as cable television, telephone, and high-speed Internet. Many of the rooms offer spectacular panoramic views of the Sangre de Cristo Mountains and the Continental Divide.

FUN FACTS

- The ornate iron elevator also served as transportation of a different sort in the early 1900s. Frozen ground during the winter months made it impossible to dig graves at the Sunnyside Cemetery. Bodies were transported by elevator to the fourth floor of the hotel, and held until springtime thawed the ground. Hotel guests have reported ghost sightings on the fourth floor. Apparitions of headless ghosts, ghosts without arms or legs, and even ghosts that appear to be doctors have been reported.

- The Victor Hotel is known for ghost stories. Perhaps the most widely told is about the ghost of "Eddie." Eddie was a miner who lived in Room 301. Leaving for work one day, Eddie fell through the elevator shaft to his death. Today, guests in Room 301 often don't stay the entire night. They report hearing footsteps and other unexplained sounds. On occasion, the well-maintained elevator mysteriously activates on its own, always stopping on the third floor.

- Colorado Governor Ralph Carr, known for racial tolerance and for protection of the basic rights of the Japanese Americans during the World War II, lived in Victor and worked for the *Victor Daily Record*. His rival and lifelong friend was radio broadcaster and writer Lowell Thomas at the *Victor Daily News*.

- There is still a wealth of gold in, around, and under the city of Victor. Although gold mining today does not bring with it the excitement or hustle and bustle of the old days, the industry continues in the form of the Cripple Creek & Victor Gold Mining Company. While operating the largest open pit and leach mine in Colorado, the company has also focused on the historic preservation of the district.

Contact Information: Victor Hotel
  4th Street and Victor Avenue, Victor, Colorado 80860
  www.victorhotelcolorado.com 719.689.3553. or 800.713.4595

REDSTONE INN – 1902
THE RUBY OF THE ROCKIES

The Beginning

An industrialist, a tycoon, a millionaire, and to some, a robber baron, John Cleveland Osgood built a family-friendly community for his employees, called Redstone, at the base of Coal Basin along the majestic Crystal River. While some called Redstone a utopian village or an experiment in social paternalism, Osgood's workers were dedicated and loyal. And Mrs. Osgood, known as Lady Bountiful, was beloved by her family, the workers, and the community. Redstone was, and still is, a picturesque Victorian mountain mining community unlike any other in the country.

John Osgood was born in 1851 and grew up in western Iowa until the deaths of his father, Samuel, and his mother, Mary, left him an orphan in 1859. He went to live with Quaker relatives in Providence, Rhode Island, where he attended the Friends Boarding School and eventually found work at various mills and produce companies.

A full moon shines over the historic Redstone Inn, located high in the Rockies along the Crystal River in Redstone. Landmark Register: NR5PT.553.1

At the age of sixteen, he got a job as a cashier at the White Breast Fuel Company where he gained knowledge that would serve him well later in life. Osgood managed to put himself through school, attending the Peter Cooper Institute—also known as the "Poor Man's Harvard"—where he earned a degree in accounting. After graduating at the age of nineteen, he became a bookkeeper for the Union Mining Company in Ottumwa, Iowa. Four years later, he was head cashier of the First National Bank of Burlington, Iowa. His strong aptitude for business was admired as he rose in position with the bank.

Osgood learned that coal, the fuel used in the growing railroad industry as well as for home heating, returned a high rate of return on investment. In 1876 he left his job at the bank and acquired controlling interest in his previous employer, the White Breast Fuel Company. By this time, White Breast Fuel had expanded and was the prime fuel supplier of the Chicago, Burlington & Quincy Railroad. In February 1882, Osgood was selected by the officers of the railroad to investigate and report on possible coal resources in the state of Colorado.

Osgood investigated nearly every existing coal camp in the state. His business knowledge and keen foresight would change the economy in the state forever. Osgood invested heavily, acquiring rich deposits of coal across the state including extensive coal bands in the western plateau region along the Crystal River. In 1884 he formed his own coal company, the Colorado Fuel Company, with seven hundred acres of coal land. Osgood systematically surveyed the land along the Crystal River, as well as the western region, including Treasure Mountain. Over a four-year period, he bought land with potential coal deposits as well as existing claims. He also invested in the rich marble claims along the river.

By 1888 Osgood controlled more than five thousand acres of land rich with coal. With the acquired assets, his company had more than $5 million in capital. The business did so well under his leadership that in 1892 Osgood bought out his competition, the powerful Pueblo-based Colorado Coal and Iron Company, which he renamed the Colorado Fuel & Iron Company (CF&I). In time, Osgood's company would extend south to New Mexico and north into Wyoming with sixty-two mines and quarries. The company produced necessities for western expansion, including iron rails, steel pipes and fencing, and the common nail.

While CF&I expanded rapidly and profited, Osgood returned his focus to the Coal Basin area, and in a big way. First, his company constructed two hundred coke ovens to carbonize the coal mined from Coal Basin. The beehive-like coke ovens were the essence of the fuel enterprise. They were used to burn and then distill the coal into coke, which was then transformed into an energy source for heating or into a component in the steelmaking process. Next, Osgood brought transportation to the isolated area with the construction of the Crystal River Railroad, completed in 1899. The narrow gauge rail line ran twelve miles climbing grades in excess of 4 percent, hauling the coke to connect with the main line of the Denver & Rio

Grande Railroad at Carbondale to be transported to the steel mills in Pueblo.

The coal miners and workers operating the coke ovens lived in tents or makeshift shacks along the river and the basin. John Osgood wanted better conditions for his employees and their families. To that end, he built them a town, which some would call a model for company towns.

The town was lavish in every way. The eighty-four cottage-style homes that Osgood built for the workers had indoor plumbing and electricity. Designed by the New York architectural firm of Boal & Harnois, each house was unique in its design and color. Some were simple, others were elaborate for the era. All included shingle roofs, a small yard and a gardening space, and a few even had neat picket fences. The tranquil beauty of the Crystal River flowing through the town added to the majestic Rocky Mountain setting of the village.

The two-story Redstone Inn is adorned by a large square clock tower with a clock on all four sides.

Particular attention was paid to proper drainage and sanitation. A water system was installed, using water from the local reservoir, which also was used for fire protection. Osgood provided a second source of jobs in the valley by hiring an auxiliary group known as the Redstone Improvement Company to provide various maintenance services.

The Redstone community amenities included horse stables, a company store, a club house, a library, a school, and churches. Osgood's employees and their families enjoyed a miner's lifestyle unlike any other in America. Osgood provided for his bachelor employees by building a grand hotel for them at the edge of the town: the Redstone Inn.

Glory Days

> There are many beautiful valleys in
> Colorado, but the valley of the Crystal,
> vies with any and all. Sixteen miles up the
> canon lies Redstone. A perfect picture of

color it is, well built, harmonious with
its surroundings and prosperous, if not
opulent, in appearance.
—*Denver Times*, September 12, 1902

John Osgood built the forty-two room Cleveholm
Manor on 200 acres south of the Redstone Inn. By the
time it was completed in early 1903, locals were already
calling it the Redstone Castle.

Denver Public Library, Western History Collection, MCC-1967

Dominating this picture-perfect mining community, the Redstone Inn stood two stories tall and was adorned by a large square clock tower with a clock on all four sides. As with the other buildings in Redstone, the inn was designed and built by Boal & Harnois. Theodore Boal, who also constructed several buildings in Denver (including the Denver Country Club), was the mastermind behind the Redstone Inn. The wood frame hotel had a red sandstone base with three wings enhanced with elaborate cross-timbering and capped by a steep pitched gable roof. An outdoor courtyard centered between the wings of the inn added to the opulence.

Inside, the finest of oak furnishings were procured from local furniture maker Gustav Stickley, who would later become one of America's better known furniture makers. There were twenty furnished rooms for the miners as well as spacious parlors, reading rooms with stone fireplaces, a billiard room, a barroom, and even a theater with hand-painted scenery backdrops. Businesses on the main floor included E. H. Williams' barbershop about which the local paper reported:

All the young men in town vote him a
master of the tonsorial art.

While protocol was somewhat relaxed in most areas of the inn, in the full-service dining room guests were expected to dress appropriately, watch their language, and drink in moderation. A curious rule that Osgood implemented was dubbed the "no treating rule." It allowed people to buy as many drinks for themselves as desired, but prohibited anyone from buying someone else a drink. Strange as it seems, there was never any drunkenness or rowdy behavior in the inn.

Although the Redstone Inn was built for the town's bachelor miners, it also catered to traveling salesmen, businessmen, and general visitors to the area. There was a second hotel built in the mining town, the Big Horn Lodge, which catered to officials and board members of CF&I. However, the lodge was not well ventilated against the constant smoke and fumes of the nearby coke ovens. In any case, within a year, the Redstone Inn was the hotel of choice for all visitors.

While the miners respected and appreciated their employer, John C. Osgood, and his extraordinary humanitarian effort in building Redstone for them and their families, it was Osgood's second wife, Alma, who touched their lives in a personal way. John was by nature a very private person, but Alma was good-natured and very outgoing.

When Osgood's first marriage ended in divorce, he reconnected with Alma Regina Shelgrem, whom he had met years before through Belgium's King Leopold. A courtship ensued, and in October 1899 Osgood and his tall, slender, blonde bride arrived in Denver, where the newspapers had quite a field day with rumor and innuendo. Alma

was said to be a Swedish countess with a "dubious" past. Although nothing was ever proven, it was enough of a scandal that she was snubbed by Denver's elite social club, the Sacred Thirty-Six. No matter for Osgood; he simply took his bride to the Crystal Valley and his own town of Redstone. Alma immediately fell in love with the mountain area and the people who lived there.

To the miners' wives and their children, Alma was not only a respected presence but a friend. She often drove her horse-drawn carriage through town, stopping at houses to check in or ask if there was anything needed. If there were needs—food, clothing, medical attention— Alma immediately attended to

Denver Public Library, Western History Collection, Z-6616

The circa 1905 photograph of the Club Room at Cleveholm Manor shows the luxurious furnishings, antiques, and art of the mansion.

The Fireside Lounge in the Redstone Inn is a cozy spot anytime, but especially during the holidays.

the task. In this way, she earned the name "Lady Bountiful." The kind sentiment from the town folks meant a lot to Alma, although she insisted it was the caring for others that mattered to her. In 1902 she organized night school for the town and later provided 250 books to the school library.

The Christmas season was the Osgoods' favorite time of year. The couple had no children of their own, but they held grand Christmas parties for the mining families and presented gifts to every child. Alma encouraged the children to write letters to Santa Claus and made sure they were delivered to her.

John and Alma Osgood were not only kind and generous to their employees—who were the citizens of Redstone—they also encouraged community involvement and support. John organized a local volunteer fire department, securing advice from Julius Pearse, the former chief of the Denver Fire Department. John provided the equipment and uniforms for the firefighters. Alma helped organize the town band, providing instruments and uniforms for the members (all miners) and even paid for a band leader, Eliseo Jacoe. Alma also composed a song for the band called the "The Redstone Waltz."

The Osgoods proved to be perfect partners, not only in their commitment to coal workers and their families, but also in business. Alma fell into her role as the wife of a multimillionaire with flair and grace. Her youth, love of life, and charm, put the guests of the Redstone Inn at ease.

The Rest Is History

In 1902, Osgood had completed building the mining town of Redstone and the Redstone Inn. CF&I had grown to more than thirty-six thousand employees. He was the fifth-richest man in America. Now he turned his attention to building a mansion for Alma in the Crystal River Valley.

The construction of Cleveholm Manor, located a mile south of the town on two hundred acres of gorgeous meadow property, began in July. The architectural firm of Boal & Harnois was again hired. The Tudor-style home contained forty-two rooms and was built of red stone brick, quarried locally. By the time Cleveholm Manor was completed in early 1903, the locals had already begun calling the mansion the Redstone Castle. To this day, it is often confused with the Redstone Inn. According to Osgood and

an account in the *Denver Republican* in July 1901, the cost of the mansion was $40,000. However, when the couple filled the mansion with their many fine furnishings, antiques, and art—acquired from their extensive travels around the world—the value of the estate was placed at $2 million. It was here that the Osgoods entertained notable guests such as J. P. Morgan, Jay Gould, John D. Rockefeller, and even President Theodore Roosevelt (in 1903).

By the time John Osgood entertained the president, he was the largest private landowner, employer, and taxpayer in the state of Colorado. During the next decade, more than one million tons of coal were mined by Redstone miners and workers. With the growth of the company, the employees and citizens of Redstone prospered as well.

With prosperity came more investors and visitors to Redstone, who stayed at the Redstone Inn. The Inn was closed for a time in 1910 while the Osgoods traveled extensively in Europe. Details are sketchy, but the couple did not return to Redstone together and divorced at some point during this time. Osgood would later say that Alma was one of the finest ladies he had ever known. Alma remained in France where she died in 1955.

The hotel received a complete renovation in 1925, when Osgood brought his third wife, the former Lucille Reid, to Redstone. A year later, John Osgood died. The entire estate and business holdings were left to his widow. Lucille Osgood ran the Redstone Inn as a resort hotel quite successfully until the Great Depression of the 1930s caused near financial ruin. By 1941 Redstone had a total population of fourteen residents.

The Hotel Today

The historic Redstone Inn remains the premier hotel in the Crystal River Valley. Standing tall and inviting among the pristine Victorian cottages, art galleries, and Colorado marble sculptures in the park, the hotel is open year-round.

Renovations and updates in keeping with the latest technology and style have been an ongoing aim at this hotel. In the 1950s, with the growth of the highway system, the hotel added another wing to accommodate tourists. The Redstone area is located along the West Elk Loop Scenic and Historic Byway of Colorado Highway 133.

Forty rooms afford guests all the charm of mountain hospitality. Another remodeling occurred in 1983, bringing the spacious parlors into a new splendor and expanding the restaurant and dining areas.

Fun Facts

- John Osgood often treated his distinguished guests to outdoor excursions around his property. On a horseback trip up McClure Pass, one of his guests commented on the difficulty of the trail and said an automobile would never reach the summit. A few days later, Osgood took his guests up the trail again by horse. To their astonishment, at the summit of the pass was an automobile! A few of Osgood's employees had been instructed to dismantle the vehicle, haul the pieces to the summit, and reassemble it. A good gentlemanly chuckle was had by all.

- Fire was ever a threat to mining towns. Due to the foresight of Osgood, who implemented a reservoir water system and a volunteer fire department, Redstone never suffered from such a disaster.

- The quarry located at the nearby community of Marble was the source of stone used to construct both the Tomb of the Unknown Soldier and the Lincoln Memorial in Washington, DC.

- Osgood's first wife, Nonnie Irene de Belote, was the author of romance novels who occasionally researched her novels by having romantic dalliances of her own. She once made quite a scandalous scene in the bar of the Hotel Colorado in Glenwood Springs when her advances toward an innocent patron were rejected. She was escorted from the hotel, and the embarrassed John Osgood soon ended the marriage.

- The entire community of Osgood's mining village of Redstone is listed on the National Register of Historic Places as an historic district.

Contact Information: Redstone Inn
82 Redstone Boulevard, Redstone, Colorado 81623
www.redstoneinn.com   970.963.2526 or 800.748.2524

River Forks Inn – 1905
A River Runs through It

Courtesy of hotel proprietor Bill Jones

Among the many crevices of the Rocky Mountains, hidden from the white man for centuries, lies a narrow gorge cut through the solid rock by what is known today as the Big Thompson River. Native American tribes, primarily the Utes, knew the river well. The headwaters of the river begin high in what is known today as Forest Canyon, at the northern edge of Rocky Mountain National Park. The steep terrain and sparse vegetation along the canyon of the Big Thompson allows for the free-flowing rush of water downstream, creating rock cliffs that rise several hundred feet toward the sky. For two miles, the water flows down the canyon and then gently meanders through a lovely mountain meadow.

It was here that many members of the Ute Mountain tribe gathered for the winter season. Later called Cedar Cove, the meadow was a natural warm valley, protected by the canyon walls and the surrounding Rocky Mountains. Ute leaders such as Tabernash and Colorow brought their tribes to winter in this area, which held an abundance of game for hunting as well as good fishing.

Westward expansion, encouraged by the government, led scouts, mountain men, trappers, and traders to follow the river and eventually make their way into the spectacular valley. Most moved on, but one who stayed was Mariano Medina.

Travelers through the Drake area of the Big Thompson Canyon are as welcome at the River Forks Inn today as they were a century ago.
Landmark Register: NRHP

The Beginning

Medina, a native of Taos, New Mexico, was an experienced trapper, trader, and bounty hunter by the time he settled in the valley in 1858. Throughout his years of trapping and trading, he kept company with notable mountain men such as Jim Bridger, Tom Tobin, Louis Vasquez, Jim Baker, Kit Carson, and the Bent brothers. When Medina and his Indian wife took up a claim along the Big Thompson River, they became the first permanent settlers in the area. Medina built a large building, fortified with natural stone, and opened a trading post that later included a community center. More buildings followed when Medina opened a trading post. His stone buildings offered refuge during the Indian scares.

Medina also built rafts to ferry travelers across the river for a hefty charge. Later, he built a toll bridge high enough to avoid the roaring river waters during the spring thaw. Known locally as "Medina's Crossing" or "Namaqua Station," it soon became the crossing point of choice for the many travelers along the trails in the area. The Texas and Overland Trails crossed here as did the Denver/Laramie Trail. Offshoots of the Platte River Trail and the Oregon Trail also passed through Medina's land.

> Mr. Ceran St. Vrain has been seen in the company of Mariano Medina at his post in the Big Thompson ... with other famous people, William Gilpin and William Bent.
> — *Rocky Mountain News*, September 5, 1859

Medina's stepson, Louis Papa, so enjoyed his childhood in the valley of the Big Thompson that he filed for a homestead at Cedar Cove, where he built a log cabin. In the cove, Papa met Frank Bartholf, a newcomer to the area, and the two became lifelong friends. Bartholf had homesteaded land a few miles north of Cedar Cove, along the Big Thompson River, at a point where the river forks north toward the Mummy Range (now part of Rocky Mountain National Park). Here, Bartholf built a respectable cattle ranch, which Papa eventually managed.

Incredible as it may seem, at the turn of the century, the original stage road through the valley had never been improved. The Larimer County commissioners took bids for road construction in early 1903. After two years of infighting, corruption, armed guards posted along the road, and scandal that resulted in a nasty lawsuit, a one-lane dirt road that followed the river was finally opened for use.

Meanwhile, Frank Bartholf had done quite well for himself. With the success of his ranch, he had gained respect throughout the valley, even being one of the county commissioners during the stage road controversy. Once the road was opened to travelers and tourists, Bartholf began building a commercial inn at the river fork.

Glory Days

The two-story log inn, built at the junction where several tributaries join the Big Thompson River, began as a stage stop along a popular road of travel. Travelers took this route to get to Loveland, which was the nearest town to a railroad, and businessmen and tourists took the route to Estes Park. The enterprising Bartholf secured a deal with the Colorado & Southern Company, which operated the stagecoach service between Loveland and Estes Park, to provide meals and personal accommodations for its passengers. The stage stopped at the inn to change horses, and allow the passengers to have a meal and relax or even spend the night, before resuming their journey.

The River Forks Inn, originally known as the Forks Hotel, opened on May 15, 1905, and before the year was out, Bartholf set his sights on expansion. After a very profitable year he enlisted the help and influence of Colorado State Senator William A. Drake to secure a post office to be housed in his establishment. With this procurement, the community had to be named. The area surrounding the river forks thereby became known as Drake, in honor of the Colorado senator.

The inn became widely known for its fine overnight accommodations and excellent meals. Bartholf improved the inn with expansions and additional buildings. The main building contained thirty guest rooms on the upper level, while the spacious main floor had a large dining area and a separate room for visiting, playing cards, or reading.

Within two years of the successful opening, a new explosion of tourist trade through the Big Thompson Canyon brought prosperity to the area and attention to the wonders of the canyon. The instant popularity of the Stanley Steamer, a new automobile invented by F. O. Stanley of

Courtesy of hotel proprietor Bill Jones

Hotel owner Bill Jones doubles as bartender at the River Forks Inn.

nearby Estes Park, not only changed the mode of transportation, but also provided a personal way to travel and sightsee. Those early days of automobile transportation brought a new set of road hazards. In an effort to avoid mishaps, the speed limit for autos driving through the canyon was twelve miles an hour, and drivers were required to honk their horns when approaching curves in the road. Horse-drawn vehicles had the right-of-way in all situations, and in general, drivers were to pull their cars over and stop the engines. By 1910 the road had been improved due to the increasing popularity of the area.

The inn easily adapted to changes in transportation, as did the Drake community. With the new influx of tourists, the hotel, as well as surrounding businesses, flourished. Among the entrepreneurs was Bartholf's daughter, Mrs. Van Bramor, who realized the economic opportunity and filed for eighty acres to establish a summer resort, which she called Rosedale. Known as the "halfway place" because its location in the canyon was halfway between Loveland and Estes Park, the resort was a popular destination.

By 1912 a few gas stations, stopping areas, and restaurants dotted both sides of the canyon road. Through all the changes, the River Forks Inn, as it came to be known, remained a favorite stop.

The Rest Is History

Throughout the history of this rustic inn, several changes have been made, including changes in ownership, yet the original intent—hospitality—has remained constant.

Frank Alderdyce eventually bought the River Forks Inn and became the postmaster, a position he would occupy off and on for two decades. Later, Ralph and Helen Hayden purchased it, making improvements over the forty years they owned the establishment. The Haydens expanded the property to include a delightful campground, the newest trend in the tourist trade. They also remodeled the original building to include a large cafe and grocery store.

The hotel was the scene of much activity during the 1930s. Under President Franklin Roosevelt's work project, known as the Works Progress Administration (WPA), highway workers widened and paved the road now known as US Highway 34. The WPA workers stayed for months at a time at the hotel. When the improved road was finished in 1938, local businesses in Drake, Loveland, and Estes Park were thrilled with the results.

Tourism became a whole new experience. The new paved highway stretched from Loveland on the east, through Drake and the Big Thompson Canyon, to Estes Park on the west and continued over Trail Ridge Road, the highest continuously paved highway in the world. Travel along the road, which once took two days, now took two hours, if the weather

Denver Public Library, Western History Collection, MCC-997

After improvements to the road from Loveland to Estes Park in 1905, the Forks Hotel became a popular stop for tourists and travelers. This photograph shows two Stanley Steamers in front of the hotel in 1909.

cooperated. Tourists marveled at the mountain scenery, the meadows filled with wild-flowers and wildlife, and the occasional snowfall in July.

Disaster struck the Big Thompson Canyon and the town of Drake in July 1976. On a Saturday night, a wall of rushing water roared through the canyon, leaving little in its wake. Nearly 150 people lost their lives, and many bodies were never recovered. More than 200 homes and businesses were destroyed, as well as the road and several bridges. When it was over, the area was nearly leveled, and debris dangled over or drifted in the river.

"Scores dead, hundreds hurt in Big Thompson flash flood," was the headline in the *Rocky Mountain News* on August 2, 1976. The article reported that "survivors told of a surge of water in the Big Thompson River and its north fork" that ranged from a "wall six to eight feet tall" to a "steady rise that took everything with it—cars, houses, everything."

When it was over, one of the few businesses left standing was the River Forks Inn. The Haydens had spent the previous night going house to house, warning their neighbors of the rushing floodwaters. Helen Hayden later recalled, "Everything was so dark without electricity. But with the lightning, which was often, we would see the debris and campers and small cabins going down the river. We were all anxious for morning to come but were dreading what we would see. As we walked to the hotel, the hummingbirds were thick, flying around our heads, and all their feeders were gone. Fish were all over the ground, and what a sight to see, no houses, no nothing."

The hotel sustained much water damage, and repairs and remodeling soon began. At the west end of the hotel, a two-story expansion was built. Inside, the rustic log décor enhanced the rock wall siding as well as the large fireplace and elaborate wooden bar. Upstairs, a comfortable and inviting lounge greeted guests.

With the new improvements to the hotel, as well as to the entire town of Drake, it wasn't long before tourists were again enjoying the sights and hospitality of the Big Thompson Canyon area.

The Hotel Today

Nestled in the beautiful, rugged canyon, the rustic River Forks Inn retains the historic splendor of yesteryear, while offering modern conveniences. Ten charming guest rooms provide a comfortable overnight stay, or visitors can simply relax and enjoy the other amenities the facility offers. The Stage Stop Event Center is a popular local attraction, with live music and karaoke nights. A large outdoor deck provides seating and a stage for concerts. A fun beer garden graces the opposite side of the hotel, where guests can enjoy an outdoor lunch or dinner and maybe spot wildlife on the property. Overnight camping by the river's edge is also available on the hotel property.

The River Forks Inn has the only restaurant in the Big Thompson Canyon between Estes Park and Loveland. The inn is located a short drive from Estes Park and Rocky Mountain National Park.

FUN FACTS

- Indications of ancient Indian camps can still be found in the area of Cedar Cove.

- Fort Namaqua Park—located nearly halfway between Loveland and Drake, at County Road 19E and the Big Thompson River—is the site of a trading post and stage station operated by Mariano Medina, who came to the area in 1858. It is one of the earliest historic sites in Colorado. An impressive stone marker with a plaque marks the site.

- Historian Ken Jessen writes in *Thompson Valley Tales*, "The Riley road was so narrow that it led to some strange events. The stagecoach from Loveland to Estes Park had the right-of-way in both directions. If the coach met a wagon at a point far from a turn-out, the men on the coach would unhitch the on-coming wagon and walk the horses around the coach. Next, the men would remove the wheels from the wagon and roll them by the coach. Finally, the bed of the wagon would be placed on the hillside allowing the stage to pass. The wagon would then be reassembled, and the two vehicles would continue their journey."

- Troy and Roy Jones brought back weekend music at River Forks Inn, a tradition started by Jerry Shaffer. Shaffer was the son of a previous owner and had a country band that played regularly for patrons of the restaurant and bar.

Contact Information: River Forks Inn
1597 West Highway 34, Drake, Colorado 80515
www.riverforksinn.com   970.669.2380

HOTEL BOULDERADO – 1909
WHERE EVERY GUEST MAY EXPECT THE BEST

The nomadic Southern Arapaho Indian tribe had wintered for years at the base of the Flatirons, the iconic rock formations that are the geological wonder of today's town of Boulder. With the discovery of gold in Boulder Creek and its tributaries during the Pikes Peak gold rush of 1858–1859, miners flocked to the area. Boulder Creek, as well as the town and county of the same name, was named for the rocky creek that flows east from the Continental Divide. With the steady population increase, eventually the Southern Arapaho, led by Chief Niwot, were forced to move off their winter land.

As the area grew in population, the Boulder City Town Company was founded on February 10, 1859. The town founders laid out a two-mile-long community along Boulder Creek. With the creation of the Colorado Territory in 1861, the new town of Boulder became the seat of Boulder County. The town grew slowly but steadily as a

The five-story Hotel Boulderado has entertained visitors to Boulder for more than a century.

Landmark Register: NR5BL.240

mining supply town, and gained a substantial foothold when land was donated for the establishment of the University of Colorado in 1876.

The Beginning

Despite having a first-class institution of higher learning, being a railroad hub, and enjoying a thriving business community, the town of Boulder only had eight thousand residents at the turn of the century. Even more surprising, Boulder lacked a luxury hotel. The citizens of Boulder rallied, and several potential backers stepped forward to bring a hotel to town.

In late 1905, with the backing of the city council, the Boulder Commercial Association was formed. The group, a forerunner to the Chamber of Commerce, pledged to raise the money for a hotel by selling shares for $100 each. "Let it be the Hotel Beautiful" was the association's slogan. After six months, with less than half of the money pledged for the hotel construction and furnishings, the *Daily Camera* launched an editorial campaign to rouse support for the money drive. It evidently worked, because

Courtesy of Silvia Pettem

by the end of the year, sales of the stock doubled and an architect was hired. On April 27, 1906, the Boulder Hotel Company was formed.

Meanwhile, suggestions for the name of the hotel were bandied about in the editorial pages of the newspaper. William R. Rathvon, president of the Boulder Commercial Association, suggested that the hotel be named Boulderado, a composite of the town name, Boulder, and the state name, Colorado.

The family firm of William Redding & Son designed the Mission Revival red brick structure trimmed in sandstone. Groundbreaking ceremonies took place on the northwest corner of 13th and Spruce Streets in 1906.

The Hotel Boulderado was five stories tall, with central parapets, each of which were flanked by four square corner towers. There were several pairs of tall narrow windows on each floor, with gabled accents, giving the hotel the look of Italian Revival architecture.

The hotel took nearly three years to build. When completed, local newspapers up and down the Front Range gave rave reviews of Boulder's finest hotel.

The Hotel Boulderado has been the site of college sorority and fraternity events for many years. These 1960s students look down on the lobby perhaps anticipating a special occasion.

Glory Days

The Hotel Boulderado put on a glorious grand opening on New Year's Eve 1908. The *Daily Camera*, in its first edition of 1909, declared:

```
Last night's visitors at the Boulderado
were charmed with the beauty ... the size
and airiness, the arrangements of rooms and
suites, and magnificence of the entirety. The
beautiful music of the orchestra added to
the sum to make a perfect total.
```

Guests entered the hotel from Spruce Street under a brick portico. The spacious lobby was nothing short of astonishing. The center rose open and airy to above the mezzanine, where a stained glass canopy, lighted by a skylight, allowed the sunshine to brighten the entire lobby. Exquisite mosaic tile flooring extended from the lobby to the dining room. The front desk, located in an alcove in a cherrywood wall, was below a false ceiling made of imported European cathedral glass and suspended from the second

Courtesy of Allison M. Fleetwood Jr. Photography

floor. Next to the front desk, a water fountain offered fresh water piped in from the nearby Arapaho Glacier, Boulder's primary water supply.

The Otis Company elevator in the lobby, the latest in technology, offered guests the convenience of quick access to their rooms on the upper floors. However, the stairway was (and is) the lobby's most elegant feature. The spectacular cherrywood stairway leading to each of the upper four floors, was tiered in such a way that as it angled upward, it actually allowed guests to peer down below at four advantageous angles. To the left of the front desk, a beautiful cherrywood balcony was large enough for a string quartet to provide music for the many college fraternity or sorority events.

Just off the lobby was the guest dining room, stunning in wood-paneled walls with half-circle windows of stained glass. The tables were covered with white linens and set with the finest china and polished silver. Dinners were served in the multicourse fashion of the day which included entrees of beef, chicken, deviled crab, lobster, turkey, pork, or ham.

The atrium of the Hotel Boulderado with its stained-glass canopy is a testament to the historic preservation of this landmark hotel.

A plush ladies parlor next to the dining room allowed for pleasant female conversation, while a smoking room and a card room, complete with an eight-foot-tall glass cigar case with a variety of brands, allowed for male bonding. A music room invited guests to play the piano or relax and enjoy as others played.

The seventy-five guest rooms provided the comfort expected of such a grand hotel. Telephones were installed in most rooms, a technology very few western hotels could claim. Each room had light fixtures that ran on both natural gas and electricity. The "engine room," located in the basement, contained the coal furnace where hotel employees worked in shifts stoking the furnace to provide heat through the hotel's steam radiators as well as hot water to the kitchen and bathrooms.

The Hotel Boulderado originally opened to attract visitors and businessmen to Boulder. Room rates of a dollar or two per night were set to attract that clientele. For fifty dollars a month, baths and meals were included.

As the hotel grew in popularity, it became the center of Boulder's social events. It hosted weddings and college graduation ceremonies. Matrons of the University of Colorado often rented rooms when potential female students visited the campus.

The Rest Is History

It is said that famed poet Robert Frost considered the Hotel Boulderado his favorite hotel. He always stayed there while traveling on lecture circuits that included the University of Colorado. Another frequent guest was jazz musician Louis Armstrong, who had his own suite on the fifth floor. Other noted guests of the hotel included Enos Mills, the Estes Park conservationist; Ethel Barrymore; Colorado native Douglas Fairbanks; and Helen Keller. Perhaps the most notable of all visitors was vice presidential candidate Franklin D. Roosevelt in 1920. On a campaign stop through the western states, Roosevelt gave a speech in Boulder and later attended a dinner hosted at the Hotel Boulderado. (Roosevelt and presidential candidate James M. Cox lost the election.)

Local businesses contributed to the prosperity of the hotel. Two storefronts were located on either side of the brick portico entrance on the Spruce Street side. Businesses included a barbershop and clothier. In later years, the Chamber of Commerce and Western Union had offices in the hotel.

The hotel's design—and the business model, for that matter—was one of practicality, thereby easily adaptable to change. For example, marketing and local ads from the 1920s included the phrase: "Where every guest may expect the best and get it."

In 1923 the hotel became the headquarters for District Attorney Louis Reed during the investigation of Boulder's most high-profile murder of the era. Boulder police officer Elmer Cobb was shot to death on Pearl Street on his way to work on November 19, 1923. Local law enforcement believed that Cobb had been murdered because he knew a great deal about the illegal gambling and bootlegging operations, and the authorities were closing in. The hotel setting was used by the investigating team as a neutral place for

holding witness interviews without fear of intimidation. The police chief was arrested for allegedly hiring a hit man but later released for lack of evidence. After several interrogations, no one was ever indicted, and the murder remains unsolved to this day.

With the downturn of the economy during the Depression years, the hotel suffered financially but never closed. The Hotel Boulderado, owned by the Boulder Hotel Company, went through a series of managers until the hotel was sold to a private investor, the Hutson Hotel Company, in 1940. During World War II, the hotel served the community in a variety of useful ways, from offering reduced room rates to soldiers to hosting events to promote War Bonds.

Following the war, the hotel underwent a series of renovations. New electric wiring was installed

Denver Public Library, Western History and Genealogy, X-11888

The photograph shows the Hotel Boulderado in the 1960s when the ground floor hosted the Chamber of Commerce and a realty business.

throughout, and the heating system was converted to natural gas. The dining room kitchen received an overhaul, including new stoves, ovens, and refrigerators. Over the years, the dining room went through several incarnations—it was a coffee shop and then a casual soda shop and diner complete with a soda fountain where ice cream sodas sold for fifty cents and prime rib dinners cost less than two dollars. Eventually, the dining room would be restored to its former glory as a fine dining area.

During a heavy snowstorm in 1959, the hotel skylight collapsed under the weight of the snow, which in turn, damaged a portion of the suspended false ceiling containing the imported cathedral glass. Unfortunately for the history of the hotel, the entire false ceiling and cathedral glass were replaced with Plexiglas in patriotic red, white, and blue.

In April 1907, Boulder residents voted to outlaw drinking establishments within city limits, long before the state of Colorado voted in 1915 to prohibit alcohol sales. It wasn't until 1967 that the city of Boulder repealed this archaic ordinance. By 1969 the Hotel Boulderado had refurbished the basement, opening the Catacombs Bar there,

and added an outside stairwell entrance.

Another improvement to the hotel occurred in 1985 with the addition of the North Wing, costing $4 million. The modern architectural design blends well with the red brick, sandstone trim, and broad symmetry of the original structure. A second expansion occurred in 1989.

The Hotel Today

In 1977 the Boulder Landmarks Board designated the Hotel Boulderado as a city landmark. This, and the listing on the National Register of Historic Places, has added to the building's historic value. As such, the hotel is very proud of its history. Relics and photographs are on display throughout the first floor of the North Wing, including framed newspaper articles and old menus. The city's first large luxury hotel, the Boulderado has continued its pledge to provide the best service in the city. It has been meticulously restored to the Edwardian era in which it was built, including a reproduction of the false ceiling (at a cost of $65,000) with glittering stained glass over the lobby.

Other improvements included the renovation of the two original storefronts on the Spruce Street side, one of which is today's popular Corner Bar. Under an inviting green awning at the main entrance from 13th Street, the lobby is nearly unchanged. The original mosaic tile flooring remains, as does the Otis elevator, which is still in service— the hotel staff manually operates the cables to move the elevator cab up and down the guest floors. At the front desk, the hotel's original safe is still in the same place it has been since 1909. To the left of the front desk is the drinking fountain, dating back to the days when the Arapaho Glacier supplied most of Boulder's water.

Today, the hotel has 160 guest rooms and suites. Amenities include complimentary wireless high-speed Internet access, flat screen televisions, an in-room coffeemaker, and express checkout. A wonderful gift shop has replaced the music and reception room, where long ago women wore long, flowing dresses while relaxing and socializing with one another.

Dining facilities include Q's Restaurant, which serves breakfast, lunch, dinner, and room service. The Corner Bar is more casual and includes patio dining. The Catacombs Bar is a friendly place with nightly drink specials and pool tables.

Fun Facts

- The large blocks of orange-red sandstone that formed the original foundation of the Hotel Boulderado are still visible at the street level.

- Thompson Pressed Brickworks, located on land that is now part of the University of Colorado, supplied the bricks used to construct the hotel. Thousands of red bricks were used in the original historic hotel, and additional bricks were intricately laid in rows four feet deep for warmth and durability.

- The hotel is noted for its stained-glass canopy ceiling. It was actually incorporated into the hotel design following the 1906 earthquake in San Francisco. That city's Palace Hotel had set a precedent for leaded glass canopied hotel lobbies. When it was destroyed, both the Hotel Boulderado and the Brown Palace Hotel took the lead in the design.

- The Arapaho Glacier provided water said to be "99.996 per cent pure." Businesses throughout Boulder installed water fountains streaming the "Pure Cold Water from Boulder Owned Arapaho Glacier." Today, the Hotel Boulderado has the only original water fountain in existence.

Contact Information: Hotel Boulderado
2115 13th Street, Boulder, Colorado 80302
www.boulderado.com   303.442.4344 or 800.433.4344

THE STANLEY HOTEL – 1909
MOUNTAIN GRANDEUR

Courtesy of Charla Fleming.

Like many fur traders and trappers of the nineteenth century, Kentuckian Joel Estes roamed the Rocky Mountains in search of beaver. In 1859, Estes and his son, Milton, were traveling across the North Park of the Colorado Rockies. Estes climbed a high promontory where the view far below and across the horizon was breathtaking. Father and son had stumbled into one of the most beautiful mountainous areas in all of America. The French trappers and early Spanish explorers had avoided that wilderness area. The green valleys, wide meadows, clear lakes, and inviting tundra meadows, were the favorite summer hunting grounds for the Ute Mountain Ute tribe. Even Major Stephen H. Long, who led an expedition of the area in 1820, avoided these rugged mountains and the threat of Indians. Long, astonishingly, was never closer than forty miles to the peak later named for him.

Thus, Estes and his son are believed to be the first Europeans to see the sweeping valleys and mountain creeks of the area. The Estes family built a log cabin in 1860 and

The legendary Stanley Hotel in Estes Park draws visitors and guests from around the world. Landmark Register: NRLR.2164

made the park their home. Charles F. Estes, the son of Milton and grandson of Joel, was the first white child born in the park. The incredible beauty of the area would eventually be preserved by an act of Congress with the creation of Rocky Mountain National Park.

During the fifty years after the arrival of the Estes family, a few ranchers and homesteaders moved into the area, but for the most part, the land remained unchanged. The area did, however, become a destination for the adventurous who learned of the pristine area primarily through word of mouth. During the 1870s, many climbed the peak that Long never ascended. In 1872, Anna Dickinson became the first woman to climb to the top of Longs Peak. Not far behind her, in 1873, the well traveled Isabella Bird made a dramatic entrance into the area now known as Estes Park. Miss Bird became enamored the area and wrote about it in her travel memoir, *A Lady's Life in the Rocky Mountains*, which remains in print and still attracts people to the area. Slowly, but surely, a tourist following was developing.

At the young age of fourteen, Enos Abijah Mills was encouraged by his parents to head west to the Rocky Mountains for his health. He settled at the base of Longs Peak, built a cabin and soon became a staunch promoter of the area. In 1887 Mills made his first ascent of Longs Peak, a climb he would repeat over three hundred times, no matter the season or weather conditions. He would devote the rest of his life to the outdoors, writing several books on nature and the park's history. Mills was an early conservationist and a naturalist. He began protesting the increasing encroachment by mining, logging, and other development interests and worked to preserve the area. In 1915 his dream came true. His beloved area became the tenth designated national park. He later wrote: "In years to come when I am asleep beneath the pines, thousands of families will find rest and hope in this park."

Indeed. For in 1903, a frail man suffering from tuberculosis came to the park, hoping for better health. His name was Freelan Oscar Stanley. Not only did he regain his health in the dry climate of the Colorado Rocky Mountains, he built the finest resort hotel in all of northern Colorado.

The Beginning

Steam was the predominant power source of the Victorian era, from moving locomotive engines to heating homes. As such, steam power was well established when twin brothers, Freelan O. and Francis E. Stanley of Newton, Massachusetts, produced the first of their famous Stanley Steamer automobiles in 1897. The Stanleys' new automotive technology provided a steam engine that was light enough to mount in a carriage-style motor vehicle. Kerosene or gasoline was used to heat the boiler, which operated the motor. The Stanley Steamer was efficient for its time and became quite popular across the country. The Stanley brothers gained enormous wealth through their Stanley Motor Carriage Company and other inventions, including advances in photographic processes and improvements in violin making.

When F. O. Stanley and his wife, Flora, arrived in Denver in March 1903, they unloaded their belongings from the railcar that also had carried a Stanley Steamer across the country. They registered at the finest hotel in the city, The Brown Palace. Stanley's Denver physician, Dr. Sherman D. Bonney, recommended the thin air of the higher Rocky Mountains for his patient's tubercular condition. On Monday, June 29, 1903, the Stanleys left Denver by train for the Rocky Mountains, via Longmont and Lyons, which was the end of the line for that section of the Burlington & Northern. F. O. Stanley insisted on traveling the last leg of the journey by Stanley Steamer. Motoring over the rugged mountain road, the hardy Stanley Steamer arrived in Estes Park in a record time of just under two hours.

The open and spacious lobby of the hotel creates an atmosphere of charm and elegance.

The Stanleys took up residence in a cabin for the summer. Throughout that summer Stanley's health improved. Grateful for his new lease on life, a rejuvenated F. O. Stanley threw his energy into formation of a resort town called Estes Park, after the lovely area of the same name. Using his own money to back the new town, Stanley built a water power plant, financed a sewer system, and funded the first bank in Estes Park, even though the town would not be incorporated until 1917. He also became a strong supporter of the natural beauty and wildlife in the newly created Rocky Mountain National Park.

Stanley built a home on the western edge of Estes Park. Built in the traditional New England clapboard, or Colonial Revival, style, it would be the architectural prototype for his grand hotel.

Stanley was taken with the beauty of the Rocky Mountains and the congeniality of the people. He conceived the idea for a grand resort hotel that would be the envy of the entire Rocky Mountain region. First, he needed a suitable site to build his dream.

The land that Stanley set his sights on not only came at a hefty price, but also brought scandal, legend, and lore that have remained to this day. The land was owned by an Englishman named Thomas Wyndham-Quin, the Fourth Earl of Dunraven. In 1872, Lord Dunraven was enjoying his second hunting expedition in the United States. Arriving in the glorious park, and quite pleased with the abundance of wildlife, Lord Dunraven purchased land with the idea of building a hunting lodge and operating a

private hunting preserve for his guests. Dunraven did not stop there. He acquired an additional fifteen thousand acres through an illegal homestead scam. When Stanley purchased the land from Lord Dunraven, even more land schemes were uncovered. While no charges were ever filed, Lord Dunraven left the area shortly after the land sale to Stanley never to be seen or heard from again in the area.

After the dust settled, Stanley soon kicked up the dust again in 1907 when construction of the grand hotel began. With architectural plans of his own design, Stanley turned the project over to T. Robert Weiger to complete his masterpiece. The *Longmont Ledger* reported this news on January 25, 1907:

> We have on good authority that F. O. Stanley, of the Stanley Automobile fame, is planning to build a $200,000 hotel at the head of Big Thompson Canyon, as it enters Estes Park.

The ground groundbreaking ceremony took place in the fall of 1907. Stanley hired local contractors and construction supervisors with experience in building in the rugged Rocky Mountain environment. With a crew of thirty-two men, the back foundation of the hotel was cut into the hillside, and the base and steel frames were in place by the time construction was halted for the winter. Over the next two years of construction, more subcontractors were brought in who hired workers—many flooding Estes Park from as far away as Greeley and Boulder. Despite intermediate work stoppages for bad weather, the hotel gradually rose amidst the grandeur of the park.

The base of the hotel was constructed of locally quarried sandstone. By June 1908, the third story of the hotel was rising rapidly. Meanwhile, construction of Stanley's overall complex was also proceeding. Twelve buildings, including the grand hotel, faced south overlooking the meadows below and offering splendid views of the mountain range beyond. Within a month, wagon loads of finished lumber, used in the flooring and siding, arrived from local sawmills, including one in Hidden Valley owned by Stanley. It is estimated that over 250,000 feet of lumber were cut, sized, and finished by local sawmills for use in the hotel construction. By July 27, the shingles had been neatly placed on the roof, and crews were laying a half-mile of pipeline for water to the hotel site.

As sidewalks and gardens were being constructed, and with plumbing and electricity in place, Stanley took a hands-on approach to the interior details. He personally designed the kitchen, which was one of the first in the state to be completely electric. The dining room was lavish and large and extended to include a separate dining room for the children. An avid pool player, Stanley paid particular attention to the design and symmetry of the billiard room. The walls were paneled in dark wood and benches with leather cushions were placed throughout the room for easy viewing of the many games

that could be played simultaneously in the room.

As the hotel complex neared completion, one major detail had not yet been worked out—the name of the hotel. "Dunraven" had been bandied about in the local newspapers. The name did not sit well at all with local citizens, some of whom had been swindled by the Englishman. *The Mountaineer* editorialized in the August 13, 1908, issue: "If it was left to the people of the Park to name the hotel, it would be called 'The Stanley.'"

In response, Stanley offered ten dollars to anyone who could suggest an appropriate name for the hotel. The media responded by circulating a petition to name the hotel "The Stanley." On October 15, the *Loveland Reporter* published an account of the petition drive, with nearly two hundred signatures:

> A petition signed by nearly everyone in the park was presented to Mr. Stanley this week, asking that the name of the hotel be named the Stanley, and he acquiesced.

With the ordeal of naming of the hotel out of the way, finishing touches were made on the construction, staff was hired, and everyone, yes, even the newspapers, eagerly awaited the opening of the Stanley Hotel.

Glory Days

On the morning of June 22, 1909, a grand fanfare and a jovial party—a parade of sorts—welcomed the Colorado Pharmacists' Association's twentieth annual convention as the first guests of the hotel. Members of the Association arrived in Loveland on the 10:45 Colorado & Southern Railroad. The guests were greeted by F. O. Stanley and a fleet of twenty-two special Stanley Steamer coach automobiles. The guests were then transported to the hotel, with a parade and band heralding them along the highway route. What a glorious site it must have been as the parade of automobiles made their way up the long driveway to the entrance of the stately Stanley Hotel! Twelve buildings, all in the New England clapboard style and all painted a lovely shade of "resort yellow," faced south overlooking the glorious mountain range. In the center of this hotel complex was the masterpiece and the finest example of Georgian Revival architecture in all of Colorado.

The hotel was four stories tall with the center of the structure fashioned in a double octagon cupola and flanked by two wings. A long and wide veranda was graced on both sides of the entrance with rocking chairs inviting guests to relax and take in the scenery with Longs Peak in the distance. Six sets of turned columns supported the veranda roof.

Guests entering the hotel stepped into a lobby bathed in light that lent an atmosphere of charm and elegance, a theme reflected throughout the hotel. The lovely carved grand

staircase commanded the attention of all.

Ascending this beautiful staircase, guests were treated to lovely rooms behind thick mahogany doors. Inside the eighty-eight rooms were tinted walls, large windows, and the finest brass beds available. Fifty of those rooms contained the luxury of porcelain bathtubs. The best of modern conveniences were available to the guests, including running water, electricity, and telephones. Heating was the only amenity lacking in the guest rooms, because F. O. Stanley designed the hotel to be strictly a summer resort.

The official grand opening to the public occurred on July 4, 1909. The Casino complex offered concerts, dancing, and gambling, while outdoor activities included a golf course, tennis and croquet courts, and music concerts. Inside the hotel, there was a bowling alley and an open alcove on the second floor where a beautifully carved grand piano could be seen and heard from the lobby below. Guests were treated to the finest dining fare in the northern mountain park range.

```
A pleasant surprise awaits the guests, for
the new Hotel Stanley, where they will be
domiciled, instead of being in the class
ordinary of mountain hostelries, is simply
palatial, equaling anything of its size in
the world.
- Rocky Mountain News, July 13, 1909
```

The Rest Is History

F. O. Stanley was not only a wealthy businessman, he was a man of vision. Having had his health restored in the clear air of the Rocky Mountains, Stanley would forever promote the area far and wide. Tourism was the reason he built his dream hotel, and he promoted both with gusto. A critical article in the *Longmont Ledger* of December 25, 1908, reported:

```
We don't mean that Estes Park is out of
civilization or anything of the kind, but
when one considers that 'Estes Park' is
thirty-four miles from Longmont and Loveland,
the two nearest cities on the Colorado and
Southern [railroad] ... of course it would
look queer to some people why so big a hotel
as that would be built there.
```

While the writer was correct in his geography and logistics, he failed to report Stanley's involvement in road building, his automobile dealerships, and the fact that

the automobile was increasing local tourism. In 1905, Stanley became vice-president of the Good Roads Association, a group formed to improve the mountain roads into the park. Under his leadership, and with his influence and financial backing, a new road was built from Lyons to Estes Park. This sparked improvements to other roads into the park, bringing greatly increased automobile tourism with it.

In 1907, Stanley set up a Stanley Steamer dealership in Loveland and operated by D. O. Osborn. The five-passenger touring Stanley Steamers sold extremely well, becoming the fad of the era. Stanley kept his own fleet of Stanley Steamers in the Carriage House on the grounds of the hotel complex. These automobiles were used to carry a dozen passengers per vehicle to and from the hotel and the railroad depots of Lyons, Loveland, or Longmont. Thus, the golden age of automobile tourism helped fulfill Stanley's exemplary vision.

Over the years, the rich and famous, international royalty, and celebrities of all sorts have stayed at the Stanley Hotel. Among the many who played and stayed at this historic setting were President Theodore Roosevelt, Margaret Tobin Brown (better known as "Molly" after her famous Titanic survivor experience), John Philip Sousa, and the Emperor and Empress of Japan.

Perhaps the most famous hotel guest was author Stephen King who was also indirectly responsible for bringing this historic hotel to the attention of countless readers throughout the world. For all the history of yesteryear that this great hotel encompasses, new history was made and has become woven into the legend and lore of the Stanley Hotel. It was here that King was inspired to write his best-selling horror novel, *The Shining*. While King and his wife, Tabitha, were enjoying a getaway stay at the hotel in room 217, he conceived the idea of a story about a man gone mad in an isolated hotel closed for the season. When the popular novel was made into a movie, it was not filmed at the Stanley Hotel. The television version of the story, which ran in the 1990s, was partially filmed at the hotel and included fine exterior shots of the hotel, as well as featuring several local citizens in the production. With the success of both productions, the Stanley Hotel gained new awareness and increased clientele. The influence of the novel in bringing tourist to the Stanley continues today.

The Hotel Today

This historic landmark hotel carries on the legacy of its builder, F. O. Stanley, as well as mystery and the lore of previous guests who have walked through this majestic mountain resort.

Originally designed as a summer resort, today the Stanley Hotel is open year round. Guests are treated to a variety of venues throughout the complex. The Concert Hall, originally the Casino, has seating to accommodate nearly five hundred guests. The building east of the Concert Hall houses the fleet of Stanley Steamer vehicles. Future plans include opening the collection to the public as a museum.

Within the hotel itself, the elegant dining room offers a menu with a wide variety of entrees. More casual dining is available in the Cascade Restaurant, and the Steamers Cafe is a great stop for a quick bite. There is even a Starbucks coffee shop located within the hotel. Complimentary wireless Internet is available throughout the hotel. There are several private rooms available for meetings and conferences.

Following a recent renovation, guest rooms now range from the spacious to even larger suites, and all include privacy, comfort, and inviting seating areas with forty-two-inch flat screen televisions. Rooms are available with either king, queen, or double beds; and many rooms feature walk-in closets. Nearly all rooms provide fabulous views of the mountain range.

With all the history and elegance of this grand hotel, the legacy of being one of the most haunted hotels in the country endures. Room 217 is, of course, the most requested room, as this was the room where Stephen King stayed. The other popular guest room is Room 401, for it is said that the ghost of Lord Dunraven himself walks the floors in this room.

For the guests who desire a relaxing and pleasant stay with or without ghosts, there is always the delightful veranda with its splendid views and clean mountain air.

Exactly what the founder F. O. Stanley intended.

Denver Public Library, Western History Collection, L.C. McClure, MCC-1007

Freelan O. Stanley's hotel under construction in 1909. Stonemasons can be seen building a rock wall.

Fun Facts

- After Stanley sold the hotel to his newly formed Stanley Corporation in 1926, several changes were made, the most visual being the color change. No longer resort yellow, today the hotel complex is painted white, lending a fine contrast to the mountain majesty.

- Stephen King did not write *The Shining* while holed up at the hotel. The idea of the novel, however, was conceived while he was a guest at the hotel.

- The original movie, starring Jack Nicholson, plays continuously on guest room televisions.

- Several Hollywood movies have been filmed at this historic hotel, including *Dumb and Dumber*. The star of the film, Jim Carey, stayed in Room 217.

- Ghost tours of the Stanley Hotel are open to the public and include a mysterious underground tunnel. However, for those looking for less spooky ghosts, it is said Flora Stanley still plays the grand piano as well as she did when the hotel opened in 1909.

- Local, national, and even international paranormal groups have conducted research at this hotel. Many of these groups have been televised and can be seen on the Travel Channel and Si-Fi Channel.

Contact Information: The Stanley Hotel
333 Wonderview Avenue, Estes Park, CO 80517
www.stanleyhotel.com   970.577.4000 or 800.976.1377

THE HOTEL DENVER – 1915
A HOTEL WITH VARIETY

The Hotel Denver is located at the intersection of 7th Street and Cooper Avenue in Glenwood Springs, which was formerly known as Defiance. Landmark Register: GFCHL.5

The small settlement of Defiance was laid out in 1883 by Isaac Cooper and grew at a very slow pace until renamed Glenwood Springs in 1885. The unique location at the confluence of the Roaring Fork River and the Grand River—later renamed the Colorado River—allowed Defiance, which consisted of only a few dugouts and tents, to become became an encampment for westbound settlers. As with most early mountain towns and mining camps, Defiance was populated with the usual crowds of bunco artists, gamblers, gunslingers, and prostitutes. Thus, the main street of commerce was where miners spent their wages in the tent saloons and brothels. The taxes and fees collected by the Defiance Town and Land Company from this popular area along Riverfront Street (today's 7th Street) were very beneficial to the growing town. Yet, as the tents were slowly replaced with buildings, the businesses along Riverfront became an eyesore. To comply with the town's improvement efforts, John Blake replaced his common-law wife's tent bordello with a brick building at the corner of Riverfront and Bennett Streets. Gussie Blake ran her successful business during the spring and summer seasons and vacationed in the East during the winter months when John would rent out the building. In 1885, Gussie returned to find her building had been leased by Garfield County officials. Undaunted, she

erected a tented lean-to structure against the county courthouse and was soon back in business. The county officials complained in town meetings and in the local newspaper, but to no avail. Gussie Blake was within her legal rights. The side-by-side arrangement continued for a year until a frustrated county official named Fred A. Barlow provided a house for Gussie and her business on Cooper Avenue. Today's Blake Avenue is named for the Blake couple, although history does not record whether Gussie Blake was present to receive the honor.

It was Isaac Cooper's wife, Sarah, who suggested a name change for the growing town. With a new name, Glenwood Springs was incorporated in Garfield County on September 4, 1885. The city began to grow in ways the first settlers such as the Coopers only dreamed about. The growth of Glenwood was in part due to the Denver & Rio Grande Railroad Depot, completed in 1887. Glenwood Springs proved to be a perfect spot for the rail station, since the railroads followed rivers in the West.

Today, the hotel features an open lobby reminiscent of a European outdoor cafe.

The Beginning

As the town grew into a city in the remaining years of the nineteenth century, certain sections of Glenwood Springs remained typical of early towns in the Wild West. Local law enforcement was ineffective, and violence was common. Gambling and prostitution continued along the thriving red light district from Riverfront Street to 8th Avenue. As the city grew, enterprising men and women came to town and more businesses opened, even on Riverfront.

An aspiring young Italian immigrant named Henry Bosco settled in Glenwood Springs and opened a bottling company in 1906. He began his business by renting the basement of a tavern on Riverfront Street. This proved to be a strategic location—there were nine taverns along the street and a dozen more within the block. Bosco was able to sell his product conveniently and with little overhead, so to speak. He did so well that he bought the building he started in and later bought the building next door. In time, he bought the adjoining buildings, including the Columbus Saloon and Sheridan Bar. The block became known as Bosco's Wholesale Liquor and

Saloon. Over time, Bosco merged the buildings and opened the Star Hotel in 1915. Businesses operated on the first floor, and the upper floors provided the finest rental guest rooms for workers and miners that Riverfront Street had ever offered. Despite the proximity of Art Kendrick's furnished rooming house at the west end of the street, which was called Denver Rooms, Bosco's Star Hotel did very well. Indeed, prosperity had arrived on Riverfront.

The prosperity was short lived. Colorado outlawed gambling in 1912, and the threat of statewide prohibition on liquor was looming. World War I was about to erupt in Europe, and the number of visiting dignitaries and tourists to Glenwood Springs diminished. In 1917, when America entered the war, young men from the Glenwood Springs area enlisted to fight in Europe.

Business in Glenwood Springs, as in towns across the country, was slowed, if not stalled. Henry Bosco began to talk business with Art Kendrick. The character of Riverfront was about to change.

Glory Days

With the end of the war in 1919, America rejoiced and rebounded, but the prosperity, free spirit, and gay parties, soon came to a screeching halt when Colorado went dry with the Prohibition Act of 1921. Tourism and population in Glenwood Springs both dropped dramatically.

Bosco and Kendrick united their hotel businesses in an effort to sustain their business through the economic downturn that Prohibition brought about. In 1921, when Bosco and Kendrick merged the Star Hotel and the Denver Rooms, The Hotel Denver was born. During this early period of the hotel's history, a Chicago gangster who had considerable connections with Al Capone, Diamond Jack Alterie, spent some time at the hotel. During one stay, an inebriated Diamond Jack got into an argument with another guest. In the hotel lobby, the argument escalated, and the man ran up the stairs to his room. Diamond Jack

The three-story brick Hotel Denver is shown here circa 1965.

Denver Public Library, Western History Collection, X-8822

173

followed the man and shot through the door. The bullet hit its target, and the man fell dead. Amazingly, Diamond Jack Alterie was eventually cleared of all charges.

Despite the gangster episode, the hotel not only survived during Prohibition and the subsequent Great Depression, it also brought in businessmen, salesmen, and small investors who were willing to invest in the area. Men like Frank Kistler, a Wyoming oilman, who bought the Hotel Colorado; New York banker, George Sumers, who bought nearly all the land around nearby Cardiff; and Oklahoma oilman, J. E. Sayre, who invested heavily in Glenwood Springs. With these investors and the strong will of the local community, the economy slowly began to turn for the better. As the Hotel Denver prospered during these times, so did the surrounding area. Gone were the brothels and gambling establishments, replaced with grocery stores and mercantiles. Riverfront, by now renamed 7th Street, had become a respectable commercial district.

The Rest Is History

With the local economy improving, The Hotel Denver was also improved and remodeled several times over the years. Reminders of the original structure are evident today from the exterior brick facade to the walls within the hotel, including the brick work surrounding the hotel bar. Other reminders of the past are the treasured framed Rock Island Railroad scenic pictures, handcrafted and inlaid with mother-of-pearl.

In 1938, Henry Brosco's partnership in the hotel passed to a nephew, who eventually acquired Kendrick's half as well. Under the nephew's ownership, the Hotel Denver expanded to the exceptional resort hotel it is today.

The Hotel Today

With new businesses and an energetic revitalization program, 7th Street is now a historic district and has become something of a center for downtown excursions. Many outdoor café patios entice visitors to enjoy a beverage or meal, while the local brew pub offers a wide selection of craft beers. From 7th Street, it's an easy walk to the downtown area. 7th Street is also the stop for the Amtrak train and serves as the entry point to the pedestrian bridge over the Colorado River.

This historic landmark hotel offers thoroughly modern conveniences, including a twenty-four-hour business center, keeping with a tradition that began over ninety years ago. Services include audio visual equipment rental, meeting room facilities, and a fax and photocopy center.

Complimentary parking is offered to guests, and a bar and lounge located on the main floor invite guests to a little relaxation. The main floor also has a full service hair salon. Among the many amenities offered are 32-inch LCD televisions with premium satellite channels and wireless Internet access. Rental car and ski shuttle services are also available. Guest rooms and suites vary widely. From single or double, to mountain views or private hot tubs, each room has a unique style.

Fun Facts

- When President William Howard Taft arrived by train in Glenwood Springs, he refused to leave the train because of the station's proximity to the red light district.

- In 1900, the Rock Island Railroad Company commissioned fifty one-of-a-kind hand painted mother-of-pearl pictures. Each depicted a different scene along the Rock Island Line. The paintings were given to certain hotels as a promotion for the railroad. The Hotel Denver and The Broadmoor Hotel in Colorado Springs were the only two Colorado hotels to receive the unique pictures.

- While the infamous dentist-turned-gunfighter, John Henry "Doc" Holliday, lay in a near coma at the Hotel Glenwood in October 1887, the Denver & Rio Grande Railroad held a banquet in the dining room celebrating the arrival of the first train. Doc Holliday died in that hotel on November 8, 1887. He is buried in the city's Linwood Cemetery.

- In June 1898, the first Strawberry Day Festival was a huge success on Grand Avenue in Glenwood Springs. The Roaring Fork Valley is famous for growing large strawberries and the annual festival is still a popular annual event.

- More recently, the notorious serial killer Ted Bundy escaped from the Glenwood Springs jail on the night of December 30, 1977. His escape was not noticed for seventeen hours!

Contact Information: The Hotel Denver
402 7th Street, Glenwood Springs, Colorado 81601
www.thehoteldenver.com   970.945.6565 or 800.826.8820

THE BROADMOOR – 1918
A WORLDWIDE RESORT

The Broadmoor Hotel in Colorado Springs shines year round, just more so at Christmas time.
Landmark Register: NREP.186

Courtesy of The Broadmoor

The Beginning

When Count James M. Pourtales set sail for America in 1884, he left behind his homeland of Germany and set his sights on a future in Colorado Springs. That move changed his life and transformed the city at the base of Pikes Peak.

Pourtales came to Colorado with a very complicated heritage. He really was a count, although by the time of his birth, the title was reduced to a respected formality. His family were Huguenots exiled from France by King Louis XIV. Settling in Neuchatel,

the family acquired a fortune under King Frederick of Prussia. Consequently, Frederick the Great, in need of political favors, granted the family nobility status. The family did well for several generations until political upheaval rolled over the European continent. By the time Count James inherited the family estate, severe drought and famine had reduced the value of the family land in what was now Germany.

A large, able man of admirable mental faculties, the Count had a plan to save his family's fortune and standing by the time he stepped foot on American soil. With a financial portfolio in hand, he sought investments with no less than an eight to ten percent return. The Count was very focused on his plan. He found investments beyond his wildest dream in an area that reminded him of home—the Pikes Peak region. Pourtales fell in love with the beauty of Cheyenne Mountain west of Colorado Springs, as well as a beauty of the human kind. His French cousin, the beautiful

The Broadmoor lobby's marble stairway and registration desk in 1918.

Countess Berthe de Pourtales, a rich divorcée, had relocated to the Pikes Peak area. Following a whirlwind courtship, the two were married and settled in Colorado Springs.

In the meantime, Pourtales had made a few investments, one of which, in 1885, was a struggling dairy farm at the base of Cheyenne Mountain. William J. Wilcox had twenty Swiss and Jersey cows on his Broadmoor Dairy Farm at the time he sold it to the Count. Within a year, Count Pourtales had purchased an additional twenty-five hundred acres of prime grazing land from the Rose brothers. Eighty dairy cows grazed the land, and Pourtales had plans for further expansion. The enthusiastic reporter for the *Weekly Colorado Gazette* reported in the February 27, 1886, issue:

```
A second stall for sixty is in construction
and will be completed by March 1st. As yet
the company is not in full operation but
improvement will be that customers have a
place where their milk can or pitcher can
be found by the driver of the milk wagon
early in the morning.
```

Within a year, Pourtales had built a cheese factory, acquired the crucial Cheyenne Creek water rights, and added five Swiss bulls for breeding. In 1890 the *Colorado Springs Gazette Telegraph* carried this clever Broadmoor Dairy Farm ad:

> Baby cries for it.
> Relatives sigh for it.
> Old folks demand it.
> All the wise ones get it.
> Daddy pays for it.
> Mother prays for it.
> Others crave it.
> Only a few don't get it.
> Remember, it pays to buy
> BROADMOOR Dairy milk and cream.

In 1889 Pourtales began buying the real estate surrounding his dairy farm, with the intention of future residential development. While a large portion of the new land holdings were divided for residential lots, Pourtales also built a community building and formed the Cheyenne Mountain Country Club. When the club opened on July 4, 1891, it was only the second country club in the nation. The club offered golf, polo, tennis, shooting, archery, bowling, and cricket to its members. Next, Pourtales formed the Cheyenne Lake, Land, and Improvement Company, which created a splendid lake on the property. Because he was unable to secure a contract with the local trolley company, Pourtales devised another way to bring people to his property. As Colorado Springs was a temperance city, and the Broadmoor Dairy Farm was outside the city limits, Pourtales began plans for a hotel and casino enterprise.

Pourtales sank $300,000 into a grand resort to promote the property. The construction contract for the new Broadmoor Casino and Hotel went to the firm of Gills and Walsh in March 1891, with the completion date stipulated as June 1, 1891. Pourtales also contracted with a Denver firm for an electric plant to provide electricity for the hotel and casino at a cost of $10,000.

The rectangular two-story Georgian-style casino, modeled after the Imperial Palace in Potsdam, Germany, was constructed at the edge of the lake. The second story veranda faced the lake and extended to stairs leading to the water's edge. The main floor contained gaming rooms, a fully stocked bar, and a ball room with polished maple-wood floors. Just south of the casino, was the hotel. The hotel was a smaller building in the same Georgian style. It boasted a stone roof, which blended nicely with the surrounding mountains.

The casino and hotel opened with great fanfare in August, thanks to enthusiastic public and media attention. The Saturday night opening was a gala with fireworks,

balloonists, and tightrope artists performing over the lake. Business was brisk, and the hotel and casino were an immediate success with concerts and liquor flowing, even on Sundays. However, within a year, faced with mounting clergy disapproval and financial difficulties, the popularity of the Broadmoor Casino and Hotel began to fade. Employee thefts from liquor to silver spoons and bookkeeping mismanagement increased the financial problems. Maître d'hôtel Kelly was in the habit of giving pretty women guests Casino spoons as souvenirs. Pourtales fired Kelly, but the financial problems continued. Heavily in debt by the time of the economic depression of 1893, Pourtales' entire holdings went into receivership. The Broadmoor Casino and Hotel suffered another setback in July 1897 when fire destroyed the casino. The hotel escaped damage, but all the guests were evacuated. The following year, with borrowed money, Pourtales built a new expanded casino on the Broadmoor grounds, this one modeled after the popular European casino in Monte Carlo.

> Many of the smart sets of Colorado Springs were in attendance and Denver also was well represented.
> - *The Denver Times*, June 16, 1898

Count Pourtales never recouped the losses from his Broadmoor investments. He made another fortune in Cripple Creek mining speculation and eventually sold his Broadmoor holdings to the estate of Cripple Creek mining millionaire Winfield Scott Stratton's Myron Stratton Estate.

Spencer Penrose, another wealthy investor with ties to Cripple Creek mining, purchased the Broadmoor property from the Stratton estate in 1916, for $90,000. His dream was to create a worldwide resort.

Glory Days

Spencer Penrose, known as "Speck" to his family and friends, came west from Philadelphia for adventure and found a fortune. After several successful mining investments in Texas and New Mexico, Penrose heard about the new gold strike at Cripple Creek in 1891. He arrived in Colorado Springs just in time to help his old Philadelphia friend, Charles Tutt. He placed Penrose in charge of managing the mining investment firm Tutt had formed in Cripple Creek. Together, the two amassed a fortune in mining investments, including ownership of the fabulously rich C.O.D. Mine.

Penrose was also instrumental in promoting transportation and tourism. Along with most Americans of the time, he fell in love with the automobile. His love led to the formation of the Pikes Peak Automobile Company in 1912. The very next year he created the first auto race to the summit of Pikes Peak. The Pikes Peak Hill Climb is a popular tourist draw to this day. By 1916, he had leased the Pikes Peak road from the US

Department of Agriculture and began building an auto highway to the top of the peak.

While his construction team was building a mountain highway, Penrose hired several more construction teams to build his dream hotel. He envisioned a hotel that would be the finest in the Pikes Peak region and possibly the finest in the country. Penrose had previously offered nearly $90,000 for the Antlers Hotel when it became available as part of the estate of owner General William J. Palmer. Dr. William Bell, Palmer's business partner and executor of the estate, rejected the offer. Penrose, in a public statement, responded to the rejection, "I beg to say my associates and myself did everything possible to acquire the Antlers Hotel, in order that Colorado Springs might have a first-class, up-to-date hotel for the future, but with little attention paid to our endeavors, we have now plans for building the best hotel in Colorado at Broadmoor."

The *Colorado Springs Gazette* was enthusiastic in their report of May 16, 1916:

> The site of the old Broadmoor casino and hotel was yesterday decided upon for the new hotel to be built by Spencer Penrose and associates. The idea is to build the hotel on the side of the lake toward the mountains. However, that idea was put to rest by architect Fred J. Sterner, who said 'By all means build the hotel so that the lake will be in the foreground when looking towards the mountains.' The site for the building is ideal. And so the matter is settled.

Along with Sterner, who had also been the architect of the Antlers Hotel, Penrose hired the New York architectural and design firm of Warren & Wetmore, which had designed many buildings for the Vanderbilt family. Construction of the main complex began on May 20, 1917. Special tracks were laid so that concrete and steel could be brought to the site by rail. The stone used in construction came from Penrose's nearby Turkey Creek Ranch.

An Italian Renaissance-style tower rose nine stories tall. On each side of the tower were two wings, stepped up in elevation to the tower, simulating the rising mountain range. In the early years of the hotel operations, the additional wings were closed in the winter. The exterior terra-cotta walls were painted a signature pink; a color to be forever known as "Broadmoor Pink." The slanting, low pitched, red-tiled roof complemented the walls beautifully and blended nicely with the mountainous backdrop, especially at sunset.

The interior was exquisite. Spencer Penrose and his wife, Julie, relied on a team of

interior designers, artisans, and sculptors hired from Italy. The result was a magnificent array of ornate pillars, moldings, hand-painted beams and ceilings, Italian tile, and paintings which decorated the entire hotel.

The 350 hotel guest rooms each had a private bathroom and were decorated in styles from French to Chinese, a touch Julie Penrose provided. Private suites were designed for those who could afford them. Among those who could, were Penrose's friends: local businessman Charles MacNeill and Cripple Creek millionaire Albert Carlton.

July 29, 1918, was the grand opening of the finest resort hotel Colorado had ever seen. Guests arrived via a brick driveway lined with lavish landscaping to the circular entrance where a splendid Italian-style carved marble fountain greeted the guests at the center of the *U*-shaped entrance to the lobby. Inside, the guests were greeted in the spacious lobby entrance, adorned with the finest furnishings in the grand Tudor style, a crystal chandelier, European furniture, and imported wallpaper. The curved marble staircase led to the dining room, lavishly decorated in Wedgewood blue and accented in ivory. Chandeliers lighted the frescoes and fine art on the ceiling. Following the elegant dinner, the guests were ushered into the ballroom for remainder of the night's festivities.

Dancing lasted well into early morning hours. The opulent event was made even more memorable and successful by the personal guests of Spencer and Julie Penrose, including his well-connected associates in the mining, banking, hotel, and investment businesses, as well as New York millionaire John D. Rockefeller Jr.

Guests at the hotel had a variety of outdoor activities available to them. Behind the hotel, the lake was stocked with 10,000 trout, and a walking path encircled the lake. To the south of the lake, Donald Ross, well known throughout the country for his master designs of golf courses, turned more than 130 acres of scrub oak, sage brush, and rolling dirt into one of the finest 18-hole golf courses west of the Mississippi

Denver Public Library, Western History Collection, X-14625

Railroad tracks along the tree-lined drive leading to The Broadmoor are shown in this photograph taken between 1918 and 1920.

River. The 1901 casino building was moved to serve as a guest house. World renowned golf pro "Long Jim" Barnes was hired away from the famous Whitemarsh Golf Club in Philadelphia to be The Broadmoor's first golf pro, where he became the world's highest paid pro at $15,000 per season!

Inside the hotel, the main floor held a variety of shops and businesses, including a cigar shop, a barber shop, a ladies boudoir shop, a pastry shop, a photography studio, a doctor's office, a brokerage office, and a newsstand. Other amenities included a valet and laundry service. Smartly dressed elevator operators were on hand to serve guests, and the switchboard was available 24 hours, with three operators working shifts to handle the house telephone calls. The hotel also had what is believed to the first underground parking garage in the state.

Italian chef Louis Stratta left the Antlers Hotel to prepare the finest American and international dishes for the guests at The Broadmoor. The dining experience was enhanced with soft music from the hotel orchestra. The Silver Grill restaurant was a favorite of locals and later became a popular site for wedding receptions and large social functions.

Penrose insisted on impeccable service throughout the hotel. The staff was trained to provide a level of service experienced in the finest hotels of Europe. All employees, from the bellhops to the managers, received extensive training. In the hotel's history, there have been only four executive chefs and six executive officers, a true testament to the loyalty of employees and the pleasures of working at the hotel. The enormous success of The Broadmoor was in no small part due to the exceptional quality.

The hotel logo change to 'BROADMOOR' helped to clearly separate the hotel from the Broadmoor Dairy Farm, which was still in business. A more colorful reason for the change may be the two legends that place Penrose himself in the creation of the new logo. As a guest at the Antlers Hotel, the story goes, Penrose was refused service or admission to his room because the desk clerk did not recognize him. Penrose approved the logo and kept the raised *A* as a permanent reminder of that rebuke and the rebuke he had received when he offered to buy the Antlers Hotel from the Palmer estate. In any case, or uppercase, as it were, the distinctive logo is recognized all over the world.

The Rest Is History

While Penrose was building his monumental hotel, he was also mindful that the political winds were about to change. Years before the Eighteenth Amendment made Prohibition a national law, Colorado was the first state to enact Prohibition in 1916. Penrose bought liquor in large quantities, knowing Prohibition would soon become the law of the land. He hid the alcohol stash in the basement and tucked into various crevices of his hotel, and even more at his home, El Pomar, and in his childhood home in Philadelphia. Penrose was not the only man in America to hoard the hooch during this era, but it is thought that he had the largest such stash in the country. It is not surprising

that Penrose advocated tirelessly for repeal of the Eighteenth Amendment. When repeal of Prohibition finally came in 1933, Penrose arranged for the shipment of his precious stash by two rail cars to The Broadmoor where he hosted one heck of a party. The liquor not consumed at the infamous end-of-Prohibition party was stored and later served at the hotel during World War II, when wine and liquors were not imported into the country. Broadmoor liquor stories have always been a favorite part of the hotel lore for guests. The Tavern at The Broadmoor exhibits a collection of dusty bottles of liquor, wines, and champagne that were once part of Penrose's stash.

Since the grand opening in 1918, US presidents, foreign dignitaries and celebrities from many cultures have stayed at The Broadmoor. Presidents include Herbert Hoover, Franklin D. Roosevelt, Dwight D. Eisenhower, John F. Kennedy, Richard M. Nixon, Gerald Ford, Ronald Reagan, George H. W. Bush, and George W. Bush. There is a colorful story of Vice President Dick Cheney's visit that involved guard dogs that broke loose from the Secret Service and mingled in the crowd near the lake.

Foreign dignitaries who have brought majestic presence to the hotel include Jordan's King Hussein, England's Princess Anne, Japanese Prime Minister Toshiki Kaifu, the King of Siam, and British Prime Minister Margaret Thatcher.

Celebrity visits over the years included World Heavyweight Champion boxer Jack Dempsey, Standard Oil president A.C. Bedford, Charles Lindbergh, Bing Crosby, Clark Gable, Jack Benny, Bob Hope, Jackie Gleason, Jimmy Stewart, Walt Disney, Joe DiMaggio, John Wayne, Sugar Ray Leonard, Terry Bradshaw, Peggy Fleming, Dorothy Hamill, Lance Armstrong, Jackie Joyner-Kersee, Sir Elton John, Cher, Stephen Tyler with Aerosmith, Jane Fonda, and Michael Douglas. Jimmy Stewart and Gloria Hatrick spent their honeymoon at the hotel in 1949.

During World War II, Bing Crosby, Bob Hope, Edward Dudley, and L. B. "Bud" Maytag played an annual exhibition golf tournament at The Broadmoor. All proceeds were used to build a driving range for military personnel at nearby Peterson Air Force Base.

In 1937, the historic ice arena was constructed. Known as the Broadmoor World Arena, the skating rink was an international training center for the sport. Olympic champion Peggy Fleming was one of the many who trained there. The Broadmoor hosted the World Figure Skating Championships five times between 1957 and 1975. A memorial on the hotel grounds commemorates the Broadmoor skaters who were members of the US Figure Skating team who died in a plane crash in 1961.

In 1938 the lobby underwent a major renovation, replacing the original Tudor design with the modern-era art deco. Fluted columns and recessed dome ceilings were added to the foyer, and art deco motifs added to the wainscoting. A necessary adaptation occurred at the hotel during World War II when a few areas on the main floor were converted into additional rooms and bathrooms to accommodate military personnel from Fort Carson. It was also during this time that the hotel added a small ski area at

the base of Cheyenne Mountain called "Ski Broadmoor." However, World War II broke out shortly after the ski area opened, and the attraction was soon closed. Ski Broadmoor reopened in 1959 and was in operation until 1991.

Spencer Penrose had a penchant for adopting rare, and even wild animals, which for a time, roamed free on the grounds of the hotel. In August 1938 Penrose created the Cheyenne Mountain Zoo on property at the southern edge of the hotel resort as a sanctuary for his beloved animals, which numbered well over 200. Then as now, it is the world's highest zoo at an altitude of 6,800 feet.

Penrose so loved his Broadmoor hotel, the beautiful surroundings, and especially Cheyenne Mountain, that in the summer of 1935, he began the construction of what he intended to be his mausoleum. During the construction of the eighty-foot, medieval-style tower built with Pikes Peak granite, word came to Penrose of the death of his friend Will Rogers. The popular humorist died in a plane crash in Alaska on August 15, 1935. In honor of his friend, Penrose named his monument atop Cheyenne Mountain the "Will Rogers Shrine of the Sun." Completed in 1937, the monument/shrine was dedicated on September 5, 1937, during the Will Rogers Rodeo held in Colorado Springs.

Two years later, Spencer Penrose, the founder of The Broadmoor and benefactor to so many in the community, died at the age of seventy-four. Following his funeral, his ashes were interred in the chapel floor of the monument overlooking his beloved city.

The Hotel Today

The Broadmoor's excellent reputation for service, attractions, and amenities has grown over the years through an amazing array of expansions in the resort's facilities. In 1948, an additional nine golf holes were designed by Robert Trent Jones Sr and joined with nine holes from the original Donald Ross design to form a new East Course, which opened in 1952. The East Course has been the host to several USGA tournaments, including the 2008 US Senior Open. Jones returned in 1961 to design an additional nine holes that were combined with remaining holes from the original Ross course to form the West Course, which opened in 1965. In 1976 golf pro Arnold Palmer and Ed Seay designed a third golf course on the hotel property—the Mountain Course—which was upgraded in 2006 by Nicklaus Design.

The hotel opened the new Broadmoor Spa, Golf and Tennis Club in 1995, offering a full-service, world-class "amenity spa" and state-of-the-art fitness center, with exercise room, aerobics studio, indoor swimming pool, outdoor heated lap pool, and a Jacuzzi. Nearby are the golf and tennis pro shops. In 2001 the north end of Cheyenne Lake was expanded with a 11,000 square-foot infinity edge swimming pool, and the Slide Mountain water slides, a children's pool, and two whirlpools.

The hotel entrance also received a modern update. The *U*-shaped Broadmoor Pink building is now approached through a brick entrance with twin gate posts, lined by a brick sidewalk laid in a herringbone pattern beside a curvilinear brick wall.

The entrance leads to the new porte-cochere, completed with new doors to the entry. Inside, the lobby is absolutely stunning. Indiana limestone is used throughout, complemented by the decorative balconies looming above. The marbled floors glisten in the soft lights scattered among the updated furnishings.

The Broadmoor Hotel mezzanine gives guests a magnificent view of the lake and mountains to the west.

The original Terrace Lounge is now the Hotel Bar, featuring three wall murals depicting the two-week visit by the Hundred Million Dollar Club in 1920. Penrose invited forty-four East Coast hoteliers and other associates to The Broadmoor in an effort to promote the hotel. The bar in this room incorporates fine hand-carved etchings in the rich wood paneling. This hotel also boasts one of only fifty, handcrafted, one-of-a-kind, mother-of-pearl pictures in the country. These unique pictures were offered to various hotels as a promotion for the Rock Island Railroad Company.

With the growth in popularity of large corporate conventions and national business meetings across the country, The Broadmoor built the International Center in 1961. An exclusive meeting center, it contained a variety of meeting facilities, only to be followed by a second conference facility built in 1982, known as the Colorado Hall. This facility houses the famous Penrose Room, the only fine-dining restaurant in the state to receive the five-diamond restaurant rating award. The spectacular 12,000-square-foot Rocky Mountain Ballroom opened in 1994, and the following year, the facility added an additional one-hundred and fifty guest rooms with the option of either lake or mountain views. The West Complex compliments architecturally and was completed in 1976, adding more guest rooms to the resort.

Broadmoor Hall, located next to the International Center, was completed in 2005, bringing the hotel meeting facilities to more than 180,000 square feet of unmatched excellence and service. Renovation, updating, and improvements are an on-going priority of the hotel. The original 1918 hotel received a major renovation in the fall of 2001. All guest rooms, the lobby, lounges and restaurants, received an electrical up-grade, including modern heat, central air conditioning, multiple phone lines, and high-speed Internet access. Further enhancements were made to plumbing, including

installation of five-fixture bath facilities with soaking tubs, separate showers, and dual basins. The hotel today is very conscious of its environmental impact and has "gone green" by upgrading the lighting to a green technology, and participating in water and energy conservation programs.

Today, The Broadmoor offers 700 guest rooms and suites and forty-four cottage guest rooms, many of which are pet friendly. The complex includes three golf courses, six tennis courts, tennis camps, children's programs, three swimming pools, facilities for horseback riding, a movie theater, and an array of eighteen restaurants, coffee shops, and cafés. Exclusive retail shops line the area between the main Broadmoor hotel and the south addition.

The Broadmoor is the only hotel in the entire country to have received the Five-Star Award from the nationally acclaimed *Forbes Travel Guide*, for 50 consecutive years.

FUN FACTS

- In the history of Cripple Creek's great gold rush, not much mention is given to Count Pourtales. After Bob Womack filed his claim in El Paso County, he talked to all his friends in Colorado Springs. In 1892, Count Pourtales was one of the first to take Womack's advice and invest in Cripple Creek.

- The Broadmoor Dairy Company used the services of the Sinton Brothers milk delivery company, which became the Sinton Milk Company and later Sinton Dairy based in Colorado Springs to this day. The author's father, C. D. Wommack, was a district manager for that company for twenty years.

- Spencer Penrose was passionate about transportation and a collector of vehicles, riding, and driving equipment. With fellow collectors, Charles Baldwin and Chester Alan Arthur (son of President Chester A. Arthur), Penrose amassed an impressive collection of carriages and wagons, as well as automobiles, including Julie's 1928 custom Cadillac. This collection is on display at the El Pomar Carriage House Museum.

- The Broadmoor Skating Club produced three Olympic champions, thirty-five world junior champions, and sixty US champions. The Olympic Gold Medalists were Hayes Alan Jenkins, 1956; David Jenkins, 1960; and Peggy Gale Fleming, 1968.

- Golf legend Jack Nicklaus won the 1959 US Amateur Championship, his first national tournament, at The Broadmoor.

Contact Information: The Broadmoor
1 Lake Avenue, Colorado Springs, Colorado 80906
www.broadmoor.com   719.577.5775 or 866.837.9520

ARMSTRONG HOTEL – 1923
A HISTORIC SURVIVOR

Courtesy of Sarah Klenk, Armstrong Hotel

The Armstrong Hotel is today an anchor establishment in the historic Old Town Fort Collins neighborhood. Landmark Register: NR5LR.1997

The Beginning

The streams were all very high and the valley black with buffalo...and I thought the Poudre valley was the loveliest spot on earth.

So wrote Antoine Janis, a French-American explorer, who was believed to be the first settler in the area today known as the Poudre Valley in Larimer County. Janis passed through the Cache la Poudre River Valley in 1844. Taken with the beautiful valley, he staked his squatter's claim on land just west of present-day Laporte. Janis forwarded a report to his former employers at Fort Laramie, where he had been an interpreter, that suggested a fort might be needed in the area. A fort would not be built until the rush of travelers along the Overland Trail began a few years later, at a site that would become Fort Collins.

With the mad dash of gold seekers to the Rocky Mountain region in 1859, the United States Army established a series of forts along well traveled westward trails, including the Overland Stage Line, which followed the Cache la Poudre River. Known as the Mountain Division, this trail was a southern route heading west to connect with the Oregon Trail leading to California and Oregon. As western migration became heavier, a trading center was established near Laporte. This soon became a hub of the mail route running north from Denver, intersecting with the Overland Mail Route coming from the east. By 1861, Laporte became a station stop-over for the notorious Jack Slade, as he made his various stops as freight line supervisor for Russell, Majors, and Wadell, owners of the short-lived Pony Express.

In July 1862, Company B of the 9th Kansas Volunteer Cavalry established a military camp to protect the emigrant trains traveling west and the many settlers moving into the area. Following Colorado Territorial status, the US military personnel were replaced by the newly formed 1st Colorado Volunteer Cavalry in October 1862. The camp was named Camp Collins, in honor of Lieutenant Caspar W. Collins, who had been ordered by President Lincoln to protect the settlers on the western frontier. His command stretched from Fort Laramie in Wyoming south to Virginia Dale and Camp Collins.

During World War II, the Armstrong Hotel was home to Army personnel stationed in the area.

Pioneer settlers such as Joseph Mason, Henry Chamberlin, and Frederick W. Sherwood, established their farms, ranches, and businesses near the camp, and often sold goods and services to the military. Elizabeth Hickock Stone was another pioneer to the area. She and her husband, Lewis, traveled west from Minnesota in a wagon pulled by a team of oxen. Arriving in Denver in 1862, the couple purchased land where the Union Station now stands.

In Denver, they met Dr. Timothy Smith, who was the military doctor at Camp Collins. Dr. Smith asked the Stones to move to the camp and operate the officers' boarding house. The Stones left their Denver property in the care of Mr. Stone's son and relocated to the military camp. Elizabeth Stone was said to be the first woman to settle in Camp Collins area. She immediately established her influence with the soldiers, creating a sense of community and caring that carried over to the founding of the town. Her carefully prepared meals for the soldiers were so appreciated that the soldiers began calling her "Auntie Stone." The Stones decided to stay and built the first civilian home at the camp in 1864.

In August 1864, Lieutenant Collins issued an order appropriating for the military an area of six thousand acres adjacent to Joseph Mason's homestead claim. The new fort built on this site was called Fort Collins. Following the Civil War, the fort was decommissioned by the Interior Department in 1867. The settlers and many of the soldiers stayed and built a town also called Fort Collins.

Auntie Stone operated the first hotel in the new town in her log cabin home. Because of her sound business acumen, she was the only woman included in the founding of Fort Collins. Auntie Stone entered into several business ventures with H. C. Peterson. Together, they built the first flour mill in Larimer County. Completed in 1868, it was the second mill in the entire territory. In 1871, they founded the first brick kiln in northern Colorado. The first firing provided enough bricks for two brick homes in Fort Collins, one of which was Auntie Stone's new home. Ever mindful of the community, she contributed to all church causes, regardless of denomination, and was a leader in the Woman's Christian Temperance Union.

Owner Ace Gillett marketed his hotel well. The Ace Gillett Lounge is located in the basement of the hotel today and offers live music.

The arrival of the Colorado Central Railroad in 1877 made the new town of Fort Collins the agricultural shipping center for all northern Colorado. With affordable transportation, produce and livestock from the area were shipped to markets across the state. Soon businesses moved in and with a sound economy, and with schools and

churches to improve the quality of life, Fort Collins became a prosperous community. By 1879, the town could boast of a small college. Colorado Agricultural College would eventually be known as Colorado State University. Wide tree-lined streets in residential neighborhoods boasted some of the finest Victorian homes in northern Colorado. Built of local quarried red or tan sandstone, or red soft brick from Auntie Stone's brick kiln, many still stand today.

One of those early homes was built in the heart of the town for Andrew Armstrong, a successful local businessman. Following his death, the property went to his daughter, Carolyn. In 1923, she and her husband, Charles Mantz, built the tallest building in Fort Collins on the site of the home at College Avenue and Olive Street. In April of that year, they opened their Armstrong Hotel.

Glory Days

> The largest and most expensive business block ever built in Fort Collins.
> – *Fort Collins Courier*

Arthur E. Pringle designed the Armstrong Hotel, with construction beginning in 1922. Built in the popular square symmetric art deco style of the 1920s, the three-story brick building had two street entrances and a distinct corner entrance with a central parapet facing College Avenue. Each corner of the building featured a tile cartouche with a carved floral motif. The restrained design of the era allowed for a flat roof, while the building's symmetrical facade lent itself well to the large display windows on the first floor. The main floor of the hotel housed businesses such as the first AAA office in the area. Inside, the south end of the main floor featured leaded prismatic glass tiles, which diffused the sunlight coming into the lobby and adjoining dining room. Forty-three rooms were available on the upper floors. The evenly spaced windows on the second and third floors allowed for streaming sunshine and wonderful views of the town and prairie beyond. Two ground level light courts, which can be viewed from the third floor hallway, allowed light and ventilation into the central guest rooms of the upper floors. Transoms over each room door allowed the hot air to escape, providing natural ventilation and a cooling effect.

While there were other hotels in Fort Collins, such as the Northern Hotel and the Linden Hotel, both built in the 1880s, the Mantz couple was more adept at capitalizing on the new tourist trade. By advertising in conjunction with AAA, the Armstrong Hotel became the popular hotel of choice from which to tour the scenic Rocky Mountain National Park and the Poudre Canyon. As the tourist trade increased in the area, the Armstrong Hotel flourished as travelers and visitors returned to stay at the stylish hotel.

The Rest Is History

The Armstrong Hotel, along with all of Fort Collins, struggled through the Depression years and the World War II years that followed. During the war, the hotel became a barracks for the United States Army personnel stationed in the area. Following the war, the hotel resumed accommodating guests and expanded to offer long-term residency. Many guests considered the hotel their home. It was about this time in the hotel's history that the iconic neon electric sign was erected. As America recovered from the war, automobile tourism, which had been a novelty, quickly became part of the American way of life. The beautiful Poudre Canyon, with Fort Collins as the gateway, became a favorite destination for tourists.

Through the years, this historic hotel has had a series of owners, and the name has changed with new ownerships. It has been known as the Empire Hotel and, later, as the Mountain Empire Hotel. All the owners have operated the establishment as a family business.

The Armstrong Hotel sits in the heart of Fort Collins, an area today known as "Old Town." Originally platted by Franklin C. Avery in 1872, the area is characterized by triangular-shaped lots and wide streets. During the 1970s, the Old Town area suffered when new businesses opened south of the area. As businesses closed and the area began to decline, the Armstrong Hotel remained.

Eventually, the City of Fort Collins focused attention on the downtown area. A revitalization movement put considerable effort into restoring the area to the Old Town historic atmosphere visitors enjoy today.

Throughout the history of Old Town, and all the hotels that operated in the area, the Armstrong Hotel, the last to open, is the only historic hotel still operating today.

The Hotel Today

In November 2002, the Armstrong Hotel went through another change in ownership. Steve and Missy Levinger bought and began restoring the hotel to its former glamour. With the help of a grant from the Colorado State Historical Fund, the Levingers were able to restore the exterior and bring a vibrant historic ambiance to the interior of the Armstrong Hotel.

Renovation began in August 2003. The exterior was refurbished with historically accurate storefronts on the main floor facing College Avenue and the exterior awnings replaced. From historic photographs, the Levingers were able to recreate the neon sign from the 1940s and reinstate some of the glamour of the art deco period.

Inside the hotel, restoring the character of yesteryear was paramount. From deteriorated wooden window frames to crumbling plaster walls and tin ceilings, all were replaced. The original fir wood floors were returned to their natural beauty, and doors throughout the hotel were replaced with reproductions of the originals. The art deco theme also included the refurbishing of the main staircase and returning the original

Courtesy of Sarah Klenk, Armstrong Hotel

This vintage postcard advertises the $1.25 hotel room rate.

O'Keefe elevator to working order. The hotel also received a long overdue update to the electrical wiring to bring the wiring into compliance with fire and building codes.

The Levinger family opened the hotel to guests and visitors in June 2004. In keeping with the hotel ownership tradition, the Levinger family proudly offers first class accommodations at Old Town's only surviving historic hotel.

Of the many attractions at the Armstrong Hotel, the Ace Gillett's Lounge is a classic example of the retro design. Located in the basement of the hotel, Gillett's is styled as a speakeasy from the Prohibition era. The lounge was named in honor of one of the previous owners of the hotel and offers live music.

The hotel contains forty-three guest rooms and each one is unique in design, amenities, and historic charm from the original 1920s setting, to retro, or modern, décor. This hotel even accepts pets.

Banquet and conference rooms are available for the business traveler, as well as Internet access and laundry and dry cleaning services.

As the last operating hotel in the historic district of Fort Collins, the Armstrong Hotel is the definite start and end when visiting Fort Collins and the scenery of Poudre Valley.

Fun Facts

- Chip Steiner, Downtown Development Director, and Steve Levinger, owner of the Armstrong Hotel, were recognized in a special ceremony at the State Capitol on April 18, 2005, by Colorado Governor Bill Owens and Lt. Governor Jane Norton for the historic rehabilitation of the Armstrong Hotel.

- The Auntie Stone log cabin, the only building of the original military post buildings to survive, was moved twice during the town's development and now sits on the grounds of the Fort Collins Pioneer Museum. The interior remains as it was at the time, lined with canvas from worn tents.

- In 1862, Ben Holladay's Overland Mail and Express Company ran several routes through Larimer County. Of the twelve station houses known to have existed in the county, the Sherwood stage station house still stands. In 1864, the Sherwood ranch was a swing station on the Overland Trail stage stop and was known across the country. Arapaho Chief Friday and his band camped at the ranch during the winter of 1865. Sherwood was commissioned in 1865 by President Lincoln as Indian agent to the Arapaho in Colorado Territory.

- Known in Colorado legend as "Mountain Jim," James Nugent was the guide and friend to adventurer and writer Isabella Bird on her famous climb to the summit of Longs Peak in September 1873. The one-eyed, rough looking, buckskin-dressed mountain man must have been a strange sight to the refined Englishwoman. Even so, according to Miss Bird's account, Jim was strong willed, harsh and keenly aware of his surroundings, and a perfect gentleman. During their journey to the top of the peak, the weather turned bad. Jim assured Miss Bird she would reach the summit, even if he had to carry her. Cold and nearly frostbitten, she did indeed reach the top with his help. During the descent, Miss Bird slipped from the rocks twice. Jim saved her life both times and saw the party safely down the mountain. On June 19, 1874, Jim was shot in the head at his cabin near Estes Park. He lingered for several months before his death in September 1874. Mountain Jim Nugent was buried in the Mountain Home Cemetery in Fort Collins. His remains were later moved to the undeveloped north end of the new Grandview Cemetery in Fort Collins.

Contact Information: Armstrong Hotel
259 South College Avenue, Fort Collins, Colorado 80524
www.thearmstronghotel.com   970.484.3883 or 866.384.3883

GLOSSARY OF ARCHITECTURAL DESIGN

arch — a curved opening such as a doorway or window

art deco — a decorative style dating to the 1920s; originating in Paris, the style was popular into the 1940s.

baluster — typically vase-shaped, a series of decorative wooden posts supporting a railing; simpler styled posts are often referred to as banisters

bay window — a semicircular window projecting outward from the exterior wall

belvedere — a structure, such as a pavilion, with a particular advantage of location or view

casement — a window frame that opens by side hinges

Chateauesque — an early French Renaissance style revived in American buildings between 1870 and 1900

clapboard — the exterior of a building with beveled wooden boards, hung side by side, with one edge thicker on one side than the other

coffer — a recessed panel in the ceiling, typically octagon or square in shape

cornice — the crowning portion of a tower or wall

cupola — a portion of the roof structure, such as a dome, usually made of glass, allowing for natural sunlight

dormer — an opening in a sloped roof, typically projecting to form a vertical wall, usually housing dormer windows

Eastlake — a decorative style named for Charles Locke Eastlake, who used English Gothic styles such as embellished walls reflective of English castles

facade — the exterior front of a building

gable — triangular edge of a wall formed by the sloping ends of a pitched roof

Georgian Revival — symmetrical composition with classical detail, dating to the 1880s

Italian Revival — a general term for Renaissance architecture revived in early nineteenth-century American structures; typically symmetrical in design, often including rounded arches, with Italian Romanesque detailing

leaded glass — cut glass pieces assembled into windows or decorative objects using strips of lead and putty to seal the glass into place

mansard roof — a four-sided roof with two slopes, known as a double pitch, on each of the four sides; used extensively by French architect Francois Mansart during the French Renaissance period of the 1660s

Palladian — a three-part design for a door or window with a round opening, flanked by columns or pilasters; named for sixteenth-century Italian architect Andrea Palladio

parapet — a low wall at the edge of a roof or balcony

pediment — a low-pitched triangular gable typically on the front of buildings and often featuring an artistic sculpture

pilasters — flat columns or narrow upright supports attached to a wall

Queen Anne — a excessively ornamental style that is asymmetrical in design and often highlighted by bay windows, gables, long porches, round turrets, and towers

Romanesque Revival — a large round building style, typically with many arches, large columns, and thick walls; America's most prominent example is Thomas Jefferson's Monticello

rotunda — a circular room beneath a dome

stucco — an exterior finish made of a plaster composed of cement, lime and sand

suspended ceiling — a lower ceiling suspended from rod hangers below the actual ceiling of a building

terra-cotta — a hard, brownish-red clay material used for decorative purposes as well as a form of fireproofing

transom — typically a horizontal bar, either fixed or movable, over a window or door; a hinged window above a door

vestibule — a small entryway between the outside door of a building and the main hall or entrance of a building

Victorian — standard term for American architecture and furniture from the nineteenth century, named for England's Queen Victoria

wainscoting — a protective as well as decorative wood paneling typically applied to the lower portion of an inner wall

BIBLIOGRAPHY

Books

Bachman, David, and Tod Bacigalupi. *The Way It Was: Historical Narrative of Ouray County.* Ridgway, CO: Wayfinder Press, 1990.

Benham, Jack. *Ouray.* Madison, WI: Bear Creek Publishing. 1976.

Blair, Edward. *Leadville: Colorado's Magic City.* Boulder: Pruett Publishing, 1980.

Brown, Robert L. *Ghost Towns of the Colorado Rockies.* Caldwell, ID: Caxton Press, 1982.

Dallas, Sandra. *Colorado Ghost Towns and Mining Camps.* Norman: University of Oklahoma Press, 1984.

Dallas, Sandra. *No More Than Five in a Bed.* Norman: University of Oklahoma Press, 1984.

Eberhart, Perry. *Guide to the Colorado Ghost Towns and Mining Camps.* Denver: Sage Books, 1959.

Feitz, Leland. *Cripple Creek! A Quick History of the World's Greatest Gold Camp.* Colorado Springs: Little London Press, 1967.

Feitz, Leland. *A Quick History of Creede.* Colorado Springs: Little London Press, 1968.

Feitz, Leland. *A Quick History of Victor.* Colorado Springs: Little London Press, 1969.

Fleming, Barbara, and Malcolm McNeill. *Fort Collins: The Miller Photographs.* Mount Pleasant, SC: Arcadia Publishing, 2009.

Gregory, Doris H. *Ouray's Beaumont Hotel: A Century of Ouray's History.* Bend, OR: Cascade Publications, 1989.

Hicks, David. *Estes Park from the Beginning.* Denver: Egan Printing Company, 1976.

Hunt, Corinne. *The Brown Palace Story.* Denver: Rocky Mountain Writers Guild, 1982.

Koelling, Janet, and Kerry Koepping. *Hotel Colorado: Fountains of Enchantment.* Glenwood Springs, CO: Hotel Colorado Non-Profit Museum Corporation, 2001.

Kreck, Dick. *Murder at the Brown Palace: A True Story of Seduction & Betrayal.* Golden, CO: Fulcrum Publishing, 2003.

Levine, Brian. *Cripple Creek: City of Influence.* Historic Preservation Department, The City of Cripple Creek, 1994.

Levine, Brian. *A Guide to the Cripple Creek-Victor Mining District.* Colorado Springs: Century One Press, 1987.

Martin, MaryJoy. *The Corpse on Boomerang Road: Telluride's War on Labor 1899-1908.* Lake City, CO: Western Reflections Publishing, 2004.

Nelson, Jim. *Glenwood Springs: A Quick History*. Fort Collins: Glenwood Springs, CO: Blue Chicken Publishing, 1998.

Nelson, Jim. *Marble & Redstone: A Quick History*. Glenwood Springs, CO: Blue Chicken Publishing, 2000.

Noel, Thomas J. *Buildings of Colorado*. New York: Oxford University Press, 1997.

Noel, Thomas J., and Cathleen M. Norman. *A Pikes Peak Partnership: The Penroses and The Tutts*. Boulder: University Press of Colorado, 2000.

Nossaman, Allen. *Many More Mountains*, Volumes 1 & 2. Denver: Sundance Books, 1989, 1993.

Pettem, Silvia. *Boulder: Evolution of a City*. Boulder: University Press of Colorado, 1994.

Pettem, Silvia. *Inn and Around Nederland*, Tourism and Recreation Program of Boulder County, Inc., 1998.

Pettem, Silvia. *Legend of a Landmark: a History of the Hotel Boulderado*. Boulder: University Press of Colorado, 1994.

Pickering, James H. *Mr. Stanley of Estes Park*. Estes Park: The Stanley Museum of Colorado, 2000.

Rohrbough, Malcolm J. *Aspen: The History of a Silver Mining Town 1879-1893*. New York: Oxford University Press, 1986.

Royem, Robert T. *America's Railroad: The Official Guidebook of the Durango & Silverton Narrow Gauge Railroad*. The Durango & Silverton Narrow Gauge Railroad, 2007.

Smith, Duane A. *Guide to Silverton and Durango*. Evergreen, CO: Cordillera Press, 1988.

Smith, Duane A. *Rocky Mountain Boom Town: A History of Durango*. Boulder: Pruett Publishing, 1986.

Smith, Duane A. *Rocky Mountain Mining Camps*. Boulder: University Press of Colorado, 1992.

Smith, Duane A. *San Juan Bonanza: Western Colorado's Mining Legacy*. Albuquerque: University of New Mexico Press, 2006.

Smith, Duane A. *San Juan Legacy: Life in the Mining Camps*. Albuquerque: University of New Mexico Press, 2009.

Smith, Duane A. *Silverton*. Lake City, CO: Western Reflections Publishing, 2004.

Smith, Duane A. *The Trail of Silver & Gold: Mining in Colorado, 1859-2009*. Boulder: University Press of Colorado, 2009.

Smith, Duane A., and Richard D. Lamm. *Pioneers & Politicians: 10 Colorado Governors in Profile*. Boulder: Pruett Publishing, 1984.

Smith, Jeff. *Alias Soapy Smith: The Life and Death of a Scoundrel*. Juneau, AK: Klondike Research, 2009.

Sprague, Marshall. *Money Mountain: The Story of Cripple Creek Gold*. Lincoln: University of Nebraska Press, 1953.

Sprague, Marshall. *Newport in the Rockies: The Life and Good Times of Colorado Springs*. Athens: Swallow Press/Ohio University Press, 1969.

Watrous, Ansel. *History of Larimer County, Colorado*. Fort Collins, CO: Courior Printing and Publishing Company, 1911; reprint Johnstown, CO: Old Army Press, 1972.

Weber, Rose. *A Quick History of Telluride*. Colorado Springs: Little London Press, 1974.

Wildfang, Frederic B. *Durango*. Mount Pleasant, SC: Arcadia Publishing, 2009.

Wildfang, Frederic B. *San Juan Skyway*. Mount Pleasant, SC: Arcadia Publishing, 2010.

Wolle, Muriel. *Stampede to Timberline*. Denver: Sage Books, 1949.

Wommack, Linda. *Cripple Creek Tailings*. Littleton, CO: JoyLin Enterprises, 1992.

Wommack, Linda. *From the Grave: A Roadside Guide to Colorado's Pioneer Cemeteries*. Caldwell, ID: Caxton Press, 1998.

Wommack, Linda. *Our Ladies of the Tenderloin: Colorado's Legends in Lace*. Caldwell, ID: Caxton Press, 2005.

Archives and Source Materials

Denver Landmark Preservation Commission; individual and district designations, and Historic Building Inventory, Denver Planning Office.

Denver Public Library, Western History and Genealogy Department.

History Colorado, Office of Archaeology & Historic Preservation, including city and county preservation records.

History Colorado, National Register record listings of the State Historic Preservation Office, http://www.historycolorado.org/oahp/listed-properties

Additional Sources

Cripple Creek Colorado: Commemorative Centennial, The City of Cripple Creek and the Cripple Creek City Council, 1992, *Gold Is Where You Find It* by Dorothy Mackin, page 67.

Cripple Creek Colorado: Commemorative Centennial, The City of Cripple Creek and the Cripple Creek City Council, 1992, *There Had to Be Gold* by Linda Wommack, page 17.

Historic Hotels of America, National Trust for Historic Preservation, Preferred Hotel Group 2011 edition. http://www.preservationnation.org/travel-and-sites/travel/historic-hotels.html

Pioneers of the San Juan Country, Sarah Platt Decker Chapter, DAR.

Romero, Tom I., II. *Last Night Was the End of the World: Prohibition in Colorado,* The Colorado Lawyer, January 2003, vol. 32, no. 1.

The Broadmoor of Cleveland Park, The Broadmoor Board of Directors, 1983.

Womack/Wommack Genealogy Records dating to 1621, Womack/Wommack Genealogy Group, compiled by various certified genealogists, including the late Joyce D. Wommack, the author's mother.

Additional Interviews and Correspondence

Brown Palace Hotel, Debra Faulkner, Historian, August 23, September 19, October 3, 8, 9 and 10, 2011.

Creede Hotel, David Toole, January 20, 21, March 21, July 20, and 21, 2011.

Cripple Creek District Museum, Steve Mackin, August 15, 31, 2010, and January 20, 2011.

General Palmer Hotel, Paula Nelson, July 26 and 27, 2011.

Goldminer Hotel, Scott Bruntjen, September 29, October 14, 16, and 17, 2011.

Hotel Boulderado, Historian Silvia Pettem, September 28, 29, October 1, 2, 10, 15, and 16, 2011.

Meeker Hotel, Vicki Cross, January 12, 2011, Kimberly Ritchie, July 26, 27, 28, August 2, 2011.

Rio Grande Southern Hotel, Sheila Trevett, June 28, 29, and July 2, 2011.

River Forks Inn, Bill Jones, July 29, 2011.

Rochester Hotel, Carley Felton, July 13, 20, and 21, 2011.

Rosemary Fetter, March 2, 2009.

Stanley Hotel, Patty Twogood, July 30, 2011.

Strater Hotel, Roy Meiworm, July 13, 14, and 21, 2011.

Newspapers

Local newspaper articles accessed for this work quoted verbatim are cited throughout the text.

INDEX

Acknowledgments

Hotels were not only welcomed in any booming mining town or growing city, they were often a statement of refinement in the community. Colorado's historic landmark hotels are a testament to the Victorian era of Colorado's early history.

Special thanks to those who believed in this project and gave freely of their time and advice. First on that list is my husband, Frank, who tolerated the many late nights of research and writing, and helped me work out the research obstacles. Long-time friend and award-winning writer/songwriter Jon Chandler has never wavered in his support and encouragement. In this particular endeavor, his encouragement sparked several ideas which have been incorporated into this work. Most importantly, four of his wonderful songs surrounding the Hotel Colorado are generously included on a CD with this book. To Connie Clayton, who diligently edited the manuscript with wit and humor and became my support line on many levels, my sincere thanks.

To assemble the initial research, I received a great deal of assistance and support. Once again, Professor Tom Noel of the University of Colorado Denver, showed his interest and steered me in the right direction. Duane Smith, Professor of Southwest Studies at Fort Lewis College in Durango, extended his time in reviewing the Durango hotels. Sandra Dallas's excellent research in several early volumes on Colorado history including her 1967 book, *No More Than Five in a Bed*, was a wealth of information in many otherwise little covered areas.

Perhaps the most fun in the research process was talking with the hotel proprietors and managers. Their enthusiasm for the history of their hotels was infectious. They include Jennifer Groves of the New Sheridan Hotel, Kimberly Ritchie of the Meeker Hotel, David Toole of the Creede Hotel, Paula Nelson of the General Palmer Hotel, Sheila Trevett of the Rio Grande Southern Hotel, Carley Felton of the Rochester Hotel, Roy Meiworm of the Strater Hotel, Bill Jones of the River Forks Inn, Patty Twogood of The Stanley Hotel, Susan Adelbush of the Hotel St. Nicholas, Scott Bruntjen of the Goldminer Hotel, and Stephanie Panico of The Brown Palace Hotel. All were eager to share the history and photographs of their historic hotels.

Hotel historians who also contributed freely to this work include Janet Koelling and Kerry Koepping of the Hotel Colorado, Steve Mackin of Cripple Creek, and Teri Johnson of the Stanley Hotel. Brown Palace historian, Debra Faulkner, graciously read, critiqued, and added to the chapter of the fabulous Brown Palace hotel history. Historian Silvia Pettem did the same with her excellent critique of the Hotel Boulderado as well as contributed photographs.

I also wish to thank friends such as Maria Cunningham who went way beyond the call by conducting interviews and taking great photographs in Cripple Creek and Victor to make this book come alive in "then and now" photos. Coi Gehrig, Linda Jones, Charla Fleming, and Lori Flemming graciously gave of their time and supplied photographs.

I extend a special thank you to Charla Fleming, whose ideas and enthusiasm for the history of Colorado's landmark hotels led me to write this book.

Finally, to Tom and Doris Baker of Filter Press, who expertly shaped the manuscript into a book of which I am very proud. My sincere appreciation for their encouragement and professionalism.

To all of you, my heartfelt thanks.

ABOUT THE AUTHOR

Colorado native Linda R. Wommack is a professional writer and historical consultant. She has written six books on Colorado history, including *From the Grave: Colorado's Pioneer Cemeteries, Our Ladies of the Tenderloin: Colorado's Legends in Lace,* and *Colorado History for Kids*. She has also contributed to three anthologies of Western Americana. Linda has been a staff writer and contributing editor for *True West Magazine* since 1995 and has contributed a monthly article for *Wild West Magazine* since 2004. She has also written for *The Tombstone Epitaph*, the nation's oldest continually published newspaper since 1993.

Linda's research has been used for documentation by the national Wild West History Association and for histories of the Sand Creek Massacre as well as documenting critical historic aspects for the Lawman & Outlaw Jail Museum in Cripple Creek, Colorado.

With a college degree in history and English, Linda feeds her passion for history by participating in activities with many local and state preservation organizations at historical venues by presenting talks, hosting tours, and through her involvement in historical reenactments across Colorado. As a longtime member of the national Western Writers of America, she has served as a judge for the acclaimed national Spur Awards in Western Americana literature for several years. She is a member of both state and national cemetery preservation associations, the Pikes Peak Heritage Society, the Gilpin County Historical Society, the Wild West History Association, and Women Writing the West.